Red Letter Days

The Christian Year in Story for Primary Assembly

Jeanne L. Jackson

Stanley Thornes (Publishers) Ltd

First published in 1995 by:
Stanley Thornes (Publishers) Ltd
Ellenborough House
Wellington Street
CHELTENHAM GL50 1YW

97 98 99 00 / 10 9 8 7 6 5

A catalogue record for this book is available from the British
Library.

ISBN 0 7487 1934 2

Photoset in North Wales by
Derek Doyle & Associates, Mold, Clwyd.
Printed in the United Kingdom by
T. J. International Ltd.

Contents

Introduction   1

Red letter days
November	*	*Advent Sunday†*	3
	30	*St Andrew†*	5
December	3	*St Francis Xavier‡*	7
	6	*St Nicholas‡*	10
	7	*St Ambrose‡*	12
	25	*Christmas Day**	14
	26	*St Stephen†*	17
	27	*St John the Evangelist†*	18
	28	*The Holy Innocents†*	21
	31	*St Sylvester*	22
January	1	*The Naming of Jesus†*	25
	6	*Epiphany**	26
	14	*St Felix of Nola*	28
	25	*The Conversion of St Paul†*	30
February	1	*St Brigid*	32
	2	*The Presentation of Christ†*	34
	3	*St Blaise*	36
	*	*Shrove Tuesday*	38
	*	*Ash Wednesday†*	40
	11	*Caedmon*	41
	14	*St Valentine*	43
March	1	*St David‡*	45
	2	*St Chad‡*	48
	*	*Mothering Sunday†*	50
	17	*St Patrick‡*	53
	19	*St Joseph of Nazareth†*	55

	20	St Cuthbert‡	57
	25	The Annunciation†	59
	*	Palm Sunday†	61
	*	Holy Week: Monday	62
	*	Tuesday	64
	*	Wednesday	65
	*	Maundy Thursday**	66
	*	Good Friday**	68
	*	Easter Day**	70
April	23	St George‡	73
	25	St Mark†	75
	27	St Zita	77
May	*	Rogation Sunday	80
	*	Ascension Day**	81
	*	Whit Sunday**	83
	*	Trinity Sunday	85
	*	Corpus Christi†	87
	25	St Bede‡	89
	26	St Augustine of Canterbury‡	91
	31	The visit of Mary to Elizabeth‡	93
June	5	St Boniface‡	95
	9	St Columba‡	97
	22	St Alban‡	99
	23	St Audrey (Etheldreda)	101
	24	The birth of John the Baptist†	103
	29	St Peter†	106
	29	St Paul (See Conv. of Paul 25 January)	30
July	15	St Swithin	108
	25	St Christopher	110
	25	St James the Great†	112
	26	Anne, Mother of Mary‡	114
	31	St Ignatius of Loyola‡	117
August	1	Lammas Day	119
	1	St Keneth	122
	6	The Transfiguration†	124
	9	St Oswald‡	126
	18	St Helen	128
	31	St Aidan‡	130
September	3	St Gregory the Great‡	132
	16	St Ludmilla (See Wenceslas 28 September)	140
	17	St Lambert	134
	21	St Matthew†	136
	25	St Cadoc	138

	28	*St Wenceslas*	140
	29	*St Michael and All Angels*†	142
	30	*St Jerome*	145
October	1	*St Theresa of Lisieux*	147
	4	*St Francis*‡	149
	18	*St Luke*†	151
	25	*Ss Crispin and Crispinian*	153
November	1	*All Saints*†	155
	2	*All Souls*‡	158
	11	*St Martin*‡	160
	17	*St Hilda*‡	162
	17	*St Hugh*‡	164
	23	*St Clement*	166
	25	*St Catherine of Alexandria*	169

The Date of Easter from 1995–2025, showing also Ash Wednesday,
  Ascension Day and Whit Sunday   171
Chronology of Saints   173
Bibliography   175
Alphabetical index of stories   177
Theme index of stories   181

* Moveable Feasts – see individual entries for dates, or refer to table showing the date of Easter to 2025.

The importance of different festivals varies from one denomination to another. The key gives a general guide:

  ** Principal festivals
   † Greater festivals
   ‡ Lesser festivals

for Val

Acknowledgements

With many thanks, as always,

to the children and staff of Cobden Primary School, who make every day a red letter day!

and

to Val, who is known for having the patience of a saint!

Introduction

Why *Red Letter Days*?

These were the high days and holy days of the Christian year, so called because of the way they were written in the early medieval ecclesiastical calendars. The Books of Hours – early prayer books – usually began with a calendar showing which days should be celebrated as feast days and saints' days. The scribes of those times (for all books were painstakingly hand written) used different coloured inks, not only for decorative effect, but to distinguish between the ordinary and the special, the lesser and the greater days. Normally the minor festivals and saints' days were written in black, whilst the principal festivals and saints' days were written in red, often embellished with gold leaf, giving sparkle and lustre to the page.

Red Letter Days tells the stories behind the main Christian festivals and many saints' days. It revives days that perhaps have been long forgotten. It attempts to put back into the year the rhythm and punctuation that our forbears experienced, but which has become lost in modern times when the seasons melt into each other. Often we would not know, but for the weather or the cards in the shops, what time of year we were in.

Each of the eighty-one stories in *Red Letter Days* is preceded by an explanatory note or a short biography.

Although this book does not concentrate on customs, it will be seen that many time-honoured traditions are connected with the Christian calendar. Many Christian festivals were celebrated at the times of earlier pagan festivals; the wiser early Christians realised that the way forward was to marry the old with the new, entwine both the pagan and the religious elements of festivals, in order to convert from the old Gods to the new Christ. The Church's own need for ritual, together with its great influence on rural and agricultural life, ensured that the calendar traditions continued almost unbroken until the industrial revolution, when the old order began to change.

Many of the legends of the saints are apocryphal. They are sometimes far-fetched anecdotes mixed with folklore, but their strength lies in the impression they give of the men and women they portray, for in almost every legend is some grain of truth, albeit allegorical, which indicates some characteristic of the saint; his or her courage, integrity, humility, generosity, cheerfulness, honesty, tolerance, trust, selflessness, obedience, consideration, loyalty, perseverance, strength of character. (In other words, all those qualities we are trying to foster in our children!)

It is hoped that these notes will help the teacher towards a greater understanding of the stories themselves, so that they are not read in total isolation. The stories, while written with an assembly 'audience in mind, will retell equally well to smaller groups of children, where it will be easier to elicit further discussion concerning the points raised in the stories.

When *Red Letter Days* is used for assemblies, it is not anticipated that schools will use every story in chronological sequence throughout the year, but rather that the book will be used as a 'dip-in-able' resource. To this end the saints' stories have also been listed under a thematic index, as teachers may well wish to use them to fit in with a particular theme or idea, almost regardless of the date of the feast, rather than in their own right on their specific day.

However, it is not anticipated that teachers will wish to retell the stories of the principal festivals at any other time of year but their own, therefore these stories have not been included in the thematic index.

Red Letter Days

Advent Sunday

4th Sunday before Christmas Day

27 November (if Christmas Day is on a Sunday)
to
3 December (if Christmas Day is on a Monday)

Advent Sunday is a moveable feast. It is the fourth Sunday before Christmas Day, its date therefore determined by the day on which Christmas falls. It is also the Sunday nearest to Saint Andrew's Day. Advent Sunday marks the start of the Christian year.

The word 'advent' means 'coming' or 'arrival', and the season of Advent – the period of time between Advent Sunday and Christmas Day – is a time of preparation for the arrival of Jesus, the Son of God.

At this time, events surrounding the birth of John the Baptist are remembered. John was born a few months before Jesus, to Mary's cousin Elizabeth. God had promised to send a Saviour for his people, and John, in adulthood, was to prepare the people for Christ's coming.

John and Jesus are promised
adapted from Luke 1:5–66

Two babies had been promised. God had promised to send two special babies to do his work when they were grown up.

Zechariah and Elizabeth were the first to know. Zechariah and Elizabeth had been married a long time. They had no children even though they had always wanted a child of their own, and now they thought they were too old to have a baby.

Zechariah was a priest, and one day whilst he was in the holiest part of the temple the angel Gabriel came to speak to him.

'I have come from God to say that soon you and Elizabeth will have a child,' said Gabriel. 'You will have a baby boy and you are to call him John. When John is grown up God has special work for him to do. Soon, God will send his own Son into the world, and John must tell the people to be ready for him.'

But Zechariah could not believe what the angel was telling him.

'We are too old now to have a child,' he said.

'Don't you believe what I have come to tell you?' asked Gabriel.

'I cannot believe it,' said Zechariah.

'Then you will be silent until after your baby is born,' said Gabriel. 'Then you will know that what I tell you is true.'

Zechariah started to speak, but found that he was unable to say anything. He went home and wrote down everything the angel had said, so that Elizabeth would understand what had happened.

When Elizabeth was six months pregnant, the angel Gabriel was sent again with a message from God. But this time he visited Elizabeth's cousin Mary, in Nazareth.

'Don't be afraid, Mary,' he said. 'I am here with a message from God. You are going to have a baby. A very special child. A baby boy whom you are to call Jesus. He will be the Son of God himself.'

'I don't understand,' said Mary. 'I can't have a baby. I am not married yet. Joseph and I haven't planned to have a baby yet.'

'You will have a child,' said the angel Gabriel. 'The Holy Spirit will come to you, and God's strength will be with you.'

'It's not possible,' began Mary, but Gabriel interrupted her.

'You know your cousin Elizabeth?' he asked.

'Yes, of course,' said Mary.

'Well, everyone thought she was too old to have a child, but she is pregnant and her baby is due to be born soon,' said Gabriel. 'There is nothing that God cannot do.'

'I know,' said Mary. 'And I will do whatever God wants me to do.'

A little while later, Mary went to stay with her cousin Elizabeth to see how she was and to tell her the news about her baby.

'I'm so pleased,' said Elizabeth. 'Jesus will be a very special baby and you will be a very special mother. You must be very happy to know that God has chosen you to be the mother of his Son.'

Mary smiled. 'I am happy,' she said.

Mary stayed for a few weeks at Elizabeth's house, then she went home again to Nazareth.

Shortly after Mary had left, Elizabeth's baby was born. He was a beautiful baby boy. When the baby was eight days old, Zechariah and Elizabeth had a naming service, and a party for all their friends and neighbours. Everyone thought that Zechariah and Elizabeth would call their baby Zechariah, after his father.

'No,' said Elizabeth. 'We are calling him John.'

'But no-one in your family is called John,' everyone said. 'Surely it would be better to name him Zechariah after his father.'

'No,' said Elizabeth again. 'His name is John.'

The friends and neighbours turned to Zechariah to see what he thought. Someone gave him something to write on, because of course he could not speak.

Zechariah wrote 'John', and everyone was surprised. But they were even more surprised when Zechariah said, quite clearly, 'Our baby will be called John'.

At that moment, when Zechariah could speak again, he knew that the angel Gabriel had spoken the truth. He knew that John would be a special baby with special work to do for God when he was older. Now that he could speak again, Zechariah told everyone at the party what the angel had said to him when they met in the temple all those months before.

'John will tell the people that the Son of God is coming,' he said. 'John will help the people to know who Jesus is.'

'This baby is a special child,' said Elizabeth, looking at John lying in her arms. 'But there will be another special child born soon. A baby even more special than this one. A baby sent from God. A baby born very very soon.'

And Elizabeth smiled with happiness because she knew that Mary's child would soon be here, and the world would never be the same again.

Saint Andrew

30 November

Andrew, an apostle, lived in the first century, in the village of Bethsaida on the shores of the Sea of Galilee. He was the first of the disciples to be called to follow Christ, and was brother to Simon Peter who also became a disciple.

Andrew is mentioned several times in the Gospels, but the accuracy of later accounts of his life, including mention of his being made first Bishop of Constantinople, and of his martyrdom at Patras, is questionable. Andrew is believed to have died c. 60.

Andrew is the patron saint of Scotland, Russia and fishermen.

Fishers of men   *Trust/working together*
adapted from Matthew 4:18–20

Andrew and Simon Peter were brothers who lived in the village of Bethsaida on the shores of the Sea of Galilee. Almost all the men in Bethsaida were fishermen, including Andrew and his brother; in fact the name of the village – Bethsaida – means 'place of fishing'.

Each day Andrew and Simon Peter would set out early in their boat and cast their nets on the waters of the lake. Some days their catch was good; the nets were pulled in bulging with glittering, silver, writhing, wriggling fish. Other days the nets were almost empty, and the men knew they would make no money in the market place.

But on the whole, life in Bethsaida was good, and busy! There was always work to do. When the fishing was finished and the fish sold, there were nets to mend, new nets to make, sails to repair, boats to clean; a hundred and one jobs always waiting to be done. Yet Andrew managed to find time to spare to go up into the hills above Bethsaida to listen to a great preacher who lived there.

His name was John the Baptist, and he told wonderful stories of a great king coming to save the people.

'His name is Jesus,' said John the Baptist. 'And he is the Son of God.'

But some of the people did not believe the words of John the Baptist.

'How would you know!' they sneered. 'Has God himself told you this news?'

'Yes,' said John the Baptist. 'And soon you will be able to see for yourselves, because Jesus is coming here, to Galilee.'

Some of the people laughed and refused to believe John, but Andrew believed him and wished he could meet Jesus.

One day, when Andrew was talking to John the Baptist, John suddenly stopped speaking and pointed to a man coming towards them.

'Look, the Lamb of God,' said John, and Andrew knew that the man was Jesus. He could not wait to get back to Bethsaida and tell Simon Peter.

'And he came as close to me as you are now,' he said. 'He looked kind and understanding. He looked friendly and ordinary, not a bit like you would expect a great king to look. I wish you could have seen him, Simon. I wish I could see him again, and meet him, and talk to him.'

A few days later, Andrew and Simon Peter were in their boat out on Lake Galilee. The fishing was good and their nets were full. Andrew pulled in the heavy nets as Simon Peter guided the boat back to shore, ready to land the fish. Both were so busy with their tasks that neither noticed what was happening on the beach.

A man, with a crowd of followers, was walking towards Bethsaida from the hills. As they walked along, more people joined in the throng until there was a great crowd on the beach. Suddenly, the noise made Simon Peter look up.

'What's this?' he said to Andrew. 'What's going on?' Andrew stopped hauling in the nets and looked.

'It's Jesus,' he said. He watched as Jesus moved away from the crowd, towards the edge of the water. He saw him look out across the water to their boat. He saw him shield his eyes against the sun, and call and beckon to them.

'He wants to tell us something,' said Andrew. 'Quick, move the boat in towards him.'

Simon Peter manoeuvred the boat nearer the shore.

'Come,' called Jesus. 'Come with me, and I will teach you to be fishers of men.'

Without waiting to be told more, Andrew dropped the nets of fish back into the water, jumped overboard and began wading towards Jesus. He turned back to Simon Peter, 'Come on,' he called. 'Jesus wants us to follow him. Leave the boat. Come on.'

And Simon Peter, too, left the boat and went with Andrew to follow Jesus, to become his first disciples.

Saint Francis Xavier

3 December

Francis Xavier was born near Pamplona in 1506 to a Basque family of the Spanish Navarre. While at university in Paris he met and became good friends with Ignatius of Loyola, and was one of the group of seven who founded the Society of Jesus (Jesuits).

In 1541 Francis Xavier was sent by Ignatius, at the invitation of the King of Portugal, to the East Indies to evangelise the people there. After a voyage of some 13 months he landed in Goa which became his headquarters. For the next seven years Francis Xavier worked in Goa, in the south of India, in Sri Lanka, and in the Malay peninsula, returning periodically to Goa.

Francis Xavier baptised many people, especially among the lower castes, but he had little understanding of the Indian religions and little success at converting the Brahman caste.

In 1549 he travelled to Japan where he was well-received, and where he made many converts. After returning briefly to Goa he set out in 1552 for China, which at that time was closed to foreigners. While waiting for transport to take him to the mainland he became ill and died alone but for a young Chinese Christian who had travelled with him from Goa.

Many of Francis Xavier's letters have been preserved and these give a clear insight into the man and his work. He is believed by many to be the greatest missionary in the history of the Christian church, after St Paul.

Francis Xavier and the people of Yamaguchi

Sharing/setting an example/kindness/ appearances can be deceptive

Francis Xavier had travelled to many countries, teaching people about Jesus and baptising those who wanted to become Christians, but now he wanted to go to Japan.

He travelled with some friends to a place called Kagoshima. Here they settled in to live with the people, to get to know them, and to talk to them about Jesus.

The people of Kagoshima were poor, so Francis Xavier and his friends gave away everything they had to help them. They shared their food with the villagers, they gave away spare clothing, they shared their money with them. And most importantly, they shared their time. They helped in the rice fields, they helped build new huts. They lived like the villagers, they slept on the bare earth floor and they ate just rice and vegetables and drank only water.

And all the time they talked to the people. They spoke of Jesus and his love for everyone. They told stories from the Bible. They talked about how to live good lives helping others, caring for others, sharing with others. The people knew they were telling the truth because Francis Xavier and his friends were teaching by example. They were showing the people how to lead good lives, not just talking about it.

Soon, many people of Kagoshima asked to become Christians, and Francis Xavier baptised them.

After a while, the friends decided to move on to another place, so they left the people of Kagoshima and travelled to Yamaguchi. But the people of Yamaguchi seemed very different from the people of Kagoshima. They seemed reluctant to talk to the friends. They listened to some of the stories of Jesus, but they didn't ask any questions. They allowed the friends to stay in their village, but they were not over-friendly towards them. They were hesitant about taking the gifts that Francis Xavier and his friends offered them.

The friends felt like giving up. They felt like being unkind to the people because they were not being friendly to them, but they knew that to do so would not help the situation. So they carried on being kind, sharing what they had, telling the stories of Jesus, even though they were not getting any response.

Eventually the friends decided to move on again. They travelled this time to the capital city of Miyako.

'I will go and see the Mikado – the King of Miyako,' said Francis Xavier, but when he arrived at the palace the guards would not let him in.

'You can't come to see the king dressed like that,' they said. 'You look poor. The Mikado can only see rich people. And where are your gifts? You can't come to see the Mikado without expensive presents. Go away.'

Francis Xavier went back to the friends and told them what had happened. 'So we can't go and see the king, and without permission from the king, we can't preach to the people. We'd better leave.'

So, dejectedly, the friends went back the way they had come, and ended up in Yamaguchi again. 'Well, there's no point in staying here,' they said. 'We weren't exactly welcomed last time we were here.'

But just then, someone came out of a house and spoke to Francis Xavier.

'What are you doing here again?' he said.

Francis Xavier told the man what had happened in Miyako.

'We'll help you,' said the man, and he called to the people of Yamaguchi to come out of their houses and help.

'You were kind to us when you were here a few weeks ago,' the people said. 'So now we will help you.'

To the friends' astonishment, the people of Yamaguchi kitted them all out in fine clothes, fit to meet a king. Then they gave them two gifts – a wonderful clock and a musical box.

'The Mikado will like those presents,' the people said.

Francis Xavier and his friends thanked the people of Yamaguchi for their help and their kindness, and promised to come back and see them again, after they had been to see the king.

Then they set off again for Miyako and the palace.

'Come in!' said the guards when they saw the friends arriving, dressed in fine clothes and bearing gifts. 'Come and see the king.'

They spent a long time talking to the king. He was interested in what they had to say. He was interested in their stories of Jesus and their information about Christianity. The king gave the friends permission to teach his people about Jesus. He gave them his protection, and he gave them a building to use as a church and a monastery.

'We wouldn't have been even allowed to see you if it were not for the people of Yamaguchi,' said Francis Xavier.

'They are a kind people,' said the king. 'But they take a lot of getting to know. They're not friendly straight away.'

Francis Xavier and the friends left the king then, and moved into their monastery. They stayed in Japan for several years, and by that time, more than 2000 people had decided to become Christians.

Saint Nicholas

6 December

Very little is known of Saint Nicholas despite his being one of the most popular saints of the east and west. He is patron of countries (e.g. Russia), towns (e.g. St Nicholas at Wade in Kent), and of sailors, merchants, pawnbrokers, young girls, children and apothecaries. He also has some 400 English churches dedicated to his name.

There are many legends of Saint Nicholas, the most well-known of which is that of his saving three girls from prostitution by anonymously giving them three bags of gold.

The custom of giving gifts to children on Saint Nicholas' feast day, common in the Low Countries, has developed into the present day custom of Christmas presents from Santa Claus, through North America and the Dutch settlers, where 'Sinte Klaas' was the dialect form of Saint Nicholas.

Nicholas, however, is known to have been a bishop in Myra in south-western Turkey, in the fourth century.

Nicholas and the bags of gold
Caring/kindness/consideration for others/sharing

Nicholas was a young man who was very kind, very helpful and thoughtful, and very rich. The fact that he was so wealthy worried him because he thought it unfair that he should have so much when he knew there were others in the world who had so little. But what could he do about it? He knew that even if he gave all his money away, there would not be enough to help all the people who needed it.

One night when Nicholas was on his way home he passed a house and heard the sound of crying. He knew that in this house lived a father and his three daughters. He knew that the father had once been a rich merchant, but that he had lost all his money in some foolish buying and selling. He knew that the father worked hard to earn a living, but that it could not have been easy to earn enough money for all four of them.

Nicholas hurried on, but as he passed the door he heard the eldest daughter say, 'I know I have to leave. I know there isn't enough money for us all to live here any more. I know I have to find work as a servant or a slave, but I'm frightened. I don't know where to go or what to do.' He heard her youngest sister say to her father 'Can't she stay? Does she have to leave?' And he heard the father reply 'There is no choice. We cannot all continue to live here in this house. You must each find work where you can. There is no hope here in this house. You must all leave.'

Nicholas heard the dejection in the man's voice and knew it was not what he wanted for his daughters. He heard the eldest daughter start to cry again.

Nicholas hurried away from the house, planning how he could help the family. He had money, they needed money. It was simple, he would give them help in such a way that they would not know it was him.

Later, much later that night, Nicholas returned to the house. There was no-one about. There was no light showing from inside the house. Everyone must be asleep. Nicholas crept round to the back of the house. There was a low wall there and Nicholas climbed on to it. From here he could climb on to the roof. Carefully, quietly, stealthily, always looking around to see that no-one had seen him, Nicholas edged his way along the roof tiles towards the chimney. He held tightly to the chimney stack with one hand and felt in his pocket with the other. He pulled out the heavy, cloth bag containing a hundred gold pieces. Enough there to ensure that the eldest girl did not have to leave home.

Nicholas dropped the cloth bag down the chimney. He heard it land in the grate with a dull thud and a chink as the metal pieces settled into the ashes. Nicholas stayed quite still for a few more minutes, checking that the sound had not woken any of the people in the house, but everything stayed quiet. Nicholas carefully climbed down from the roof and went home.

He could only guess at the surprise of the merchant and his daughters the next morning when they found a bag of gold in their fireplace.

The next night Nicholas went back to the house. He had decided that one bag of gold was not enough. There were, after all, three daughters. Surely that meant there should be three bags of gold. He dropped another bag down the family's chimney.

When the merchant discovered the second bag of gold, his surprise of the first day was nothing compared to his astonishment on the second.

'Two bags!' he said. 'Yet I have three daughters … surely it won't happen again? Tonight I must wait up all night just in case the visitor returns. I must thank him. If it were not for this unknown helper, our family would by now be split up and who knows if we would ever see each other again.'

That night when the girls had gone to bed, their father sat in the corner of the dark living room, watching, waiting, listening. It was hard to stay awake, but in the early hours of the morning the man heard a sound. A scraping, scrabbling sound like feet on tiles, slipping, sliding. Then silence. Then a rattle and a thud and a chink as a heavy, cloth bag came clattering down the chimney.

Quickly as he could the man leaped from his chair, across the room and out of the door, to catch the helper, to thank him and to find out who he was.

But he was too late. The mystery helper was already running down the road, and all the merchant could see was his long red cloak flapping behind him as he ran.

The next day the girls' father searched the town to try to find the man who had helped them, but without success. No-one seemed to know of him, or to have heard of him. Nicholas was nowhere to be found.

Yet, in the days that followed, there were more stories of people who had been helped, but by whom, they didn't know. But each time, the way they had been helped was the same. Gold pieces in cloth bags were dropped down the family chimneys.

Saint Ambrose

7 December

Ambrose was born in Trier, then in Gaul, c. 340, studied Law and became Governor of an area whose capital was Milan, in 370. In 374 the Bishop of Milan died and Ambrose, while appealing for peace at a meeting to elect a successor, was asked to take his place.

But Ambrose was unwilling. He was not a baptised Christian, and the post held great responsibilities and much political involvement, since Milan was the centre of the Western Roman Empire at a time when there was much paganism and yet many newly-converted Christians. However, Ambrose was baptised and consecrated, and with his strong character and capacity for hard work, proved to be an inspired preacher and a successful bishop, always accessible to his people. He was the first preacher in the West to use hymns as a popular means of praise.

Ambrose became one of the four great Latin doctors of the Church (together with Augustine, Gregory the Great and Jerome). There are many stories showing Ambrose's strength of character, of which the following is one.

Ambrose died in Milan in 397.

Ambrose and the emperor

Courage/standing up for what you believe to be right/honesty

Ambrose was Bishop of Milan, and not afraid to speak his mind.

'One of these days he'll get into trouble for being so honest,' the people said. 'One of these days Ambrose will open his mouth once too often and it'll be the worse for him!'

But Ambrose couldn't stop speaking up for what he believed was right, no matter who he was talking to.

One day there was a terrible event in Salonika in Greece. A crowd of people became angry and they killed the Roman governor there. When the emperor heard about it he was outraged.

'How dare they kill one of my men,' he shouted. 'How dare they kill a Roman officer. Well, they'll not get away with this. I'll get my own back.' And without further ado, he ordered a legion of soldiers to sail to Greece and kill all the people there; men, women and children, to pay them back for killing the Roman governor. The soldiers killed 7,000 people.

When Bishop Ambrose heard what had happened, he was too late to do anything to save the people.

'There's nothing you could have done anyway,' said his friends. 'Emperor Theodosius is a powerful man. You couldn't have stopped him.'

'He may be a powerful man,' said Ambrose. 'But he had no right to kill those people. He's supposed to be a Christian. He's supposed to belong to the Church. If he wants to be a Christian he must behave like one. I shall speak to him and tell him what I think.'

'You can't do that,' said his friends, appalled. 'He'll most likely kill you, too, if you go airing your views to him.'

'I have to tell him what I think,' said Ambrose. 'It isn't right to kill people, no matter how angry you feel.'

Ambrose wrote to the Emperor Theodosius immediately. He told him how horrified he was to hear of the massacre of the people at Salonika. He told him how wrong it was to kill people. He told him how disgusted he was that a Christian could do such a thing.

Emperor Theodosius wrote back to Ambrose straight away.

'I'm sorry you feel as you do,' he wrote. 'I'll come to Milan and visit you in your cathedral and we'll talk about it.'

'He can come if he wants to', said Ambrose to his friends, 'But I shan't let him into the cathedral.'

'You can't stop the Emperor from entering the cathedral!' said his friends, horrified at what might happen if Ambrose did.

'Can't I!' said Ambrose.

The day of Emperor Theodosius' visit arrived. People lined the streets to see him. He came in procession with all his entourage. He walked up to the big west door of the cathedral. Ambrose stood in the doorway.

'Good day Ambrose,' said the Emperor. 'Let me come in and see your cathedral.'

'No,' said Ambrose. 'You can't come in here until you have apologised, in front of all these people, for ordering your soldiers to kill the people of Salonika.'

There was silence.

No-one moved.

No-one spoke.

Then, 'He's done it now,' whispered one of Ambrose's friends.

Ambrose spoke again.

'It's wrong to kill. You say you are a Christian, so you know that this is true. If you are a Christian you must behave like a Christian, and act like a Christian.'

Again there was silence.

The crowd waited, breath held, to see what Emperor Theodosius would do. The silence was long and heavy.

Then Emperor Thoedosius turned to face the people.

'He's going to leave,' some of the crowd thought.

'He's going to kill Ambrose,' others whispered.

'He's going to order his soldiers to kill *us*,' some of them feared.

But Emperor Theodosius did none of those things. He spoke.

'Ambrose is right,' he said. 'You people are lucky to have a bishop who is brave enough to speak out, to speak up, to speak his mind. I say I am a Christian, yet I did something Christ would never have done. Jesus taught us to love one another. Jesus taught us not to kill. But I killed, 7,000 people. I am sorry. I am truly sorry for what I did.' And Theodosius put his head in his hands and wept.

Ambrose threw open the great door of the cathedral.

'Come in,' he said. 'Come in and say you are sorry to God.'

Theodosius went in, and the people said 'Wasn't Ambrose brave. Wasn't he courageous to speak up and say what he believed. Aren't we lucky to have such a strong and forthright bishop.'

And they nodded wisely to each other.

Christmas Day

25 December

Christmas Day is one of the principal holy days of the Christian year, while Christmas Eve is a day of preparation for Christmas Day.

It is now generally accepted that Jesus was not born on 25 December. In the Gospels neither Matthew nor Luke recorded the time of year Jesus was born, but some three hundred years after the birth Christians recognised the need for a generally accepted date on which to celebrate. This day was chosen since it was already a winter feast day throughout the Roman Empire. However, orthodox Christians begin their Christmas celebrations on 6 January.

The word Christmas is derived from Christ's Mass Day, where Mass takes the old meaning of festival.

The world's special baby is born
adapted from Luke 2:1–20

Mary was going to have a baby. She knew her baby was going to be a special baby and she knew he was going to be a boy. Mary had a name already chosen for the baby, she would call him Jesus.

Mary lived in Nazareth and was engaged to be married to Joseph, the village carpenter. One day as Mary and Joseph were talking together in Joseph's workshop, they heard a commotion in the market place. Joseph looked out of the doorway and saw some soldiers speaking to the villagers.

'It is a law passed by Emperor Augustus', the soldiers said to the startled villagers. 'You all have to be counted. You must go back to the town of your birth, and report. You must set off this week to be registered,' and the soldiers marched away to deliver the message to the people of the next village. Joseph and Mary went to join the crowd of people outside.

'What does it mean?' asked Joseph.

'It means what it says,' answered one of the men. 'We must each go back to the town where we were born, to have our names entered on the census form. We all have to be counted.'

'But I come from Bethlehem, in the city of David,' said Joseph. 'I can't go back there. It's too far! And what about Mary? The baby is due to be born soon.'

'You'll have to go,' said the man. 'We all have to go. It's the law.' And he moved away as the rest of the people started to go home to prepare for the long journeys ahead.

The next day Joseph and Mary packed a few belongings into the donkey's saddle bags, and set off for Bethlehem. It was a long way. By the time they arrived in Bethlehem it was evening and they were both very tired. Mary was looking forward to finding a room at an inn, where she could lie down and sleep. She knew that her baby would be born very soon.

Joseph was surprised to see so many people in Bethlehem. He had not thought there would be so many to be registered there. The main street was crowded, and all the inns looked full. He knocked at the door of one.

'No room here! Try down the road,' said the red-faced innkeeper.

Joseph tried again.

'Sorry, we're full,' said a woman.

Joseph tried again and again, but everywhere the answer was the same.

'Sorry!'

'No room.'

'Full!'

He turned away from the last inn and saw tears in Mary's eyes. She was sad, frightened and unhappy.

'Just a minute!' shouted the last innkeeper from his doorway. He too had seen Mary's face. 'I haven't a room in the house, but there's a stable at the back,' he said. 'It's not much, but it's better than nothing. It's warm and dry. It'll take your donkey too.'

'Thank you,' said Mary.

A few hours later, in the quiet of the dry, safe, stable, Mary's baby was born. She smiled at Joseph. They wrapped the baby warmly and put him in the animals' manger, because they did not have a cradle for him.

A short way away from Bethlehem, some shepherds were out in the fields looking after their sheep. The night was cold and dark, and the men had just walked round the field to check that all was well. Everything was quiet and still and just as it should be. They sat down on the grass to talk and to eat their meal.

Suddenly, a bright light appeared in the sky. It glowed whiter until the whole sky was as bright as day.

'What is it?' said the shepherds. 'What's happening?'

'I don't like it,' said one of them. 'Let's hide.'

'I'm scared,' said another. 'Let's go!'

But before the shepherds had chance to move, an angel appeared in front of them and said, 'Don't be afraid. I have good news for you. Tonight, in Bethlehem, a special baby has been born. A baby who will help the world. A baby who is Christ the King. You'll find him in a stable, lying in a manger. Go and see him.'

And then the angel was surrounded by other angels, who sang a beautiful song, 'Glory to God in the highest and peace on Earth to all men.'

The shepherds crouched on the grass, still afraid, still wondering what it all meant. Then slowly the singing faded away, the bright sky dimmed, the darkness returned and everything looked as it had done before.

'Did we dream it?' said a shepherd.

'Was it real?' they asked each other.

'Let's go and see,' said one. 'Let's go to Bethlehem and see if there's a new baby lying in a manger in a stable, then we'll know if it's true.'

They left their sheep in the field and went to Bethlehem. There in a stable they found Mary and Joseph, and the new baby lying in a manger, just as the angel had said.

They told Mary and Joseph what had happened to them. They explained about the angel speaking to them, and they said that they knew now that it was true; they knew the world's special baby had arrived.

Saint Stephen

26 December

Stephen was the first Christian martyr, believed to have died in Jerusalem c. 35.
All that is known of him is recorded in The Acts of the Apostles, *Chapters 6 and
7. He is thought to have been a Greek-speaking Jew who, after his conversion to
Christianity, was chosen by the Apostles to be one of seven men responsible for
the distribution of charitable funds to widows.*

*Stephen was a forceful, eloquent speaker who on one occasion denounced the
Jewish Council, accusing it of resisting the Holy Spirit and of killing Christ as their
fathers had killed the Prophets before him. The Council, already annoyed, was
further angered when Stephen claimed to see a vision of Christ while addressing
the Council members. At this point they threw him out of the city and stoned him
to death. Saul, a persecutor of the Christians, but later to become the missionary
Paul, stood by while Stephen was killed.*

*Stephen is the patron of several French cathedrals, and some 50 English
churches are dedicated to his name.*

The stoning of Stephen

Courage/standing up for what you believe
to be right/forgiveness

adapted from Acts 6:8–15 & 7:54–60

Stephen was a strong and brave Christian. He was chosen by the disciples to help
them with their work. There was much work to do; many people to talk to, to
teach, to help.

Stephen was a good man. He believed very strongly in God and in the way of
life that Jesus had taught. He believed very strongly in the work he was doing,
and because of this he was often outspoken. He often argued with people about
the right way to live. Some people liked his strong views and the way he was
prepared to stand up for what he believed in, but others did not like his ways,
and did not like him telling the crowds about Jesus and God.

One day Stephen's enemies saw their chance to show him up. They started to
argue with him, but Stephen gave such intelligent, wise and clever answers to
their questions that they could not win their argument. So the enemies paid
people to tell lies about Stephen. They said he had spoken against God and was
planning to destroy the Jewish Temple. Eventually the leaders of Jerusalem
heard what Stephen was supposed to have said, and they arrested him and
brought him in front of the Council.

'What is the meaning of your lies?' they asked.

'I haven't told any lies,' said Stephen. 'It is you who have lied! You say you are
men of God, but you are not. You haven't listened to God when he has tried to
speak to you. You didn't listen to Jesus when he was alive, and Jesus was the Son

of God. All you could do was kill him. You have always killed the people who have been sent from God, you and your fathers before you, and their fathers before them. No,' said Stephen. 'It's not me who is wrong, but you.'

The members of the Council were so angry when they heard what Stephen had to say they were speechless. They expected Stephen to hang his head in shame at the way he had spoken to them, but he stood there, straight and proud and defiant, and looked them straight in the eye.

Then Stephen looked up at the sky.

'Look!' he said, pointing. 'I can see a gap in the sky. I can see Jesus standing at the right hand of God. Look!'

The members of the Council looked, but could see nothing.

'That's it!' shouted one of them. 'He's trying to make a fool of us. Well, I'll show him!' The man stood up, grabbed hold of Stephen and pushed him out of the Council room. The others joined in and together they pushed and shoved Stephen out of the building and down the road. They picked up stones from the road and threw them at him.

Stephen ran as fast as he could, trying to dodge the flying stones. He reached the city gates and ran through, but the men followed him. One of the stones hit Stephen on the head and he fell, dazed, to the ground.

Some people who were watching what was going on took off their coats and gave them to Saul who was standing nearby, to hold. Then they too picked up stones and began hurling them at Stephen. Stephen knew now that there was little he could do to save himself from this angry mob. He knew there was nowhere for him to hide. He knew that as each new stone hit him he was in more pain and growing weaker. He knew that he would soon die.

Stephen began to pray out loud.

'Lord Jesus, receive my spirit,' he said. And then, 'Lord, forgive them. Do not hold this sin against them.'

Then Stephen died.

The people who had stoned him began to walk away, leaving Stephen's body in the dust and dirt of the road. The men who had given their coats to Saul to hold, took them back and put them on. Saul knew he had watched and done nothing to help the man who was killed, and Saul knew that the man had been killed because he had stood up for what he believed to be right.

Saint John the Evangelist

27 December

John, son of Zebedee and brother of James (St James the Greater), was a Galilean fisherman when he was called by Jesus to be a disciple. The brothers were called

'Boanerges' (sons of thunder) by Jesus because of their quick tempers, but John was also called 'the disciple whom Jesus loved' and was with him on many important occasions.

John is believed to be the author of the fourth Gospel, three Epistles and The Book of Revelation, *although the style of writing of the latter has caused scholars to doubt his authorship.*

John is believed to have lived to a great age, some say 100, spending his last years at Ephesus, where he died late in the first century. He is the patron saint of theologians, writers and all who work with books.

Saint John and the band of robbers

Caring/keeping your word/honesty/ trust/forgiveness/working together

For a long time, John lived in a place called Ephesus, where he preached to the people and tried to help them understand the teachings of Jesus. John used to say, 'Even if you can't remember any of the things that Jesus said, just remember to love one another. That is the most important thing to remember. If you do that, it will be enough.'

John was a good man, a caring and kind man, who was able to help other people be as kind and caring as him.

While he was living in Ephesus, John adopted a boy. He looked after him, fed him, clothed him, cared for him, taught him to read and write, and treated him as though he were his own son. He loved the boy very much and wanted the best for him. So John was very upset when he knew he had to leave Ephesus for a while.

'What am I to do about my boy?' he said to himself. 'I cannot take him with me; he is too young and I will be gone too long. What will become of him? Who will take care of him?' John worried about the problem for many days, and then he had an idea.

'I'll ask the bishop to look after him. The bishop is a good man. He will take care of my son.'

The bishop agreed to have the boy live at his house and to look after him until John came back to Ephesus, and John set off on his journey, sure that the boy would be safe.

At first all went well. The bishop enjoyed spending time with the boy; he taught him new things, listened to him read, played games with him, told him tales of when he was young. But soon the bishop realised that he didn't have time to spend in playing and talking and reading. He was, after all, a very busy man, with many important things to do. He started leaving the boy more and more on his own.

The boy became bored of having nothing to do and no-one to talk to. He began to go out more and more. And then he met a rough crowd of boys who asked him to join them.

'Come with us,' they said. 'You don't want to stay in that great big house with that gloomy old man. Come and live with us. We'll have good fun together.'

So the boy left the bishop's house, and the bishop hardly noticed that he had gone. He joined the gang of youths, and together they rushed about the town, shouting and yelling. Then they started stealing things.

One day a band of robbers saw the boy taking some money from a house.

'Hey. You're good at that, aren't you?' they called. 'Come and join our gang. We'll make you rich if you join us.' The boy joined the band of robbers and was soon involved in stealing and lying and even murder. The robbers saw that the boy was not afraid of anyone or anything, and they made him their leader, even though he was younger than most of them.

At about this time, John came back to Ephesus from his travels. As soon as he arrived in the town he went straight to the bishop.

'How is my boy?' he asked. 'Is he well? Is he all right?'

'Oh yes,' answered the bishop. 'He's fine.'

'Then where is he?' asked John. 'Let me see him.'

'Oh, well, he isn't here just now,' said the bishop, beginning to feel worried, for he knew what had happened to the boy and he had heard where he was living.

'Then where is he?' asked John.

'He's … he's … gone!' said the bishop.

'Gone?' said John. 'How can he have gone when I left him in your care?'

'It wasn't my fault,' said the bishop. 'I couldn't do anything to make him stay. He just left. He went to live with some robbers on the hill above the town. There was nothing I could do to stop him.'

'You have betrayed my trust,' said John. 'I left the boy in your care and you have not cared for him. I must go and find him.'

'Don't go,' said the bishop. 'The robbers are wild and not to be trusted. They will kill you.'

'But you were not to be trusted,' said John. 'So why should I be afraid of a band of robbers!'

The bishop looked ashamed as John set off to find the robbers' hideout on the hill. He found it with no difficulty.

The robbers were astonished to see their leader – the bold, brave, courageous, fearless young boy, suddenly try to run away and hide from this man walking up the track towards them.

'What do you want?' they shouted to John.

'I want to speak to my son, and to you, too,' answered John.

The robbers, and John's son, stood in front of him. They waited for his anger, for his shouts, for him to strike his son and to demand that he come home again. It is what most fathers would have done, but John did none of these things. He said quietly, 'It's not too late to change your way of life. It's not too late to say you are sorry. Oh, I don't mean sorry to me; I mean sorry to God, the father of us all. It is he you have disobeyed. He taught us to love one another. You have shown no love for other people, but it is not too late to change your ways.'

'Come home with me. All of you. Come and follow Jesus. Come and help your neighbours instead of stealing from them and killing them. What do you say?'

And his son, and the rest of the robbers, said yes. They returned to Ephesus together and worked together to make it a good place, a friendly place, a safe place to be.

The Holy Innocents
28 December

Holy Innocents' Day, once known as Childermas, commemorates the time when Herod had all the male children aged two years and under killed, in his quest to be rid of the baby he was told would be the Messiah.

Herod kills the boy children
adapted from Matthew 2:13–18

After the wise men had visited the stable and left to go back to their own country, Joseph had a dream.

In his dream an angel came and said, 'You are in danger. You must leave this place at once. Herod is going to come looking for the baby; he's jealous of him and wants to kill him. Take the baby and his mother and go to Egypt. You will be safe there. Stay in Egypt until I tell you to leave.'

Joseph knew the angel in the dream had come from God. He knew he must do as the angel said. He woke Mary and told her they must leave.

'Shall we set off in the morning?' asked Mary.

'No,' said Joseph. 'We must go now. There is no time to lose, Herod might already be searching for us.' And so they packed up the few possessions they had with them, wrapped the baby up warmly, and set off in the darkness for Egypt, where they would be safe.

But King Herod was not yet searching for the baby, he was waiting in his palace for the wise men to return. He was waiting impatiently and angrily for them. He was waiting for news of this new baby king so that he could kill it. He was not going to have another king living nearby. He, Herod, was king around here.

Herod paced up and down the palace. He looked down the road to see if there was any sign of the wise men returning. He asked his palace guards if they had seen the men. He asked some of the local people if they knew where they were.

'Yes,' said someone. 'I've seen them. You mean those men from the East who followed the star.'

'Yes,' said Herod. 'Where are they?'

'They've gone,' said the man. 'They've gone home to their own country. They took that road out of Bethlehem,' and he pointed to a road curving east past Jerusalem.

When Herod realised that the men from the East had tricked him he was furious.

'How dare they not come back here to see me,' he shouted. 'How dare they not tell me where the baby is,' he raged. 'Well I'll get my own way. I'll make sure that baby doesn't grow up to take my place as king. I'll find it and kill it, and if I can't find that baby, I'll kill them all. Every baby in the land.'

Herod remembered the conversation he had had with the wise men about when they had first seen the star. From this, Herod worked out that the new baby must be less than two years old. He knew the wise men were looking for a king, therefore the baby must be a boy.

Herod gave orders to his guards to kill all the boys in and around Bethlehem who were two years old or under. Herod's orders were carried out, for his men did not dare disobey.

Saint Sylvester

31 December

Sylvester was elected Bishop of Rome in 314, only months after the Edict of Milan (313AD) recognised Christianity and ended the persecution of Christians.

Little is known of Sylvester's life, but legends abound which make him appear to have been an extraordinary character, well-suited to his position of governing the Church in her new position following the Edict of Milan, and to his position of dealing tactfully with the first Christian emperor.

Sylvester died in 335 and was one of the first non-martyrs to be venerated as a saint in Rome.

There appears to be only one church dedicated to his name in England – that of Chevelstone in Devon.

Timotheus' treasure

Courage/caring/patience/greed/
standing up for what you believe to be right

It was in the days when Christians could be killed just for being Christians, when Sylvester found Timotheus in a tree.

Sylvester was walking home. He had been visiting a friend and had stayed longer than planned. Now it was nearly dark and he was hurrying back across the fields.

In front of him was a man, also hurrying, looking anxiously behind him and around him, as if he was frightened of being seen, of being followed. Sylvester wondered who he was. It was difficult to see clearly in the dark, but Sylvester did not think he had seen the man before. He wondered why the man was hurrying across the field.

Suddenly, the man vanished.

'That's impossible!' thought Sylvester. 'A man can't just vanish into thin air. Where is he!' There was no house nearby that the man could have gone into. There was no hedge or bush that the man could be hiding behind; just an old, gnarled, half-dead tree standing alone in the middle of the windswept grass.

'Then he must be hiding behind it,' said Sylvester to himself, walking over to the tree to find out, for he was now curious to know where the man was.

He looked behind the tree. Nothing. He looked up into its branches. No-one. But there, sticking out from the tree roots was a foot. The man was huddled into a tiny hollow space at the bottom of the tree trunk.

'What on earth are you doing in there?' asked Sylvester.

'Please don't kill me,' begged the man. 'Please don't hurt me. I've done nothing wrong. Please let me go,' he pleaded.

'I'm not going to hurt you,' said Sylvester. 'But I think you'd better tell me what all this is about.'

The man told Sylvester that his name was Timotheus. He explained that he was a Christian and that some Roman soldiers had been following him all day. He knew they were out to get him. He knew that they would kill him, just as they killed all the Christians they met.

'I am a Christian as well,' said Sylvester. 'You will be safe with me. Come along. You can stay at my house until you decide what you're going to do.'

The two men went home to Sylvester's house, and Timotheus stayed there for several days. He told Sylvester that he had hidden some treasure in the hollow tree where Sylvester had found him, and that he wanted to use it to help other Christians to build a church. Sylvester and Timotheus both knew that it would be impossible to build a church just yet because although there were more and more people becoming Christians, the Roman soldiers were killing as many Christians as they could.

After almost a week Timotheus left Sylvester's house to continue on his travels. And almost a week after that, Sylvester heard that he had been caught and killed by the Roman soldiers.

'It's not fair,' said Sylvester. 'He was a good man. He should not have been killed for believing in Jesus.'

A few days later, one of the Roman prefects came to see Sylvester.

'I understand you had that Christian, Timotheus, to stay with you. Is that right?' he asked.

'Yes,' said Sylvester.

'We think he had some treasure,' said the prefect. 'Where is it?'

'I can't tell you that,' said Sylvester.

'Do you know where it is?' asked the prefect.

'I can't tell you that either,' answered Sylvester.

'If you don't tell me where the treasure is, I shall beat you up,' said the prefect.

'You won't get any information out of me by bullying me,' said Sylvester. 'You can threaten me with whatever you like, but I'm not going to give you Timotheus' treasure.'

The prefect shouted at Sylvester, he threatened him and bullied him and frightened him, although Sylvester tried not to show that he was afraid.

'Just you wait,' shouted the prefect. 'I'll *make* you tell me where it is!'

But nothing that the prefect did to Sylvester made him tell where Timotheus had hidden the treasure. In the end the prefect gave up. He realised that Sylvester was not going to tell him anything.

The prefect thought about killing Sylvester to be rid of him, but feelings towards the Christians were beginning to change. Some people said that there would soon be laws to protect the Christians from persecution. Some even said that the Christians would soon be accepted by the Romans and would be able to build their own church and worship openly.

No, there was nothing else that the prefect could do. He left Sylvester alone.

Sylvester waited. He was a patient man. There was no hurry. He, too, had heard rumours about the Romans beginning to accept the Christians and allowing them to build their own church.

Sylvester waited.

Eventually the law was changed. The Christians were to be allowed to worship Jesus. They could build their own church if they wanted to.

'But we have no money to build a church with,' said some of the Christians.'

'Yes we have,' answered Sylvester. And he went to the old, gnarled, twisted, half-dead tree in the middle of the field near his home. There, pushed high inside the hollow trunk, was Timotheus' treasure.

'This will pay for our first church,' said Sylvester. 'It's what Timotheus wanted his treasure to be used for.'

The Naming of Jesus or
The Circumcision of Christ

1 January

The feast of the Naming of Jesus, or the Circumcision of Christ, is eight days after his birth. It is the day of celebration of Christ's submission to the Jewish law.

Jesus is named
adapted from Luke 1:26–38, Luke 2:21 and Matthew 1:18–21

On the eighth day after Jesus was born, the time came for him to be named. Mary and Joseph had no difficulty in choosing a name for their new baby – they knew they would call him Jesus, because Mary and Joseph had both had a message from God telling them to give him this name.

Some time before her baby was born, Mary was walking in a garden when she became aware of someone standing near her. Mary turned to see who it was and was astonished, and a little afraid, to see an angel standing there.

'Don't be frightened,' said the angel. 'I have come with news from God.'

'But who are you?' asked Mary. 'What do you want?'

'My name is Gabriel,' said the angel, 'and God has sent me with a message. Please listen.'

Mary sat down and listened quietly to what the angel had to say.

'God is very pleased with you and has a special job for you to do,' said Gabriel. 'Soon you will have a baby boy. You are to call him Jesus. He will be a special child, a holy child. He will be a king, a king for all the world, for he is the Son of God himself.'

'But I cannot have a baby yet,' said Mary.

'God says that you will,' said the angel.

'Then I will do what God wants me to do,' said Mary, and she hurried away to tell her cousin Elizabeth the news that she was going to have a baby.

A little while later, Joseph was thinking about the baby and about Mary. He was worried because he and Mary were not yet married. Joseph fell asleep thinking about these things, and while he was asleep he had a dream.

In his dream, the angel Gabriel came to speak to him.

'Don't be afraid, Joseph,' said the angel. 'Go ahead and marry Mary as you planned. She is soon to have God's child, a wonderful child, a special child, a child who will save the world from sin. You must call the child Jesus – Emmanuel, which means God is with us.'

When Joseph woke up, he went to see Mary, and they were married.

Later, when the baby was born, Mary and Joseph remembered the words of the angel Gabriel, and they named their baby, Jesus.

Epiphany
6 January

The Feast of Epiphany occurs the day after Twelfth-night, and celebrates the visit of the wise men to the stable in Bethlehem.

The word Epiphany means 'manifestation' or 'showing' and the festival represents Christ's manifestation to the non-Jewish world. The manifestation to the magi was a message that Christ was to be a man for all people, not only for those of his own country.

The Feast of Epiphany occurred originally only in the Orthodox Eastern calendar, but appeared in the Western Church calendar in the fourth century. In the Orthodox Church, Epiphany is still of greater important than Christmas.

Visitors from the East
adapted from Matthew 2:1–12

Just before the time that Jesus was born, a new, shimmering, shining, mysterious star appeared in the sky.

'Look!' said a wise man to his friends who studied such things, 'I've never seen that star before.'

They got out their books and their charts and their maps and began their research.

'It says here,' said one, 'that a new star means the birth of a king.'

'It says here,' said another, 'that there will be a new king for the world and that a star will lead people to him.'

'Let's go!' said a third. 'Let's follow the star and be the first to find the baby king.'

The wise men prepared for the journey. They had no idea how long they would be away, or where the star would lead them. They packed everything they thought they would need, together with gifts for the new king.

They set off.

After a journey of many miles, many days, many nights, they came to the city of Jerusalem. They saw the palace of King Herod.

'The new king will probably be at the palace,' they said. 'That's a likely place for a new king to be born. Let's ask to see him.'

They spoke to the palace guards. 'Where is the baby who is born to be king of the Jews? We have seen his star in the east and we have come to worship him.'

The guards were worried. They knew nothing of a new baby. Herod was king of the Jews round these parts. These visitors could only mean trouble if they were looking for another king. They went to tell King Herod of the arrival of the visitors from the East.

'A new king?' shouted Herod. 'There is no king here but me! Where are these men? Show them in! I want to speak with them.'

King Herod talked with the wise men from the East, and found out from them exactly when the strange star in the sky had appeared. He talked with his own chief priests and teachers, and found out from them that it had been predicted a new king would be born in Bethlehem.

Herod spoke to the wise men again, this time quietly. 'Go to Bethlehem,' he said, 'and find the new baby. But when you find him, come back here and tell me where he is, so that I can go and worship him too.'

'We will,' said the wise men.

On the way to Bethlehem, they saw the star again, this time shining even more brightly than before. It seemed to stop over a stable near to an inn.

'This can't be the place?' they said. 'A new king wouldn't be born in a stable, would he?'

They went into the stable, and there they saw Joseph, and Mary with the child in her arms. They knelt down and worshipped him.

They brought out their gifts and gave them to the baby: gold – to show he was a very special king, frankincense – a sign that he was from God, and myrrh – to show he would suffer for his friends and followers in the future.

The wise men knew they were not the first to see the new baby; the shepherds had visited the stable already, but they knew they were the first people from another country to see the world's special baby.

After they had seen Jesus, the wise men prepared for their journey home.

'We must remember to call in and tell King Herod we found the baby,' said one of them. 'He wants to come and see the new king for himself.' But that night the men each had a dream in which God warned them not to return to King Herod's palace. A dream that told them that Herod meant to harm the new baby.

'We'll go home a different way so he'll not see us,' they said. 'We won't tell him where the baby is.'

And the wise men went home a different way, happy that they'd seen the world's new king.

Saint Felix of Nola

14 January

There are no fewer than 66 saints by the name of Felix in the Roman martyrology alone, but Felix of Nola is the one associated with the legend of the spider.

Felix was born at Nola, near Naples, the son of a soldier. He became a priest and was arrested and tortured by the Emperor Decius, as part of the Christian persecution. However, according to legend, Felix escaped from prison and hid in a ruined building while the soldiers searched for him. They thought no-one would be in the building because of the number of dusty webs across the door, and thus Felix avoided capture.

Later, Felix was asked to succeed Maximus, Bishop of Nola, but he refused, preferring to remain a priest and live a simple life. Felix died in Nola c. 260.

Felix and the spider   *Friendship/sharing/generosity/loyalty*

Felix was a Christian. He lived in the days when it was dangerous to be Christian; in the days when Christians were persecuted for believing in Jesus.

One day the Emperor Decius ordered his soldiers to arrest the Bishop of Nola who was Felix's friend. The bishop was an old man and Felix pleaded with the soldiers to let him go, but the soldiers would not listen. They threw the bishop into a dark, damp, dungeon.

But the bishop, despite being old, was very clever, and in no time at all he had escaped.

'We can't tell the emperor that a Christian has escaped,' said the soldiers. 'We'll have to arrest another Christian instead.' So the soldiers caught Felix and threw him into the dungeon in place of the bishop.

Somehow, and no-one quite knows how it happened, Felix also escaped from the prison. He followed the bishop and eventually caught up with him, but when he did he was dismayed by what he saw. The bishop was ill and starving. Felix gave him some bread that he had in his pocket, then picked up his friend and carried him on his back to the nearest house.

Felix had no idea whether the people in the house would be helpful to him or not, but he knew that it was more important for him to save the bishop's life, than to save his own. Luckily the people were friendly and helpful, and promised to care for the bishop and look after him until he was well again. Felix gave them some money then left quickly. He had to find a hiding place because he knew the Roman soldiers would be looking for him.

Early next morning, whilst Felix was searching for somewhere to hide, he bumped into the very men who were searching for him.

'Have you seen a man called Felix?' they asked.

'No, sorry,' said Felix. 'I don't know where he is!' Then he ran away as quickly as he could, enjoying his joke, but knowing that the soldiers would soon discover he'd played a trick on them, and that they would no doubt be even more angry because of it.

Sure enough, the soldiers soon found out and came galloping after him, in force this time, 30 of them at least, on horseback, chasing him. They were not far behind. They would soon catch up, soon have him and soon kill him.

Felix looked round. He had to find somewhere to hide. And quickly.

Just ahead was an old building. It was disused and tumbledown – an old house probably. The walls were crumbling and broken. There was a narrow crack in one of the walls – a thin crack for a thin person. Felix was thin. They had not fed him much in prison. He squeezed through the gap. On the other side of the wall was a deep, dry well. Felix climbed down the walls. He stayed at the bottom, quite still, quite silent.

Above him he could hear the sound of the horses' hooves. First galloping and then stopping. He heard voices.

'He must be in this building. There's nowhere else for him to go. Let's look.'

Felix froze at the bottom of his well. He heard another voice.

'Yes. Look. A gap in the wall. He could be inside. Help me in.'

And then a different voice.

'No. He can't be in there. Look, the crack's all covered in spiders' webs. They're old and dusty. No-one's been in there for years. Come on. While we're talking here, he'll be getting further and further away from us. Come.'

Felix heard the galloping hooves becoming fainter as the soldiers rode away. But he dare not come out of his well.

A Christian family who lived nearby found him and brought him food and water and blankets. Felix stayed there, in the bottom of the well, for six months.

Then one day the family brought him some good news with his dinner.

'It's stopped,' they said. 'The cruelty to the Christians has stopped. You're free to come out now. You can go home. You can go anywhere you want. No-one's going to stop you, or hurt you, or persecute you.'

They helped Felix climb up the steep walls of the well which had become his home, his house, his sanctuary. They helped him back to Nola, his real home.

The people there cheered him and welcomed him, and asked him if he would become their bishop – sadly the old bishop had died. But Felix said no. He wanted to live in his own house and be a priest. He wanted to live a simple life where he would have time to think, time to rest, time to just be. And he wanted to share his house with ... spiders, as a way of saying thank you to them for somehow saving his life.

The Conversion of Saint Paul

25 January

Paul, originally named Saul, was born to a Jewish family of Tarsus, in what is now Turkey. His year of birth is not known, but he is believed to have died in Rome c. 67. He is the only apostle not to have met Christ in his lifetime on earth.

Saul, a devout Jew and a Roman citizen, was active in the persecution of the Christians. He was present at and consented to the stoning to death of St Stephen – believed to be the first Christian martyr.

On his way to Damascus to persecute Christians there, Saul had a vision of Christ that altered the course of his life. Saul was baptised and took the name Paul. Later in Damascus Paul's enemies attempted to assassinate him, but he escaped by having his friends lower him over the city walls in a basket.

Paul travelled extensively, and while on these missionary journeys wrote the Epistles which became such a major influence on Christian theology and on the development of Christianity.

Tradition maintains that Paul was martyred in Rome. He and Saint Peter share the same feast day of 29 June, and this has led to the belief that they died on the same day.

Paul is the patron saint of tent makers and saddlers.

The Conversion of Saul   *Trust/tolerance*
adapted from Acts 9:1–23

Saul was a Roman, and like most of the Romans, Saul hated the Christians.

He did not believe that Jesus was the Son of God. He did not like the Christians to talk about Jesus and to say what a good man he was. He did not like Jesus' disciples preaching to the people and asking them to become Christians too. He wanted rid of the Christians.

Saul and his friends persecuted the Christians. They went round from house to house in Jerusalem, finding out which people believed in Jesus, then they captured those people and threw them into prison. They did not care if they hurt the Christians, or even if they killed them.

One day Saul heard that there were some Christians living nearby in the city of Damascus.

'We'll go and get them,' he said to his friends. 'We'll capture them and bring them back here and throw them into prison.'

Saul went to see the High Priests of Jerusalem to get a letter of authorisation – a letter which would give him permission to capture the Christians. The High Priests were pleased with Saul. If his journey went well there would soon be a few less Christians for them to worry about. But Saul's journey was to turn out very differently from the way everyone expected.

Saul and his friends set off in the morning. They walked, of course, to Damascus and at first all went well. The weather was good, they had food with them to eat, and they talked and laughed and joked amongst themselves on the way. Around mid-day they were thinking of stopping for a picnic, when suddenly a blinding flash of light lit up the sky. Saul fell to the ground, covering his head with his arms, afraid of what was happening.

Then he heard a voice, 'Saul, Saul! Why are you persecuting me?'

Saul looked up but could see nothing. The others, too, looked round, but although they could all hear the voice, no-one could see where it was coming from.

'Who are you?' said Saul.

'I am Jesus,' said the voice. Saul said nothing, but felt even more afraid.

'Go into Damascus,' continued the voice. 'Go into the city and you will be told what to do.' Then the bright light faded and the friends were left standing, puzzled, on the road.

'What is it?'

'What does it mean?'

'Why did it happen?' they asked.

But Saul said 'I can't see. Even with my eyes open, I can't see anything. The light has blinded me. Take me to the city. Lead me there.'

And so the friends led Saul by the hand into the city of Damascus and took him to the house where they were to stay.

'What is to become of me?' asked Saul. 'What is going to happen?' He felt so afraid that he did not leave the house, or eat or drink anything for three days. Paul did not know that God was about to send someone to help him.

Ananias was a Christian living in Damascus at the time. He had heard of Saul and of the way he persecuted the Christians, and he was afraid of him. Ananias felt even more afraid when he had a dream in which God spoke to him.

'Go and find Saul,' said God in the dream. 'You will find him in a house in Straight Street. Go to him and touch his eyes so that he can see again.'

'But he will kill me,' answered Ananias. 'Everyone knows what terrible things he does to the Christians. If he knows I am a Christian he will at the very least throw me into prison.'

'Go,' said God. 'I have chosen Saul to do a special job. He will not harm you. Go.'

So Ananias went to the house on Straight Street and found Saul. He said 'Saul, God has sent me so that you can see again, and so that you can have the gift of his Holy Spirit.' Then Ananias touched Saul's face. Straight away Saul could see again.

'Now I understand,' said Saul. 'Now I understand that Jesus is the Son of God. I don't want to persecute the Christians any more. I want to be a Christian. I want to tell the world that Jesus is the Son of God.'

Saul stayed a few more days in Damascus and went into the temples to tell everyone about Jesus. Everyone who heard him was astonished to hear what Saul was saying.

'Isn't he the man from Jerusalem who's been persecuting the Christians?' they said. 'But listen to him now. He's on the side of the Christians.'

'I don't understand it,' said someone. 'I heard he'd come to Damascus to arrest all the Christians he could find.'

'And I heard that he was cruel to the ones he captured,' said someone else. 'Yet listen to him. He can't stop talking about Jesus. I can't believe he's really become a Christian.'

But it was true. God had chosen Saul to tell the news of Jesus to the world. Later, Saul became known as Paul and he travelled far and wide telling everyone he met about the life of Jesus.

Saint Brigid

1 February

There is much folklore but little fact concerning Brigid's life, yet she is a patron saint of Ireland, second only to Patrick. Brigid (also known as Bride) was probably born c. 450 near Dundalk, to humble parents believed to have been baptised by Patrick. When she was about 18 she became a nun, then founded the first convent in Ireland at Cill-Dara (later Kildare). This later developed into a double monastery over which Brigid presided as abbess. Brigid contributed greatly to the spread of Christianity in Ireland.

Brigid was known for her compassion, great generosity, charity, liveliness and strength of character. She was concerned for the spiritual and physical needs of people, and was dedicated to improving mind and body. Her monastery became a house of learning, a place renowned for art and for beautifully copied manuscripts. A school of art is reputed to have been founded there.

Brigid died at Kildare c. 525.

There are many churches dedicated to Brigid, especially in Wales, showing the strong link between Welsh and Irish Christianity. Brigid is also venerated in Portugal, Flanders and Alsace, and is the patron saint of Sweden.

Brigid and the wolf

Generosity/fair play/consideration for others

One day Brigid was busy in the dairy, churning milk to make butter, when her mother came in and said, 'There's bad news today. Someone has accidentally killed the king's pet wolf. There's a dreadful to-do about it.'

'What happened?' asked Brigid.

'A woodman was working in the king's forest, cutting down trees as he always does, when one fell the wrong way and caught the king's pet wolf as it was walking by. The wolf was killed outright.'

'That's awful,' said Brigid. 'The poor wolf.'

'Never mind the poor wolf!' said her mother. 'You should be saying "the poor woodman". The king has thrown the man in prison for what he has done.'

'But it wasn't the woodman's fault,' said Brigid, indignantly. 'Surely the king can't blame him.'

'The king says the woodman was responsible,' said her mother. 'The king says it's his fault.'

'Well I don't think it's fair,' cried Brigid, and before her mother could stop her, Brigid ran out of the dairy, and into the yard to fetch her father's horse and cart. 'I'm going to see the king,' she called, as she climbed into the cart.

'You can't …' shouted her mother. But she was too late. Brigid had already set off.

The way to the palace took Brigid through the forest, and there, between the trees Brigid saw something slinking, skulking, waiting to see who would pass by. The something had beady black eyes and a tangled brown coat. It had sharp pointed ears that swivelled and turned at every sound. The something was padding now softly towards Brigid's cart. The something was a wild brown wolf.

'Come and ride with me,' Brigid called to the wolf. 'I'm going to see the king.'

The wolf jumped up into the cart and sat next to Brigid, looking for all the world like a tame dog instead of the fierce wild wolf that he was. As Brigid drove into the palace grounds, the guards sprang forward to stop her entering, but when they saw the wild wolf they stepped back and allowed her through.

Brigid walked into palace and asked to see the king. The wolf walked quietly by her side. She was shown into the king's library.

'I have brought you this wolf to replace the one that was killed,' said Brigid.

The king laughed loudly. 'You silly girl,' he said. 'My pet wolf can never be replaced. It was a special animal. It could do tricks.'

'Well this wolf can do tricks too,' she answered. 'Go on wolf, do a trick for the king.'

The animal looked at Brigid but stood still. He knew no tricks. He didn't know what to do.

'Come on,' said Brigid. 'Dance with me.' She held out her hands and the wild brown wolf stood on his hind legs and held her hands with his paws. Together Brigid and the wolf danced all round the king's library.

'You're right,' said the king. 'He can do tricks. I suppose you want me to buy him, don't you. I suppose that's why you've brought him here. All right then. What do you want for him?'

'I don't want any money,' said Brigid. 'I want you to set free the woodman who accidentally killed your pet wolf this morning.'

'You're a very brave and generous girl,' said the king, 'coming here to speak on behalf of that man without wanting anything in return. And since you've been generous, I will be generous too. The man can go free, and you can keep your wolf. I won't take it from you.'

'Thank you,' said Brigid to the king, and she turned round and went home again, taking her new friend with her.

The Presentation of Christ in the Temple, The Purification of the Blessed Virgin Mary, or Candlemas Day
2 February

It was the custom in Biblical times for the parents of a Jewish baby boy to take him to the temple in Jerusalem, 40 days after his birth, to 'present' him to God and to offer their thanks for his safe delivery. At the same time there was a service of purification – or blessing – for the child's mother, hence the first two names for this festival.

When Mary and Joseph took Jesus to the temple, they met Anna and Simeon. Simeon, on seeing Jesus, realised that here was the Messiah who would be 'a light to lighten the Gentiles'. Christians often speak of Jesus as the 'Light of the World' and candles are lit in churches as a reminder of this. Thus we have the popular name of Candlemas for this festival.

On Candlemas Day (the festival day of the candles), the candles to be used during the forthcoming year are often brought into church and blessed.

At one time popular custom held that the Christmas season lasted forty days and ended on Candlemas Day. An old country belief is that Candlemas Day will decide the weather for the remainder of the winter:

> *'If Candlemas Day be fair and bright*
> *Winter will take another flight.*
> *If Candlemas Day be cloud and rain*
> *Winter is gone and won't come again.'*

Jesus is taken to the temple
adapted from Luke 2:22–38

It was 40 days after Jesus' birth, and the time for Mary and Joseph to take him
to the temple to be presented to God. It was the custom in those days for all new
baby boys to be taken to the temple and 'shown' to God, and for their mothers
to be blessed.

Mary and Joseph set off for Jerusalem.

When they got there, it was early afternoon, a quiet time of day with not many
people about. Mary was pleased that the temple was not crowded and noisy. She
had hoped it would be quiet and still so that she could think and pray peacefully.
She saw two people as she walked into the building; one was an old woman
called Anna, and the other an old man named Simeon. Both Anna and Simeon
were good, kind people, holy people, who spent their days helping in the temple
and praying to God.

When Simeon saw Mary, Joseph and the baby, he looked at them and then
walked towards them.

'He's a lovely baby,' said Simeon.

Mary smiled. She knew that all babies are lovely to their mothers.

'May I hold him?' asked Simeon.

Mary smiled again and carefully handed the baby to the old man. Simeon held
Jesus in his arms and said, 'This is a very special baby. God promised me that
one day before I die, I would see the special baby he had sent for the world. And
here he is.'

'This baby is chosen by God to save the people of the world. This boy will
grow up to be a light to lighten the world. This child will show us the way to live.'

Mary and Joseph were astonished to hear what Simeon said. They knew that
Jesus was a special baby and that he was sent from God, but they were only just
beginning to realise how special.

Simeon handed the child back to Mary.

'I think there will be some sad times ahead for you,' he said. 'But sorrow as
well as joy is part of God's plan for his people. And now I must go and say thank
you to God for letting me see the world's special baby before I die. Bless you,'
he said to Mary and Joseph, 'I cannot tell you both how pleased I am to have
seen you and your baby.' And Simeon went away to pray.

Mary and Joseph looked at each other, and again were surprised at what had
been said.

When they had finished their prayers in the temple, Mary, Joseph and Jesus
went back to their home in Nazareth, and there Jesus grew up from a baby, into
a fine strong boy.

Saint Blaise

3 February

Little is known about Blaise, but he is said to have been Bishop of Sebastea in Armenia, born of wealthy Christian parents. Legend has it that when the Governor of Armenia began persecuting the Christians, Blaise hid in a cave where he established a rapport with wild animals. It is thought that the Emperor Licinius ordered his execution c. 316, however there is no known cult until after the eighth century.

Blaise is the patron saint of wool combers.

Saint Blaise and the animals   *Caring/friendship/generosity/sharing*

Blaise was in danger. He lived in the town of Sebastea, in Armenia, at the time when the Governor of Armenia was trying to get rid of all the Christians. And Blaise was a Christian.

He had already left his own house and had gone to stay with a non-Christian friend, but Blaise knew he was putting his friend's life in danger by staying there.

'I'll go and hide in the caves,' he said. 'There are caves up in the mountains. I'll shelter there until it's safe to come back to the town.'

'But you can't live in a cave,' said his friend. 'What about the freezing cold nights? What about the wild animals? You can't live in a cave.'

'I can't live here,' said Blaise. 'So I must go.'

It was grey and bleak in the mountains. The cave Blaise found was dark, damp and bitterly cold. He could hear wild dogs barking at night, and rats and wild pigs scratching, scrabbling amongst the stones by the cave mouth.

But Blaise was not afraid of the animals, only of the men who might come and find him. During the day he sat at the mouth of his cave, watching, listening, thinking, praying. Sometimes his friend would struggle up the mountainside with food for him, but mostly he was alone except for the animals.

They became used to his being there. Used to this man living in their midst, on their mountain, in their territory. They learned that he was not going to harm them, or hunt them, or eat them. They learned that he was gentle with animals, that he liked animals and cared for them. They learned that he could help them.

One day Blaise removed a thorn from the paw of a great brown bear. Another time he bathed the swollen ear of a wild cat. And once he cleaned the paw of a large black rat when it got trapped between two boulders. A buzzard with a broken wing lived for a time in Blaise's cave, until its wing was strong enough for flight again.

In return for this care, the animals brought him food – some choice berries, some ripe fruits, a few hazel nuts.

Blaise and the animals developed a partnership, a friendship, based on trust and respect. Often the animals would sit at the mouth of his cave and Blaise would sing to them, or talk to them, knowing they could not understand the words, but knowing that they knew he cared for them.

Blaise was singing to the animals the day that the hunters found him.

They came crashing through the bushes and scrub near the mouth of Blaise's cave. They had heard there was a Christian hiding in the mountains, but did not expect to find him. They did expect to find wild animals, plenty of them, that they could capture and take back to the amphitheatre for the amusement of the Romans.

When the three hunters found Blaise sitting in front of a crowd of wild animals, talking to them, they decided he must be some sort of magician. Why else would the animals not attack him, savage him, eat him? And the hunters knew full well what the emperor would do with a magician. Kill him.

The men grabbed Blaise and dragged him down the mountainside. When they got to the road, they tied his hands behind him and pushed him along from behind. Blaise stumbled and fell, but the men shoved him back on his feet.

Just then a woman came running out of a house, shouting and crying. 'He's got my piglet. Look he's stolen it out of the pigsty.'

The hunters and Blaise stopped, and saw a great grey wolf running along the fields at the back of the woman's house, her piglet gripped in its jaws.

'Stop!' called Blaise to the wolf.

The hunters sniggered, but then they stared in astonishment as the wolf stood still and turned to look at Blaise.

'Leave it be,' said Blaise to the wolf. 'Drop it. Put the piglet down.' To the hunters' amazement the wolf gently dropped the piglet on the ground, then slunk away to the hills.

'He is a magician,' they said.

'No,' said Blaise. 'Just a Christian who cares about animals as well as people.'

The hunters ignored this and pushed Blaise along the road again. The woman ran to pick up her piglet and take it back to the pen.

In the city of Sebastea, the hunters explained to the Roman prefect what they had seen, both at the cave and on the road.

'He must die,' said the prefect. 'He's a Christian. A Christian who can speak to animals. We'll show him how we treat animals. Throw him in a pit and leave him to starve to death.'

The hunters did as they were told. Blaise was put into a deep pit and left there to die. But, unknown to the Romans, the woman whose pig Blaise had saved came to help him.

'I'll bring you food,' she said. 'You're a good man, you don't deserve to die.'

Each night the woman brought food. Each day the Roman prefect checked to see whether Blaise was dead. It should not take him long to die. A man could not live for long without food or water.

After a week Blaise was still alive. After two weeks the prefect became angry. After three weeks he said, 'This man must be a magician. No-one can stay alive this long without food and water. Kill him.'

And so Blaise was brought out of the pit and killed; because he was a Christian, because he was kind to animals, and because a woman had helped him when he had helped her.

Shrove Tuesday

3 February (if Easter Day is at its earliest of 21 March)
to
9 March (if Easter Day is at its latest of 25 April)

Shrove Tuesday, being linked to Easter, is a moveable feast. It is a carnival day, a time for enjoyment before the solemn period of Lent begins. The name comes from the medieval word 'to shrive' – to confess one's sins and be forgiven, and is the day on which people submitted themselves to the priests for this purpose.

All over the world, Shrove Tuesday or Mardi Gras (fat Tuesday) is celebrated as a carnival. It literally means 'farewell to meat' and marks the beginning of Lent and its 40 days of abstinence from luxury foods, such as meat and dairy produce. All foods which would not keep for the duration of Lent were eaten up on this day.

Many customs have evolved surrounding Shrove Tuesday. In Venice, the 'Carnevale' lasts for almost a week. In Trinidad, planning for the next carnival starts as the last one ends. In Rio de Janeiro the carnival processions – probably the biggest in the world – last for three days. In the north of England, Collop Monday and Pancake Tuesday serve the same purpose of using up fat, eggs and milk.

At midnight on Shrove Tuesday the festivities end, and the first day of Lent, Ash Wednesday, begins.

The pancake bell

'Pancake Day is a very happy day;
If we don't have a holiday we'll all run away!'

Those were the words of a rhyme sung by children in the north of England a hundred years ago. On Pancake Day, children and apprentices – young people who were learning a trade, learning to be carpenters or cooks or blacksmiths or dressmakers, would all have a half-day holiday. And the church bell told them when the holiday could begin.

But the church bell told other people when it was time to do things, too.

The church bell in the village of Barcroft was always rung at 11 o'clock in the morning on Shrove Tuesday. It was a single bell, a monotonous bell, a tolling on … and on … on the same … note … sort of bell.

When the bell started ringing, the Vicar of Barcroft said, 'There! They'll soon be here.' And he went into the church to wait for his people to come and see him. They always came on Shrove Tuesday. They came to say sorry to God for all the wrong things they had done during the past year. The vicar was able to help them by saying that God forgave them. The people would then go away feeling happier, and everyone would be able to enjoy the rest of the day.

At 11 o'clock, when the bell started ringing, the housewives of Barcroft, and the cook in the big house on the hill said, 'Ah, Eleven o'clock! Time to make the batter for the pancakes.' They got out milk and flour, eggs and salt, and they stirred and beat and whisked and mixed the batter so that it would be ready for the pancakes at twelve o'clock. Everyone in Barcroft had pancakes for dinner on Shrove Tuesday, and everyone had dinner at twelve so that they could go out and enjoy the fun in the afternoon.

When the children in school heard the church bell ring at 11 o'clock, they wriggled and squirmed and twisted and turned in their hard wooden seats. 'Soon it will be time to go,' they whispered. 'She'll let us out soon,' they nodded, waiting for the word from their teacher that said they could go and start their half-day holiday. The sooner the better today, pancakes for dinner then fun in the afternoon with everyone from the village. They just could not wait.

The apprentices heard the church bell at eleven, and they did not wait to be told they could go. They stuffed their tools into bags, their aprons and overalls on to pegs and dashed outside. A half-day holiday, pancakes for dinner and the football match this afternoon. Life could not be better than on pancake day. 'See you later,' they shouted to each other as they ran home. 'See you at the match.'

The match was like no other football match in the whole year. Everyone turned out for it. And everyone could join in if they wanted to. There was no limit to the number of players on each side. The goals were three miles apart, and there were no rules. The whole village remembered that last year the winning team had tipped the whole of the losing team in the river in the middle of the game. That was the way they had won. But everyone took it in good fun. Everyone was a good sport. No-one complained. After all, it was Shrove Tuesday!

The eleven o'clock bell tolled on and on. The Shrove Tuesday bell, the pancake bell, the half-day holiday bell. The same bell, but reminding different people of different things; but all of them to do with the special time of Shrove Tuesday, the fun day before the start of Lent.

Ash Wednesday

4 February (if Easter Day is at its earliest of 21 March)
to
10 March (if Easter Day is at its latest of 25 April)

Ash Wednesday marks the first day of Lent – the solemn 40 day period before Easter (the period excludes Sundays), commemorating Christ's 40 days in the wilderness. Christ's 40 day fast took place when he was about 30, immediately before he began his work of teaching and healing. The word Lent comes from the Anglo-Saxon 'lenctendid' meaning the lengthening of the springtime days.

Lent, while not a fast proper, was a time when meat, eggs and dairy produce were not eaten, hence the reason for 'eating up' on the eve of the start of Lent. Nowadays, many Christians give up some food or activity during Lent as a way of disciplining their minds, and in memory of Christ's fast.

Ash Wednesday became so named when priests sprinkled ashes on the heads of penitents wearing sackcloth. Later, priests made the sign of the cross on the foreheads of the repentant, using ashes from the palm crosses kept from the previous year's Palm Sunday.

Jesus is tempted in the wilderness

Jesus knew that it was now time to begin the work that God had sent him to do; the work of teaching people and healing them, the work of showing people the true way to live, the work of telling people to love each other and care for each other. Jesus knew that the work would be hard. He knew that people would not always want to hear what he had to say. He knew he would have to be strong to do the work God wanted him to do.

'I need time to be alone before I start my work,' he said to himself. 'I need time to think. Time to pray. Time to be still and quiet.'

Jesus went away by himself into the desert – a wild and desolate place, a wilderness – so that he could be quite alone, where there would be nothing to distract or disturb him.

He stayed in the desert for forty days and forty nights, and during that time he ate nothing. He slept on the bare ground using a stone for a pillow. The days were long and hot, and the nights were cold and dark and frightening. Jesus could hear wild animals crying and howling in the distance.

Towards the end of his forty day stay in the wilderness, Jesus was very tired and very hungry. And that is when the devil came to see him.

'Tired, eh?' said the devil. 'And hungry too, I bet. Then why don't you do something about it? You say you are the Son of God? Then prove it! Show me that it's true. Turn those stones over there into loaves of bread. Go on. Do it.'

'I am hungry,' said Jesus. 'But life's not just about eating. It's about doing what you know is right. I know it's right for me just now to have no food. So no, I'll not turn those stones into bread.'

'Then let me show you something else,' said the devil. 'Come with me.'

He took Jesus to the very top of the great temple in Jerusalem.

'Look down there,' said the devil. Jesus looked. It was a long, long way down to the ground.

'Now, jump off!' said the devil. 'If you really are the Son of God, like you say, then God will save you. Just think how impressed all the people will be when they see that God has saved your life. You'll be a hero.'

'No,' said Jesus. 'I don't need to test the power of God. Now go away.'

But the devil would not leave Jesus alone. He was determined to make him give in to him. He tried again, for the third time, to make Jesus give in to temptation.

'Look at that,' said the devil, and he made Jesus look at all the countries of the world, all spread out below them like a map. 'You could be the ruler of all those countries, all those kingdoms. I'll give them all to you. All you have to do is kneel down and worship me. That's all.'

'Go away,' said Jesus. 'I want nothiing to do with you. The only one I will worship is God. I will not listen to you, and I certainly will not worship you. Go away and leave me in peace.'

At last the devil knew that it was useless to try and tempt Jesus. Jesus was too strong. He could say no to the things he knew werc wrong. He would not agree to do something he knew was wrong, just because someone else told him to.

The devil went away and left Jesus alone, just as he had asked him to. Later, Jesus left the wilderness, feeling ready to start God's work.

Caedmon

11 February

The only information we have of Caedmon is from Bede. Caedmon was a herdsman of Whitby who suddenly discovered he had a gift of singing and poetry. He became a monk under the Abbess Hilda at Whitby, and devoted much time to composing songs based on the books of Genesis and Exodus. Although virtually none of his work has survived, he has become known as the first English ecclesiastical poet. It is believed he died c. 680.

Caedmon's song   *Doing your best/humility*

Caedmon lived in the monastery at Whitby. He was not a monk, but a herdsman – a worker who looked after the farm animals while the monks were busy at their prayers, and their books, and their study.

Every evening, when the jobs were done, the workers would gather together in the big hall of the monastery to eat their supper, and after supper they would sing or talk, or tell and listen to stories.

Caedmon liked to listen when someone was telling a story, but he did not like it when people wanted to sing. On those evenings someone would take a harp down from the wall and it was passed from one person to another. Each person in turn had to sing a song. Usually it was a song that everyone knew, but sometimes someone would make up a new song and everyone would listen to it.

Caedmon could not sing. He felt embarrassment and shame when the harp was passed to him, so on the evenings when singing was chosen, he used to creep away to the cowshed, to hide, so that he would not have to join in.

'There he goes,' his friends would say. 'Poor old Caedmon, can't sing a note,' and they would laugh as Caedmon disappeared out of the hall.

One night when Caedmon was hiding in the cowshed, he heard a voice.

'Caedmon? Sing to me.'

Caedmon looked around but could see no-one. He thought it was someone playing a joke, then he heard the voice again.

'Sing to me, Caedmon.'

'I can't sing,' stammered Caedmon.

'Sing to me,' said the voice again, gently.

'But what shall I sing?' asked Caedmon. 'I don't know any songs.'

'Make one up,' said the voice. 'Make up a song about the beginning of time, the beginning of the world, the creation. Go on. Sing.'

Caedmon thought of the story he had heard the monks tell, of how God made the world and everything in it. He began to sing, hesitantly at first, then stronger, braver.

The words seemed to come easily to him and were as beautiful as poetry. The tune fitted the words perfectly, smoothly, beautifully. When Caedmon had finished his song, he sighed happily, lay down in the straw of the cowshed and fell asleep.

In the morning when he woke, Caedmon could remember quite clearly the words and the tune and the song he had sung.

'But it must have been a dream,' he thought, 'for I know I can't sing.' Nevertheless, Caedmon tried out his voice and discovered again the wonderful song of the night before.

Just then the foreman came into the cowshed.

'Who was that singing?' he asked.

'It was me,' admitted Caedmon.

'You?' said the foreman. 'But you can't sing.'

'I know,' said Caedmon. 'But something happened to me last night,' and he told the foreman about the voice he had heard and the song he had sung.

'Come with me,' said the foreman. 'We must go and tell Abbess Hilda about this.'

Hilda listened to what they had to say. Then she listened to Caedmon's song.

'It's beautiful,' she said. 'It's a gift from God.'

Then she asked Caedmon if he would like to come and live inside the monastery with the monks.

'You can spend your time composing songs, instead of looking after the animals,' she said.

'But I can't read or write,' said Caedmon.

'That doesn't matter,' answered Hilda. 'We'll find a way round that.'

And find a way they did. The monks would tell Caedmon one of the stories from the Bible and he would go away to think about it. He would turn the words around in his head and play with tunes in his mind. Then he would return to the monks with the story changed into the most beautiful poetry, which the monks would then write down.

Caedmon lived in the monastery at Whitby for many years, composing wonderful poetry and songs in praise of God, but he never grew conceited or big-headed about his gift for words and music.

Saint Valentine

14 February

Valentine is believed to have been a third-century martyr, although there is some confusion as to his identity. There are two Valentines listed in the Roman martyrology on 14 February – one a priest and the other a bishop, but it seems likely that they were in fact the same person.

Despite the lack of evidence regarding Saint Valentine, and the fact that there appears to be no English church dedicated to him, his feast day is noted in most calendars.

The idea of sending 'Valentines' on 14 February may have arisen from an old belief that birds were supposed to pair on that date, or be a surviving remnant of the Roman Luperculia festival held in mid-February

Valentine is the patron saint of beekeepers, engaged couples and the young.

Saint Valentine and the Roman emperor

Consideration for others/caring/kindness/ standing up for what you believe to be right

The Roman army, nearly 2000 years ago, was very strong. It was led by an emperor called Claudius, who was determined that the Roman army should be the best army there had ever been. No sooner had Claudius defeated one country than he led the soldiers into battle in another, then another and another.

The Roman army won all its battles, except one. No matter how hard the Roman soldiers fought, they could not defeat the Goths who lived to the north of the Roman Empire, and the fact that the Roman army was beaten by the Goths made Emperor Claudius extremely angry.

'I will *not* have my army beaten by the Goths,' he shouted. 'The soldiers must fight harder. From now on no soldiers are to be allowed time off to visit their families. I will cancel all leave. In the next battle every soldier must be there.'

'But sir,' said one of the officers, 'the soldiers need time off to visit their families. They will be unhappy if you stop them seeing their wives and children.'

'Wives and children!' bellowed Emperor Claudius. 'Soldiers shouldn't have wives and children. They should concentrate on fighting, not families.'

'But sir,' said the officer again, 'many of the soldiers do have families. It is only right that they should be allowed time off from fighting to go and see them.'

'No!' said Emperor Claudius. 'I shall make a new law as from tomorrow. No soldier shall have time off to go home. And furthermore, in future no soldier will be allowed to get married. We shall have a whole army of soldiers without wives and families, and then they won't want time off to go home.'

And so it was that the new law was passed. All leave was cancelled, and no more soldiers were allowed to marry.

The priests and bishops were told of the new law, but one of them refused to take any notice of it. His name was Bishop Valentine.

'It's a stupid law,' he said. 'Everyone should have the right to get married and have a family if they want to. And that should include soldiers too. I am not going to obey the new law. Soldiers can come to me to be married, and I will marry them secretly. Emperor Claudius will know nothing about it.'

Word quickly spread amongst the soldiers that they could go to Bishop Valentine if they wanted to be married. Many soldiers took their girlfriends to see the bishop, and they were married in secret. But word also reached Emperor Claudius that there was a bishop who had disobeyed the law.

'Find this Bishop Valentine,' he said to the guards. 'Bring him here.'

The guards brought him to Claudius.

'You must obey the law,' said Claudius.

'I will not,' said Valentine. 'I believe that men and women have the right to get married if they want to. I believe that this is what God wants, and that they should be married with his blessing. I do not believe that you should treat soldiers differently from any other people.'

'Then if you will not obey my law, you shall be killed,' said Claudius.

Bishop Valentine was arrested and taken to prison. He was put in a cold dark cell and was allowed no visitors and very little food. But the daughter of the prison guard, who could come and go without anyone taking any notice of her, felt sorry for Bishop Valentine, and secretly visited him in his cell every evening. Some days she brought him extra food, other days she brought him fresh water, or a bundle of clean, dry straw to spread on the floor for his bed. One day she brought a bunch of wild flowers, and on another day a pretty, blue pebble she found on the road.

On the day she took him a bunch of dried grasses tied with a green ribbon, she found the cell empty. Valentine had gone. There was no sign that he had ever been there except for a scrap of paper pushed into the bars of the cell. The girl carefully pulled out the paper and smoothed it. The message on the paper was not signed, but it read 'Thank you for bringing me joy. Thank you for helping me and making me happy.' The girl knew then that Claudius had carried out his threat, and that Bishop Valentine was dead.

The girl went to find her father to see if what she believed was true.

'He disobeyed the law,' said the prison guard. 'Claudius has the right to kill anyone who does not obey him.'

The girl felt sad that Bishop Valentine had been killed for believing that people should be allowed to marry if they wanted to; for wanting people to be happy together. She kept Valentine's unsigned note, in memory of him, for the rest of her life.

Saint David

1 March

David was born in Cardigan c. 520. Legend has it that he was the son of Sant – a Cardigan chieftain, and Saint Non, and that he was educated by St Paulinus.

David is believed to have founded some twelve monasteries, amongst which are Glastonbury and Menevia, where the community led a harshly disciplined life. Food was strictly basic and comprised of only bread and vegetables, and the men worked the land using no animal help.

It is believed that David was elected Primate of Wales at the Council of Brefi, Cardigan, c 550. David apparently lived to an old age and died at his monastery in Menevia, c. 589. He is the patron saint of Wales.

David and the robber

Perseverence/patience/forgiveness/friendship/
standing up for what you believe to be right/tolerance

David had been at the monastery for quite a long time when he decided that he would like to build a monastery of his own. He had always wanted to be a monk, even from being a very small boy, and during his years in the monastery he had worked hard and studied well, and made sure that he learned everything the older, wiser monks could teach him.

But now it was time to move on. Now it was time to accept a new challenge, to do something new, to start a monastery of his own so that he could tell even more people about God and his Son Jesus who had come to save the world.

David went to see the abbot – the monk in charge of the monastery.

'I have been very happy here, working with you and the other monks,' said David. 'But now I feel the time has come for me to build a monastery of my own. I know it will be hard work. I know it will take a long time. I know it will take so long that I might even die before the new monastery is finished, but it is something I feel I must try to do. I feel it is God's work that I should do this.'

'Then you must do it,' said the abbot. 'You must build your new monastery. I wish you every success in your venture.'

So arrangements were made for David to have a piece of land. It was in a beautiful green valley quite near to where David had lived as a child. And arrangements were made for David to have people to help him with the building; monks who were happy to work for nothing, for none of them received any payment for building the new monastery. They did it to serve God.

The work was hard. The men had only bread and vegetables to eat. They had only water to drink. But no-one complained. No-one grumbled. They all knew they were building the new monastery to the glory of God.

At first the work went well. The men cleared the ground ready for the foundations of the building. They cut down trees and trimmed the trunks and branches. They stacked the logs ready for use in the monastery's roof and walls. They uprooted the tree stumps using their bare hands, and began to move the stones and boulders that were embedded in the ground. They did all the work themselves. They had no machinery to help them and no animals to pull the loads. They worked hard during every minute of daylight, then ate and slept when it was dark.

But someone else stayed awake during the hours of darkness. Someone else watched the work that the monks were doing, and felt angry.

His name was Gruffydd, and he was a robber.

'I can't have monks coming to live in my valley,' he said to his gang. 'I can't have good people living here. How can I be a robber with good people as my neighbours?'

'Then get rid of them!' said one of the gang.

'Yes!' said Gruffydd. 'I will.'

So the robbers planned to sabotage the work of the monks. Every night when the monks were asleep the robbers undid all the work of that day. They scattered the logs that the monks had stacked, and rolled back the rocks and boulders that the monks had pulled out of the ground. They filled in the foundations with soil and knocked down the walls that had been built.

Every day the monks redid the work … and every night the robbers destroyed it.

'What shall we do?' the monks asked David when this had been going on some weeks. 'Shall we do something to them to get our own back?'

'No,' said David. 'We just work harder during the day. That's all.'

So they did. They patiently worked harder. Luckily the days were lengthening as summer approached, so the monks were able to work longer as well as harder. But it was not easy. The monks were exhausted by the end of each day.

Gruffydd realised that getting the monks to leave the valley was not going to be as easy as he had thought.

'Still,' he said to the others, 'they'll not keep on building when they see that we are going to destroy their work every night.

But Gruffydd was wrong. No matter what he and the robbers did to David and the monks, they never gave up. They did not look for revenge, they did not pack up and leave. They simply carried on working hard and doing their best, in the knowledge that what they were doing was right and was for God. And slowly, surely, the monastery was taking shape. Each day David and the monks were doing more work than the robbers could undo each night.

Gruffydd knew now that the monks would never leave the valley. He went to see David.

'All right!' he said. 'You win. You won't leave the valley, so I suppose I'll have to. I've just come to say you can live here in peace. I'm leaving tomorrow.'

Gruffydd expected David to be pleased to hear this news. He expected that David would angrily tell him to go; that he had caused trouble enough, that he would be glad to see the back of him and the rest of the robbers.

But no. David welcomed Gruffydd to the monastery and showed him round as though he had never seen it before. He explained what the monks were doing and why they were doing it. He talked a little to Gruffydd about God's love and forgiveness, and Gruffydd listened.

'You need not leave the valley,' said David. 'We could live in the same place together, you and I, your men and mine. We don't have to be enemies, we could be friends. We could even work together, instead of against each other.'

'We could?' said Gruffydd. Then, 'We could!' he added.

Gruffydd gave up his life of robbing and stealing and went to work at the monastery with David and his men, and discovered to his amazement that he was far happier than he had ever been before.

Saint Chad

2 March

Chad (Caedda) was born in Northumbria c. 620, and for a time was a pupil of Saint Aidan at Lindisfarne. He succeeded his brother Cedd as Abbot of Lastingham, Yorkshire, then was called to be Bishop of York. However, in 669 Chad's consecration was judged to be irregular by Theodore, Archbishop of Canterbury, and Chad retired to Lastingham, only to be reconsecrated as first Bishop of Mercia by Theodore, who was impressed by Chad's character.

Chad lived only three years as Bishop of Mercia, but during that time established two monasteries – one near Lichfield Cathedral and the other at Barrow upon Humber, for which he was given land by Wulfhere, King of Mercia.

Chad died at Lichfield in 672 and, according to Bede, was venerated as a saint immediately.

Chad and the King of Mercia

Humility/doing your best/ obedience/kindness

King Wulfhere of Mercia had two sons, one called Wulfade and the other called Rufini. King Wulfhere did not believe in God, and did not see why anyone else in his kingdom should do so.

'All this talk about God and Jesus is utter nonsense,' he used to say. 'I won't hear of it.'

In the nearby kingdom of Northumbria was a man who did believe in God. His name was Chad and he was Bishop of York. Chad was a good man, kind and gentle and caring.

One day, Saint Chad was sitting quietly beside a beautiful pool in the middle of a forest when a red deer came stumbling through the trees. It was obviously being hunted and was running in fear away from whatever was chasing it. The animal had plunged through the undergrowth in panic and its front legs were now cut and bleeding. It blundered past Chad, tripped on a tree root and fell into the pool. It was by now so afraid and in such panic that it was unable to get up, but thrashed about in the shallow water.

Chad moved quietly towards it. He spoke softly, gently, reassuring the deer that he would not hurt it. The deer became still, quiet, calm, and Chad led it out of the water on to the grass, where he stood, stroking its velvet head.

Suddenly a man came crashing through the trees. The deer flinched and moved closer to Chad. The man stopped and looked, and Chad recognised him as Prince Wulfade of Mercia, visiting York on a hunting trip.

'There it is,' said Wulfade. 'That deer's led me a merry dance. It wouldn't let me anywhere near it. How come it lets you stroke its head?'

'Perhaps it knows that I won't hurt it,' answered Chad.

'Rubbish,' said Wulfade. 'It can't tell whether a man is going to hurt it or not!' But even as he spoke, Wulfade knew that was not true. Wulfade knew that the deer could tell that this quiet man would not harm it. There was something gentle, something trusting, something kind about this man.

Wulfade sat down and began to talk to Chad. He asked him who he was and what he was doing by the pool. Chad told him he liked to sit there because it was a quiet and beautiful place, a good place to go to pray to God.

'God?' said Wulfade. 'Tell me about your God.'

So Saint Chad told Wulfade about God and about Jesus, the Son of God. Wulfade listened thoughtfully. When Chad had finished speaking, Wulfade said he would like to become a Christian, too.

'Go and think about it,' said Chad. 'Then if you want to be baptised, come and see me again.'

Wulfade left then and went to tell Rufini, his brother, what had happened at the pool. He told him about Chad and the deer. Rufini looked up as Wulfade was speaking, and there, standing near, was the red deer. Rufini followed it, and it led him back to the pool, back to where Chad was waiting.

Rufini walked up to Chad. 'Tell me about God,' he said. Chad told him what he had told Wulfade. He told him about God and about Jesus, the Son of God. Rufini listened thoughtfully. Then Rufini said that he, too, wanted to become a Christian.

'Think about it carefully,' said Chad. 'Then if you and your brother want to be baptised, come and see me again.'

When the king heard that his two sons were about to become Christians, he was enraged. He flew into a violent temper and attacked Wulfade and Rufini. He badly hurt both his sons. Then, like most people who have lost their temper, he bitterly regretted what he had done. He went to find Saint Chad and he, too, was led to him by the red deer.

'I am so sorry for what I have done,' said King Wulfhere. 'I cannot tell you how sorry I am.'

'It is not me you need to apologise to,' said Saint Chad. 'You need to say you are sorry to your sons, and you need to say sorry to God.'

'Tell me about God,' said King Wulfhere. Saint Chad spent a long time talking to the king. At the end of the conversation, King Wulfhere wanted to be baptised a Christian.

'You have taught me a great deal,' he said to Chad. 'You are a good man. You are kind and gentle. You have helped me and my sons to see that there is a better way of life than the one we lead. We have a great deal to thank you for. Perhaps one day I will be able to repay you.'

Surprisingly, that day came sooner than either King Wulfhere or Chad expected.

Not long after the incident with the deer, Theodore, the Archbishop of

Canterbury, came to visit York. He met Chad and told him he could no longer be the Bishop of York. Theodore said that the people who had asked Chad to be bishop had no right to do so.

'I am sorry,' said Theodore. 'You must leave here. You cannot be bishop here any longer.'

Chad was disappointed and upset, but he did not argue. He did not grumble or complain. He knew he must do as he was told, so he began to pack his things ready to leave.

Theodore noticed how obedient Chad was. He saw that he was ready to do as he was told without arguing or questioning. He saw how disappointed the people were that Chad had to leave. He heard how much everyone liked Chad, how they liked his qualities of kindness and gentleness. He could see for himself how much good Chad had done in York since he had been working there. Then Theodore heard from King Wulfhere about how he had helped the royal family to understand God.

'Please let him stay,' said King Wulfhere. 'Please let him continue his work as bishop.'

'I cannot do that,' said Theodore. 'But I will make him bishop in your kingdom. I will make him Bishop of Mercia.'

So it was that Chad went to be the first bishop of the kingdom of Mercia. King Wulfhere gave him a large piece of land on which to build a cathedral and a monastery, and Chad continued his work as a bishop, always treating his people in a kind, gentle, caring way.

Mothering Sunday

4th Sunday in Lent

28 February (if Easter is at its earliest of 21 March)
to
4 April (if Easter is at its latest of 25 April)

Mothering Sunday is always the fourth Sunday in Lent, the third Sunday before Easter. It is also known as Mid-Lent Sunday, Refreshment Sunday and 'Laetare' Sunday, this latter name from the beginning of the Roman Catholic service for this Sunday – 'Rejoice ye (Laetare) with Jerusalem and be glad with her.' 'Rejoice' because the joy of Easter will soon be here, and because the mid-point of Lent has been reached.

Mothering Sunday is a long-established celebration, believed to date from the Middle Ages when people visited their mother church – usually the cathedral of their diocese or the main church of a cluster of parishes – to give thanks for it.

Towards the eighteenth century, well before the days of statutory holidays, it became customary for young people in service and apprentices to be given time off in mid-Lent to visit their mothers. Thus the day became one for giving thanks for earthly mothers, in addition to giving thanks for the mother church.

Many churches nowadays give the children in the congregation a small bunch of flowers to give to their mothers as a thank you for all their care and love throughout the year.

Jesus is lost in the temple

Caring/consideration for others/obedience

adapted from Luke 2:41–52

Every year at the time of the Passover, Mary and Joseph went back to Jerusalem for the Passover Festival.

When Jesus was about 12, all three travelled to Jerusalem for the Passover Festival as usual. Jesus had been looking forward to it. Jerusalem was always busy for the festival, there were always lots of people to talk to, lots of people to meet. Mary and Joseph looked forward to going, too. They met friends there that they saw only in Jerusalem, and only at that time of year. It was a good chance to catch up on all the news, a good opportunity to find out how everyone was. They were all looking forward to the visit.

The festival of the Passover lasted eight days, but in no time at all it seemed to be over; it was time to go home again.

Mary and Joseph were to travel part of the way home with some of their friends and relatives. It was a large group of people, so Mary and Joseph were not really worried at first when they could not find Jesus.

'Where can he be?' asked Mary.

'He'll be all right,' said Joseph. 'Don't worry about him. He'll be up ahead with his friends. You know how they like to get everywhere first. He's enjoyed being with the other boys this week. They've had lots to talk about. Don't worry about him, after all, he's 12 now. He'll be all right.'

'Yes, I suppose so,' said Mary.

Much later in the day, when Jesus still had not been seen by his parents, Mary began to feel concerned.

'He should be here by now,' said Mary. 'Even if he was with his friends earlier, he'd have waited for us to catch up with him by now. Wherever can he be?'

'He won't be far away,' said Joseph. 'Look, I'll ask around all our friends and relatives. Someone will know where he is. He'll be walking along with someone. I'll find him. He'll be all right, you'll see.'

So Joseph walked to the front of the group, asking everyone he passed if they had seen Jesus.

'No. Sorry,' they said. 'We've not seen him since we were in Jerusalem.'

Joseph hurried back along the straggling, moving line of people.

'Have you seen my boy?' he asked everyone.

'No,' they said. 'Sorry. The last time we saw him he was with you in Jerusalem. We haven't seen him since.'

Joseph again hurried among the people, this time running, anxiously looking at each person's face as he passed, and calling to Jesus as he went.

'Jesus? Jesus? Where are you? Come on now, walk with us. We've been worried about you.'

But Jesus didn't reply. He was nowhere to be found, nowhere to be seen.

Joseph went to find Mary again.

'When did you last see him?' he asked.

'This morning, just before we set off. I've not seen him since. Oh Joseph, you don't think he's been left behind? You don't suppose he's still in Jerusalem do you?'

'There's only one way to find out,' said Joseph grimly. 'We'll have to go back and search there.'

So Mary and Joseph left their group of friends and began to walk back to Jerusalem. By the time they got there it was well past midnight and too late to start looking for Jesus, even if they had known where to begin. But early the next morning they began to search. They went to all the places they had been together. No sign of him. They asked everyone who might remember him. Nothing. They walked up and down all the streets, in and out of the courtyards, everywhere they could think of. Nothing.

They spent the whole day looking for Jesus, but with no success. By now Mary and Joseph were so worried they could not eat or sleep or do anything but search frantically for him.

They spent that night and the whole of the next day looking, asking people, searching, but with no luck. They tried to sleep a little on the second night of their search, knowing that if they were exhausted they would not be able to carry on.

Then, on the morning of the third day they found him.

He was in the temple talking to the priests and the teachers. These men were astounded at his knowledge of God, astonished that a boy so young should know so much about God, and be able to talk so intelligently to them about him.

Mary and Joseph were equally surprised to find Jesus in the temple, talking like this to the temple leaders, but his mother rushed up to Jesus and said, 'How could you do this to us? Have you any idea how much worry you have caused us? Do you know that we've been searching for you for three whole days? How could you go off like that, without a word, and just disappear? How could you cause us so much worry? We thought something terrible had happened to you.

We thought you were dead.' Mary burst into tears at the thought of what might have happened; and with anger that Jesus has caused so much trouble; and with relief that he was found again, safe and well.

'I'm sorry,' said Jesus. 'I didn't think you'd be worried. I thought you'd know that I was in my Father's house.'

Mary and Joseph did not understand what Jesus said. They did not understand what he meant, but Mary remembered the incident for the rest of her life.

The three of them said goodbye to the priests and teachers, and left Jerusalem and went home to Nazareth, where Jesus tried to be good and to do what Mary and Joseph told him, so that he did not cause them any more worry or sadness.

Saint Patrick

17 March

Patrick was born c. 385 on the western coast of Scotland. He was carried off by raiders when he was 16 and taken to Ireland as a slave where he was made to care for herds of farm animals. He escaped to France, and it is believed that he trained for the priesthood in Auxerre. He returned to Ireland as a missionary bishop, possibly in 432, believing that God had called him to this work.

Patrick was not the first Christian in Ireland, but it was he who established the organised church and who was responsible for the widespread knowledge of Christ. He died c. 461 in County Down and is the patron saint of Ireland.

Saint Patrick   *Trust/standing up for what you believe*
and the Christian fire   *to be right*

When Patrick was a boy he lived in Scotland with his parents on a farm near the sea. He had a happy childhood, but when he was 16 years old he was kidnapped.

Pirates landed near Patrick's home. They stole cattle, took prisoners and killed anyone who tried to stop them. They kidnapped Patrick, carried him off to Ireland in their ship and sold him as a slave. They made him look after a herd of pigs, and gave him a pigsty to live in and pigswill to eat.

Patrick hated his job. He hated the people who had taken him away from his family and friends and he became very unhappy, but Patrick had been brought up a Christian and to believe that God cared for everyone. Patrick prayed that God would care for him and find a way of letting him go back home.

One night Patrick managed to escape. He found his way to the coast and saw a huge ship in the harbour. He was sure the ship was going to Scotland, and he persuaded the captain to let him travel on it.

The ship did not go to Scotland. It took him, instead, to France.

'I can't stay here,' said Patrick. 'When will there be a ship to take me to Scotland?'

'Not for several weeks,' said the captain.

Patrick went to a nearby monastery to ask if he could stay there until a ship bound for Scotland came into harbour.

'You can stay,' said the abbot. 'You can use the time to think.' Patrick thought it was a strange thing for the abbot to say, but he found that the peace and quiet of the monastery did help him to think clearly. The more he thought, the more he knew he should stay in France and become a priest.

Patrick worked hard and decided that when he became a priest he would go back to Scotland. But a voice seemed to say to him 'Go to Ireland. The people there need you. They need you to tell them about God.'

'No!' shouted Patrick, remembering how unhappy he had been in Ireland. 'I will not go back there.'

But the feeling that he should return to Ireland stayed with Patrick all the time he was in France training to be a priest. It stayed with him when he went back to Scotland, and even when he travelled to Rome to become a bishop.

Eventually Patrick could ignore the feeling no longer.

'I will go back,' he said. 'I know there is work there for me to do.'

He asked a group of monks to go with him, and together they travelled to Ireland.

They arrived at night. It was dark and no-one noticed them landing.

'What shall we do?' asked one of the monks. 'Where shall we go?'

'We'll light a fire,' said Patrick. 'Someone will see it and they'll come to see what's happening. Then we can tell them who we are and why we're here.'

The monks did as Patrick said. Soon the bonfire was blazing brightly. The monks felt more cheerful and less afraid … but not for long.

A huge crowd of people suddenly surged down to the beach.

'Put that fire out!' they yelled.

'Don't you know you'll be killed,' they shouted.

'Only the Druid king can light a fire now, at the time of the spring festival. It's against the Druid law for anyone else to light one.'

'Put it out. You'll be killed. Put it out. You'll be killed,' the people chanted. The monks trembled and cowered, sure that they would soon be dead.

Only Patrick stood brave, sure and resolute.

'I am not afraid,' he said. 'I come in the name of God.'

Suddenly the crowd grew silent as the Druid king strode up to Patrick.

'No-one lights a fire before mine,' he said. 'Put out the flames.'

'I cannot,' said Patrick. The people gasped to hear this man defy their king.

'I cannot,' said Patrick, 'because this fire lightens the darkness. We come in peace to tell you of Jesus, the Light of the World, and to show you his light in your darkness.'

'Who is this Jesus?' asked the king.

Patrick told the Druid king of Jesus the Son of God, and of his life on earth. The Druid listened patiently.

'I was ready to kill you,' he said, when Patrick had finished speaking. 'But I see you are peaceful men. Your story sounds interesting. I will hear more of it tomorrow.' And with that, the Druid king turned and left Patrick and his men on the beach unharmed. The crowd also began to leave.

'We've never seen anyone stand up to the king and live,' they said. 'We expected him to kill the lot of you. We'll come and listen to your stories of Jesus again.'

And they did. Every day they came. Every day Patrick and the monks told the Irish people about God and the life of Jesus.

'You have taught me a great deal,' said the Druid king. 'Now I would like to become a Christian. Will you baptise me?'

Patrick agreed, and baptised not only the king but many of his people as well. The king gave Patrick land, and a building to use as a church until a real one could be built.

Patrick remained in Ireland and to him it became home – a country he loved and which loved him in return.

Saint Joseph of Nazareth
19 March

All that is known of Joseph of Nazareth, the foster-father of Christ and the husband of Mary, is written in the Gospels in Matthew *Chapters 1, 2 and 13:55, and in* Luke *Chapters 1, 2 and 4:22. Joseph was descended from King David, yet was a poor man who earned his living as a carpenter, some say as a master builder. The belief that he was an old man at the time of the birth of Jesus is unfounded. There is no mention of Joseph after the incident of Jesus being left behind at the temple when he was 12 years old, and it is assumed that Joseph died before the crucifixion. The biblical impression of Joseph is of a kind, dignified, level-headed man; a practical man but self-effacing; a protector and contributor rather than an originator; 'an upright man' according to the Gospels.*

Joseph is the patron saint of carpenters, fathers and workers.

Joseph of Nazareth

*Kindness/humility/caring/
working together/doing your best*

Soon after Jesus was born, his mother and father took him to Egypt, out of the way of King Herod who was jealous of the new baby king and wanted to kill him.

Mary and Joseph stayed in Egypt for a time, then they heard that Herod had died.

'It'll be safe now to go to Israel,' said Mary. But Joseph was not sure, and it was while he was wondering what to do that he had a dream.

'Herod is dead,' said the angel in the dream. 'You can go back to Israel now. But Joseph was still unsure. He knew that Herod's son had become King of Judea and he was afraid that the new king might also want to kill Jesus, just as his father had wanted to do. Joseph did not want to do anything that would put his family in danger.

Then he had another dream. This time the angel told him to go back to Nazareth in Galilee.

'We'll go,' he said to Mary. 'I'm sure we'll be safe back in Nazareth.' So Mary, Joseph and the young Jesus set off again, this time back home to Nazareth.

Joseph and Mary were not rich; they moved into a small house, but it was a home full of love and laughter and happiness. Joseph was not just a carpenter but a master craftsman, skilled at building and in making things out of wood, and soon the small house was filled with beautifully made pieces of furniture – tables, chairs, cupboards, beds, even wooden plates and beakers.

As soon as Jesus was old enough to be taught how to handle tools, Joseph began to show him how to make things. In those days children did not go to school, but every boy was expected to learn some craft or trade so that when he grew up he would be able to earn a living. It was natural that Joseph should teach his son to be a carpenter.

One day, Jesus and his friends were watching Joseph as he worked. He was smoothing the top of a table he had almost finished. It had to be rubbed with sand and smoothed with oil time and time again until it was as level and even and sleek and polished and glossy as a piece of stretched silk. The work needed patience and time. Joseph knew that if he tried to hurry the work or if he missed out some rubbing or smoothing, the table would not be his best work, and Joseph always tried to do his best no matter what job he was doing.

The boys watched.

'You're very good at doing that, aren't you?' said one of them. 'You're the best carpenter in Galilee, everyone knows that.'

Joseph looked at the boy and said, 'It's hard work that's needed. Hard work and elbow grease,' and he smiled, wondering if the boy had understood what he meant. Joseph was proud of his work, but he was not conceited or big-headed. He never boasted about a piece of furniture even when he knew it had turned out well, or even when it fetched a good price in the market.

A few days later, Joseph had reason to remember that conversation with the boy about hard work. Several things all seemed to happen at once that week. Mary was not very well and Joseph was looking after her as well as looking after Jesus, who was still a young child. Then there was the set of chairs to be finished that a rich merchant had ordered and wanted within the next few days. Then there was the matter of the new furniture for the synagogue that Joseph said he would help with. As if that was not enough, he had promised a friend over in Nain that he would help him with the extension he was building on to his house.

Joseph sat down to work out which job he could leave. If he could miss out just one, it might help him to fit in all the others. Well, he had to help Mary, now she was ill. Of course he had to look after Jesus; he could not possibly not look after his own child. He decided he could not let down the merchant who was waiting for his new chairs, and he could not let down the people at the synagogue, after all the whole village was working together on that project. That just left his friend in Nain; well he had to help a friend. Joseph would never want to let down a friend.

After great consideration, Joseph realised that there was only one thing to do – he must do all the jobs. Somehow he must fit them all into that week.

Joseph did not complain or grumble. He did not tell everyone how hard his life was. He just got up earlier each morning, worked all through the day and went to bed later each night. Somehow all the jobs got done. Mary became well again, and Jesus said how much he had enjoyed helping his father during the difficult and busy few days.

'Thank you,' said Mary. 'I don't know how we would have managed without you.'

'I don't know how he did it,' said the next-door neighbour. 'I'm sure he never slept all last week. Every time I saw him he was working. Work, work, work, all week long, because he was determined not to let anyone down.'

'He's a very special man,' said Mary. 'And I'm very proud of him.'

'I'm just a carpenter,' said Joseph, and he hurried off to do some more work.

Saint Cuthbert

20 March

Cuthbert was born in the north east of England c. 634, and was a bright, lively sports-loving boy. When he was 17, he had a vision that led to his becoming a monk at Melrose Abbey in Scotland, where he later became prior.

In 664 he went to Lindisfarne and made journeys to preach to the people of Northumberland and Durham. While at Melrose he made many lengthy journeys on foot to preach to people in remote areas of Scotland and northern England.

Cuthbert was known for his eloquence, but was by nature a solitary man with a great affinity for wildlife. In 676 he went to live as a hermit on Farne. He was called to be Bishop of Hexham in 684 but soon returned to the Farne Islands where he died in 687.

Saint Cuthbert and the eagle   *Trust/sharing*

One day Cuthbert was travelling over the hills of Scotland to a remote village, to talk to the people there about Jesus. He had with him a young boy called Cedda, who was showing him the way from Cuthbert's monastery at Melrose to the village. The boy had lived in the village all his life and knew the hills near his home very well, but the monastery was a long way from the village, and the boy was soon lost.

'I think it's this way,' he said, as they followed a rocky track in the biting cold wind. But a few miles further on the boy said, 'I think we're going the wrong way. I think we should be over there,' and he pointed in the opposite direction.

By now the boy was nearly in tears. He was shivering and hungry. He had no idea where they were and he knew that it would soon be dark. He was sure that Cuthbert must be angry with him.

'I'm sorry,' he said. 'I thought I knew which way it was.'

'Don't worry,' said Cuthbert. 'It's easy to lose your way in the hills. We'll go a bit further and then find a rock to shelter behind until morning. We'll be quite safe. God will take care of us.'

'But we've nothing to eat,' said the boy, starting to cry. 'And I'm so hungry. We might die of cold and hunger in the night.'

'God will take care of us,' said Cuthbert again. 'He cares for all his creatures. Look!' and he pointed to an eagle soaring high in the sky above them. 'The eagle doesn't worry about spending the night in the hills. God provides him with food and shelter, and God will take care of us, too.'

As Cuthbert and the boy watched, they saw the eagle hover in the air, its wings stretched out like fingers above them.

Then suddenly the eagle dived towards the surface of the river. It used its powerful wings to control it as it swooped low over the surface of the water. It extended its sharp talons and tipped its body backwards, then, with a splash of silver spray it lifted a huge fish, a salmon, out of the river.

The eagle tried to rise again into the air, but the fish was too big, too heavy, and it fell back to the rocks at the riverside. The eagle soared upwards and hovered, ready to try again to seize the fish.

'Quick!' said Cuthbert. 'Go and see if you can get the salmon.' But Cedda was already running across the grass and scrambling over the rocks to reach the fish.

He grabbed it before it could flip its way back into the water, and he held it high above his head, turning to grin at Cuthbert. 'Look!' he said excitedly. 'Now we can eat. I'll gather some wood. There's a dead tree over there. We can light a fire and cook the fish. There's plenty for both of us. We'll feel better when we've eaten.'

'Yes,' smiled Cuthbert. 'But you mean there's enough for all three of us! Look,' and he pointed to the sky, where the eagle still hovered, watching the man, the boy and the fish. 'He deserves his share of the food too,' said Cuthbert. 'After all, he caught the fish. God has provided enough food for all three of us.'

Cuthbert divided the fish into three portions. He took one part and put it back on the rocks at the edge of the river. Then he went to help Cedda gather wood for their fire. The eagle swooped to the rock and carried the fish off easily in its talons. Cedda and Cuthbert cooked and ate their portions of the fish.

As they were eating, Cedda suddenly pointed to a cluster of tiny lights, twinkling in a valley between the hills.

'There it is,' he said. 'There's the village we've been looking for.'

'God has indeed showed his care for us today,' said Cuthbert. 'He has provided food, and now he has shown us the way to shelter. He has answered our prayers.'

The Annunciation of the Blessed Virgin Mary or Lady Day

25 March

The Annunciation of the Blessed Virgin Mary celebrates the day on which Mary was told she was to have a baby by the Holy Spirit, and that the baby would be called Emmanuel, meaning God is with us, thus fulfilling the prophesy of Isaiah.

The day became commonly known as 'Lady Day', and was one of the quarter days of the agricultural year; days on which quarterly payments for farms, rents, land and so on were due. (The other quarter days are Midsummer on 24 June, Michaelmas on 29 September, and Christmas on 25 December.) The quarter days were also used to denote the passage of time, and people would place events with reference to them, for example a death would be remembered as so many years ago last Michaelmas, or a birth so many years come Midsummer.

Mary met an angel   *Trust/obedience*
adapted from Luke 1:26–35

Mary lived in a town called Nazareth, in Galilee. She was engaged to be married to a man called Joseph, a carpenter who also lived in Nazareth. They hoped to be married soon, and were busy making plans for the future. There was a lot to arrange. They had to decide where to live, when to be married, who to invite.

One day while Joseph was at work, Mary was walking in a garden near where she lived, daydreaming a little, thinking about the future, when she suddenly became aware of someone standing very near her. She turned to look, and there beside her was the angel Gabriel. Mary felt frightened.

'Don't be afraid,' said the angel. 'I come in peace.'

'But what do you want?' asked Mary. 'Why are you here?'

'I am here with a message from God,' said the angel Gabriel. 'I have to tell you that God is very pleased with you. He wants you to know that he has blessed you.'

'I don't understand,' said Mary, feeling even more afraid.

'God has chosen you, Mary, to be the mother of a special child. You will soon have a baby boy, and you will call him Jesus. He will be special, an important person. He will be a king, just as David was a king before him. But the kingdom of Jesus will never end. He will be the Son of God himself.'

'But I still don't understand,' said Mary, worriedly. 'I can't have a baby. We've not planned a baby so soon. I'm not married yet. Joseph and I are going to get married, but we haven't made all the arrangements yet.'

'You will have the child,' said the angel Gabriel. 'The Holy Spirit will come to you, and God's strength will be with you. The child will be called the Son of God. Don't be afraid, Mary.'

'But it's not possible ...' began Mary, but the angel interrupted her.

'You know your cousin Elizabeth?' he asked.

'Yes, of course,' said Mary.

'Well, everyone thought she was too old to have a child, but she is pregnant, and her baby is due to be born soon,' said the angel. 'You see, there is nothing that God cannot do.'

'Yes,' said Mary. 'I know.'

Then she said, 'I will do whatever God wants me to do.'

'God is pleased with you Mary,' said the angel Gabriel, then he left her, alone again in the garden.

Palm Sunday

Sunday before Easter

14 March (if Easter is at its earliest of 21 March)
to
18 April (if Easter is at its latest of 25 April)

Palm Sunday is the Sunday before Easter Day and the first day of Holy Week. It is the day which celebrates Christ's triumphant entry to Jerusalem, when the people welcomed him as a king by waving palm branches and spreading them at his feet.

The custom of churches blessing and distributing palm crosses amongst the congregation has been known in England for some 1500 years. In the early years the crosses were made from spring greenery, especially willow, which became known as English palm in some areas. Nowadays the crosses are made from imported palm leaves.

Jesus enters Jerusalem
adapted from Matthew 21:1–11 and Luke 19:28–40

Jesus had spent three years travelling round Palestine, teaching and healing the people he met. But he knew it was now time to go back to Jerusalem, time to face whatever God wanted him to do next.

Jesus and his friends stopped near a hill called the Mount of Olives.

'Go down into that village,' said Jesus to two of the disciples, pointing to a village a short distance away.

'When you get there you will find a donkey and her colt tied up near a house. Untie them and bring them here to me. If anyone says anything to you, say that the Master needs them, and they'll let you bring them to me without any problem.'

The two disciples did as Jesus asked and found the mother donkey and her young one tied to the door of a house. They were just untying the animals when some people walked by and said, 'What are you doing with those donkeys? They're not yours! Leave them alone or we'll go and tell the owners.'

'The Master needs them,' said one of the disciples.

'Then that's all right,' said the man. 'Take them and go.'

The disciples led the animals back to where Jesus was waiting. 'We must go now into Jerusalem,' he said quietly. Jesus knew that there were men in Jerusalem who would kill him, but the disciples did not know this.

The disciples threw their cloaks over the back of the older donkey and helped Jesus get on. Then they walked along the road into Jerusalem.

As they got nearer the city, more and more people joined in the procession.

'What's going on?' asked the onlookers. 'Who is that man riding on the donkey?'

'It's Jesus,' people answered. 'Jesus of Nazareth. The one who has come to save us. The one who is King of the Jews.'

The procession grew larger and became a crowd, and the crowd became so big it could barely move along the road. The people were jubilant, joyful, happy, excited and elated. They shouted and cheered to welcome the king they believed would save them from the Roman army.

They spread their cloaks on the road to make a carpet for the king. They cut down branches from the palm trees and waved them like flags.

'Hosanna! Hurrah! Welcome to our city!' they called. 'God bless the king who comes in the name of the Lord! Praise be to God! Welcome! Hurrah! Hosanna!' they shouted.

The streets leading into Jerusalem were now packed with people waving and cheering. The procession itself was as long as a street, with people at the front pushing the crowds apart to make way for Jesus on the donkey.

'Jesus is coming! The king is here,' they called. 'The prophets of old said that our king would ride into Jerusalem on a donkey. Now he's here! Jesus is here. Make way. Make way for him!'

The people of Jerusalem had never been so happy. They greeted Jesus as their king and their hero. They were sure that this man would save them. This man who came riding into Jerusalem on an ordinary donkey, not on a fine horse or in a golden carriage, would make their lives better. This man who looked just like an ordinary person would be their king. The people sang and danced and cheered and waved until they were exhausted.

But not all the people of Jerusalem were pleased that Jesus had arrived. Some of the leaders of Jerusalem pushed their way through the crowd to speak to Jesus.

'There's too much noise and fuss,' they complained. 'Tell all your friends and disciples to stop shouting and cheering. Tell them to be quiet!'

'I cannot do that,' said Jesus. 'If the people are made to be quiet, then the stones themselves will shout and cheer instead.' And he walked with the procession towards the temple.

Holy Week
The week before Easter Day

Holy Week starts with Palm Sunday, and is the week leading up to Easter Day. Jesus spent this period of time, the last days of his earthly life, in Jerusalem. The week commemorates the events leading up to and including the crucifixion.

Although Maundy Thursday and Good Friday are two of the principal Holy Days of the Christian year, Monday, Tuesday and Wednesday of Holy Week are also observed as great Holy Days, on which solemn church services are held.

Jesus goes to the temple
adapted from Matthew 21:12–17 and Mark 11:15–19

Soon after he arrived in Jerusalem, Jesus made his way to the temple. The crowds were still surging round him, but he hoped they would stay outside the temple. He wanted to go into the temple alone, to think and to pray, to be quiet and still, to be peaceful and calm.

When Jesus walked through the temple gateway, the sight that met his eyes horrified him. Instead of seeing a place of peace and quiet and calm and stillness, he saw a market-place; a place where there was noise and bustle, buying and selling, cheating and dealing going on. He saw stalls selling everything you could think of – cheese, cloth, meat, carpets. He saw money-changers and money-lenders dealing with their customers. He saw birds in cages and sheep in pens all being bought and sold.

'These people have forgotten that this is God's house,' he said. 'Stop,' he called to everyone. 'This is not a market-place, it is a temple. Treat it with respect!'

But no-one took any notice of him and the noise and bustle went on.

Jesus strode into the courtyard. He grabbed the two nearest tables and flung them aside. He ran to the other stalls and overturned them. He threw money on to the ground. He untied the pens of the animals. Within seconds the courtyard of the temple was in chaos. Adults, children, cats, dogs, goats, hens and horses ran in all directions. Pigeons and other small birds rose into the air in fluttering clouds. Debris of all kinds was scattered on the ground; broken tables, scraps of food, empty boxes, golden coins. Then, slowly, a sort of stillness and quiet came to the courtyard again, and settled uneasily on the wreckage.

And through the wreckage came striding the chief priests of the temple.

'What do you think you're doing?' they shouted. 'How dare you do this in our temple!'

'And how dare you spoil God's house by turning it into a market-place,' said Jesus. 'The temple should be a house of prayer, but you have turned it into a den of thieves.'

The chief priests did not reply because they knew that Jesus was right. They turned away and began to pick up some of the things that were scattered on the ground.

Jesus walked back to the gateway of the temple. There were many people waiting there. Some were old and sick. Others were lame or blind. Jesus spoke kindly to them all, and healed them and made them well again.

Jesus came each day to the temple, and each day he talked to the people there. Everyone listened carefully to what he had to say; they did not want to miss a single word of his teaching.

But the chief priests and leaders of Jerusalem became more and more angry.

'No-one listens to us any more,' they grumbled. 'The only person anyone listens to around here is that Jesus of Nazareth. He's dangerous now that he has so many people on his side, so he'll have to go. We'll have to get rid of him. Somehow we'll have to kill him.'

Jesus answers questions
adapted from Mark 11:27–33, Mark 12:13–17 & 28–34

Jesus and his disciples went to stay in a village called Bethany, just outside Jerusalem, but each day they went back to the temple in Jerusalem where Jesus taught and talked to anyone who would listen to him.

The priests and leaders watched and waited. They did not like the way Jesus came into the temple every day. They did not like the way Jesus talked to the people. They did not like the way everyone listened to him and took notice of him.

'We'll catch him out,' they said. 'We'll ask him some questions he won't be able to answer, and then he'll look stupid in front of all the people. Then they'll stop thinking he's quite so important. Then it will be easier for us to get rid of him.'

They prepared their questions. They were sure they would be able to catch him out. They waited for Jesus to come to the temple the next day.

'We want to ask you something!' they said, as soon as they saw Jesus coming. Jesus stopped and waited to hear what they would say.

'Who gave you the right to destroy the market in the temple? Who gave you the right to order everyone out?' the priests asked.

Instead of answering their question, Jesus asked another one. 'Who gave John the right to baptise people?' he asked. 'Did God tell him to, or was it someone else?'

The priests started to argue amongst themselves. They dared not say that it was God, otherwise Jesus would ask them why they had not been baptised. But they dared not say it was a person, because everyone was listening, and the priests knew that the people believed John the Baptist was sent by God. The priests were afraid of disagreeing with the crowd, so they said, 'We don't know!'

'Then if you won't answer my question, I won't answer yours,' said Jesus, and he walked away.

The priests were angry that Jesus had been too clever for them. They tried again to trick him. They tried to make him break the law by saying something against Caesar, the Roman emperor.

'Tell us,' they said, 'What do you think about paying money to Caesar? Should we pay our taxes or not?'

Again Jesus saw through their trick. 'Bring me a silver coin,' he said. The priests gave him a coin.

'Now, whose face and name is on the coin?' asked Jesus.

'The emperor's, of course,' said the priests.

'Then pay the emperor what belongs to the emperor, and pay God what belongs to God,' answered Jesus.

The priests and leaders felt even more angry that they had been unable to trick Jesus. They had been unable to turn the crowd against him. They had been unable to make him look foolish.

One of the teachers of the law asked another question.

'Which is the most important commandment?' he asked.

Everyone waited to hear what Jesus would say.

'The most important commandment is to love God,' said Jesus. 'And the second most important commandment is to love your neighbour as much as you love yourself.'

The teacher of the law agreed with Jesus that these are the two most important commandments. After that, no-one dared ask Jesus any more questions, and he and the disciples went back to Bethany.

The plot against Jesus
adapted from Matthew 26:1–3 & 14–16 and John 11:45–53

The priests and leaders plotted and planned to find a way to kill Jesus.

'We've got to get rid of him,' they said. 'Look at how popular he is. Look at the way everyone listens to every single word he says. Look at the miracles he performs. If we don't stop him soon he'll be known throughout the whole land. The Roman authorities will hear of him. They might believe the things he says, and then it will be the end of our empire. The end of our country as we know it. The end of our jobs. The end of us being important! He'll have to go.'

It was not easy to find a way. The priest and leaders were afraid that if they killed Jesus, the people would turn against them.

Then Caiaphas, the High Priest, spoke.

'He must die! It is better to let one man die, even if the people are not pleased, than to risk having the whole country destroyed by him. He must die!'

Caiaphas called a meeting in his palace of all the chief priests and elders.

They decided to arrest Jesus secretly, then nobody would know and there would not be a fuss.

'How are we going to arrest him without anyone knowing?' asked one of the priests. 'We need some help from someone who claims to be his friend.'

Just then there was a knock at the door. A guard came to Caiaphas with a message. 'There's a man outside who says he can help you with this Jesus business.'

'Send him in,' said Caiaphas.

The door opened again and in came Judas Iscariot. Caiaphas and the others were astonished, for this man was one of Jesus's friends, one of the twelve special friends, one of the twelve disciples.

'What do you want?' asked Caiaphas.

'What will you give me if I help you to get Jesus?' said Judas.

'If you help us to arrest him,' said Caiaphas, 'We will pay you thirty pieces of silver.'

'I will do it for thirty pieces of silver,' said Judas.

The chief priests paid Judas his money and he went away, planning how he could hand Jesus over to them.

The chief priests waited, knowing that it would now not be long until Jesus would be killed.

Maundy Thursday
Thursday in Holy Week

Maundy Thursday is the day on which Jesus had his last meal – the Last Supper – with the 12 disciples. By this time in Holy Week Jesus had many powerful enemies, and it was necessary for him to meet with his friends secretly in an upper room. While sharing bread and wine during the meal, Jesus gave the commandment 'Do this in remembrance of me' which is now at the heart of Christian Mass, also known as Communion (meaning sharing) or Eucharist (meaning thanksgiving).

The word Maundy is derived from the Latin 'mandatum' meaning a commandment.

Jesus washed the feet of the disciples before the Last Supper as a means of communicating God's wish that his followers should serve others. Today, the Pope washes the feet of 12 men in memory of this. In Britain this custom has not been carried out since the reign of King James II, but the reigning monarch gives purses of money to old people in need; the number of purses given is equal to the age of the monarch.

The Last Supper and the arrest of Jesus
adapted from Matthew 26:17–56

At the beginning of Holy Week, Jesus had been welcomed into Jerusalem as a king. But long before the week was over Jesus knew that many of the people had turned against him, and that his enemies were plotting to kill him.

Jesus arranged for the disciples to meet together for the special Passover meal; he knew it would be the last meal they would have together. They arranged to meet secretly in an upstairs room, and in the evening, when the meal was ready, Jesus and all 12 disciples sat down to eat.

While they were eating, Jesus said to his friends, 'I know that soon one of you will betray me. One of you will give me away to my enemies.'

'We wouldn't do that!' said Peter, indignantly. 'We are your friends. We won't give you away.'

'One of you will,' said Jesus sadly.

'We won't, we're your friends,' said the disciples. But while they were talking among themselves, the one called Judas Iscariot crept away; away from the upstairs room – away to earn his thirty pieces of silver – away to tell the priests how they could catch Jesus. Jesus saw him go, but he said nothing.

Instead, Jesus picked up some bread from the middle of the table. He said thank you to God for the bread, then he broke it into pieces and gave some to each of the disciples.

'Take this and eat it,' he said. 'Soon I will die, and my body will be broken for you, just like this bread.'

Then Jesus picked up a cup of wine. He said thank you to God for the wine, and gave some to each of the disciples.

'Drink this,' he said. 'Soon I will die, and my blood will flow for you, just like this wine.'

The disciples did not fully understand what Jesus meant, but they listened to him and finished their meal with him.

After the meal, they all walked together to the olive garden at Gethsemane, just outside Jerusalem. On the way, Jesus talked to the disciples again. 'Soon you will all run away and leave me,' he said.

'I will never leave you,' said Peter, 'Even if the others do, I won't.'

'Yes, even you,' said Jesus. 'Before tomorrow morning you will say three times that you don't know me, that you've never met me.'

'I won't, I'm your friend,' said Peter. But Jesus knew that it would happen.

By now they had arrived at the garden of Gethsemane. They went inside and Jesus asked the disciples to wait for him. He took Peter, James and John further into the garden with him.

'Please stay here and pray with me,' said Jesus. 'I need to pray to God my Father.' He knelt on the ground and began to pray. The three disciples also knelt on the ground, but when Jesus looked at them again, he saw that they were fast asleep. 'Could you not even stay awake with me for a little time?' he asked.

Just then there was a noise and a commotion near the entrance to the garden. The disciples looked up to see Judas, and with him a crowd of Roman soldiers all waving swords and sticks. Some carried lighted torches which flamed and flared in the cold night air. The soldiers pushed and jostled, pointed and shouted, and then became quiet as Judas Iscariot walked away from them and towards Jesus. The disciples realised that Judas was showing the soldiers which man was Jesus.

As soon as Judas spoke to Jesus the soldiers pushed forward. They grabbed Jesus and began to drag him away. The disciples were so afraid at what they saw that they ran away, into the darkness. But Peter turned back and watched to see what the soldiers would do to Jesus. He saw them take him to the house of Caiaphas, the chief priest, and take him inside.

Peter waited outside. He hadn't been there long when a servant girl came past. She looked at Peter.

'Haven't I seen you before?' she asked. 'Aren't you one of Jesus' friends?'

Peter felt very afraid. If he admitted that he knew Jesus, he might be arrested too.

'No,' he said quickly. 'No, I've never even met him,' and he hurried away from the house. But another servant girl was coming towards him.

'Look!' she said to a man standing near. 'That's one of Jesus' disciples.'

'No I'm not,' said Peter. 'I don't know Jesus of Nazareth,' and he hurried away again.

A little while later, a man looked at Peter and said, 'I recognise you. You're one of the disciples of Jesus, aren't you?'

'No I'm not,' said Peter. 'I swear I'm telling you the truth; I don't know him at all.'

Just then Peter heard a cockerel crow. It was now nearly daylight, nearly morning, and Peter knew that he had done what Jesus said he would do; he had denied him three times. Despite his promise, Peter had told people three times that he did not know Jesus, that he had never known him, that he had never even met him. Peter felt ashamed of himself and he went away and cried.

Good Friday
Friday in Holy Week

Good Friday is the most solemn and Holy day in the Christian calendar. It is the day which commemorates Christ's crucifixion. Jesus was sent for trial before the Roman Governor Pontius Pilate, who sentenced him to death despite finding no criminal offence, but in fear of the crowds who were calling for execution.

Condemned prisoners who were to die by crucifixion were made to walk to their place of execution carrying the heavy crossbeam – the upright would have already been positioned. The route Jesus walked (the Via Dolorosa or Way of the Cross), is marked by the fourteen 'stations', where key points of the journey are remembered. Many Christians today re-enact this journey in procession on Good Friday.

Churches today emphasise the solemnity of Good Friday by a total lack of decoration, a stripping of altars, and silence; no bells are rung, unless tolled in mourning. The term 'Good' Friday acknowledges that Jesus resisted evil to the end, and that despite the sadness of the day, the resurrection is to follow.

Jesus is crucified
adapted from John 18:28–40 & 19:1–30

Early in the morning Jesus was taken from Caiaphas' house to the palace of the Roman Governor, Pontius Pilate.

The priests who had brought him there pushed Jesus forward. 'This man says he is the King of the Jews,' said the chief priest to Pontius Pilate. 'He must die. It is against the Roman law to claim to be a king; you know that. You must sentence him to death.'

Pontius Pilate turned to look at Jesus. 'Are you the King of the Jews?' he asked.

'My kingdom does not belong to this world,' said Jesus. 'You say that I am a king, but I only came to tell the world the truth – the truth about God.'

Pilate went outside the palace, to where a great crowd had gathered.

'There is no reason to kill this man,' he said to the crowd. 'He has done nothing wrong. I can let him go free. I always free a prisoner during the Feast of the Passover, and it is the time of the Passover now. Shall I let him go free?'

'No!' shouted the people. 'Kill him! Crucify him!'

'But I can set him free for you,' said Pilate again.

'No!' shouted the crowd. 'Crucify him!'

Then someone said, 'If you want to free a prisoner, then let Barabbas go. He's a murderer, but we want him to be free, not Jesus.' The crowd all took up the shout, 'Set Barabbas free. Crucify Jesus. Set Barabbas free. Kill Jesus.'

Jesus heard the crowd shouting for his death; the same crowd that had welcomed him into Jerusalem only a few days earlier. Jesus said nothing, but he heard Pilate say to the priests, 'Then *you* take him and crucify him, for I see no reason why he should die,' and Jesus knew then that Pilate was afraid of going against the people and the priests.

Soldiers led Jesus away and made him carry his cross to a place called Golgotha. There was a notice pinned to the cross which said 'Jesus of Nazareth, King of the Jews.'

When the soldiers saw this notice, they teased and mocked Jesus. 'So you think you're a king, eh?' they said. They made fun of him; dressed him up in a long purple cloak and put a crown of thorns on his head. 'See what a fine king he is!' they laughed. 'Look at his crown and his cloak!'

Jesus said nothing. He did not shout or fight or ask God to save him. He remained dignified, despite the undignified things which were done to him.

The soldiers soon tired of their unkind game. They fastened Jesus to the cross and left him there to die, but one of them said, 'We shouldn't have done this. He was a good man.'

Jesus looked at all the people around him; his friends were there, and his mother, and so too were many of his enemies – those people who had been determined to have him killed. He spoke quietly to God and said, 'Forgive them, Father. They don't know what they are doing.' And then he died.

People began to move away from the cross. John took Mary, Jesus' mother, back to his house to care for her. The disciples all felt very sad, believing that they would never see Jesus again; not yet knowing that in two days' time Jesus would live again.

Easter Day

21 March (Easter's earliest date)
to
25 April (the latest date on which Easter can fall)

Easter Day is the moveable feast on which the rest of the moveable feasts depend. It can fall anywhere between 21 March and 25 April, and is calculated as the first Sunday after the full moon which occurs on or after the vernal equinox (21 March). However, if the full moon falls on a Sunday, then Easter Day is the following Sunday. Easter Day has been celebrated on the day thus calculated since the Synod of Whitby in 665, when it was agreed to adopt the Roman way of calculating Easter, and dispense with the Celtic way.

Easter is the principal festival in the Christian year, and celebrates the Resurrection of Christ, the forgiveness of sins and the triumph of good over evil. Christians believe that Christ's death atoned for the sins of humankind, and that his resurrection proves that good can conquer evil.

Easter is a gloriously happy celebration of life; symbols of new life and rebirth abound, churches are decorated with flowers, altars decked in celebratory gold and white, and bells pealed triumphantly. The happiness and joy of the festival are in direct contrast with the sombre days of Lent and the dark days of the end of Holy Week.

Jesus is alive
adapted from Luke 24:1–35 & John 20:1–18

Early on Sunday morning, while it was still dark, Mary Magdalene and some of her friends went to the tomb where the body of Jesus had been placed. There had not been enough time on the Friday to prepare the body in the way that was the custom, and on Saturday, the Sabbath, they were not allowed to do work of any kind. So now, on Sunday, they hurried to finish anointing Jesus' body with myrrh and other oils and spices.

They talked as they hurried along to the garden where the tomb was.

'But how will we move the stone that covers the entrance to the cave?' one of them asked. 'It took several soldiers to roll the stone in front of the cave. How will we move it away without any help?'

'Perhaps there'll be someone there who can help us,' said Mary. 'Or perhaps the stone won't be as heavy as we think, and we'll be able to move it ourselves. Or perhaps ...'

But Mary got no further with what she was going to say. She stopped where she was in the middle of the path and pointed ahead without another word. The others looked where she pointed and stared in amazement. The stone was already pushed aside. The entrance to the cave was open.

The women crept nearer and peered into the cave. It was empty. The body of Jesus had gone.

Mary Magdalene started to cry, believing that someone had stolen the body of Jesus. The other women ran quickly, back the way they had come, to tell John and Peter what had happened.

The disciples could hardly believe what they were told, and hurried back to the empty cave to see for themselves.

John arrived first, but was afraid to go into the cave. Peter came then and walked straight inside. He saw the rocky shelf on which Jesus' body had been placed. He saw the linen cloths that had been wrapped round him, but there was no sign of Jesus. He had gone.

Sadly, Peter and John left the cave and went back home, convinced that someone had stolen the body of Jesus.

Mary Magdalene stayed by the cave. She knew Jesus had gone, but here in the quiet garden she felt near to him.

Mary had been sitting there for some time before she became aware of someone else in the garden. Someone was walking towards her, a man. The gardener, she thought.

He came up to her and said, 'Why are you crying?'

'They have taken Jesus away,' answered Mary through her tears. 'And I don't know where he is.' Then she looked at the man and said 'Do you know where he is? If you do, please tell me so that I can go to him.'

The man looked at Mary and realised that she did not recognise him. She did not know who he was. He wondered for a moment how to tell her. How to explain. How to say it all in a way she would understand. In the end he said only word – 'Mary!'

'Mary,' spoken in a gentle voice, the voice she knew so well.

As soon as she heard him say her name, Mary knew that this man was Jesus. This man was not the gardener, but was Jesus. Jesus was not dead, but was alive again.

'Go and tell the others I am alive,' said Jesus. And Mary, feeling happier than she had felt for a long time, ran to tell the others what had happened.

Later that same day, two of Jesus' friends were walking home to Emmaus, a short distance from Jerusalem. They talked together as they walked along.

'There's no point in staying in Jerusalem now that Jesus is dead,' said one of them.

'No,' agreed the other, 'we might as well leave.'

Just then, another man joined them.

'What are you talking about?' he asked.

'We're talking about Jesus and the things that have been happening in Jerusalem during the past few days,' said one of the friends.

'What things are those?' asked the stranger.

The two friends stared at him. 'You must be the only person in this part of the world who doesn't know what's been going,' said the other friend.

'Tell me about it,' said the stranger.

So the two friends explained about Jesus of Nazareth, his work, his friends, and his death. Then, to their surprise, the man began to explain to them why Jesus had to die. By this time the three men had arrived in Emmaus, and the two friends asked the stranger if he'd like to come and have supper with them.

The man agreed, and in a few minutes they were all sitting down to a meal together.

The stranger took some bread, and said thank you to God for it, and shared it between the three of them. As soon as he did this, the other two realised who he was. They recognised him. It was Jesus, no longer dead, but alive and here in their house with them.

'We must go and tell the others,' said the friends. 'We must tell them it is true that you are alive.'

Jesus left the house then, and the two friends hurried back to Jerusalem to tell the disciples they had seen Jesus.

'First Mary Magadalene, now you two,' said the disciples. 'Then it is true. Jesus is alive. This is a happy day.'

Saint George

23 April

*George is perhaps the most well-known and most legendary of the British Saints,
yet is one of whom we know very little in terms of historical facts. He is believed to
have been martyred c. 250 in Palestine.*

*There are many legends of Saint George's brave and chivalrous deeds, the most
famous being the killing of the dragon. The story is believed to have first appeared
in* The Golden Legend, *translated into English and other European languages in
the late Middle Ages. However, it is interesting to note that earlier legends of Saint
George make no mention of a dragon.*

*Saint George is the patron saint of England, of soldiers and of the scouts. How
he became patron saint of England is unclear, though there is a story of Richard
the Lion Heart having a vision of Saint George leading the Crusaders to victory,
and thus adopting him as their father-figure.*

Saint George and the dragon
Working together/courage

Once upon a time, near the city of Silene in Africa, a shepherd boy was sitting by
a beautiful lake looking after his flock of sheep.

Suddenly, the still waters of the lake stirred and rippled, then boiled into a
frenzy of crashing waves. Out from the waves rose a great dragon, lashing its
tail and breathing long tongues of fire. The boy jumped to his feet and ran.

From the safety of a hilltop, the boy saw the dragon lunge out of the water,
seize two sheep in its huge jaws and disappear under the waves again. In
minutes, the surface of the lake was calm again and there was no sign of anything
being wrong, except for the distress of the flock of sheep which was now
unsettled and restless.

Shaking with fright, the boy ran back to the city to tell what he had seen. As
soon as the king heard the news he sent soldiers armed with swords and spears
and bows and arrows to kill the dragon.

But the soldiers were beaten, and returned dejected to the city.

'It's no good,' they said. 'The dragon is too strong and fierce for us. As soon as
we get anywhere near, it drives us back with its scorching breath. We're sorry,
but we can't get near enough to kill it.'

'Then we must stay inside the city walls,' said the king, and he ordered the
gates of the city to be locked and bolted. Then he said, 'But we must find a way
of feeding the dragon and keeping it near the lake. If it comes here to the city, it
will burn down our houses with its fiery breath.'

The king met with his ministers to decide on a plan.

'We're all right for a few days,' said one man, 'because the dragon still has the shepherd's flock of sheep to eat. But what happens when all the sheep are gone?'

'We must send our cattle and our horses, our goats and our donkeys down to the lake,' said the king. 'The dragon must eat our animals.'

'But we haven't many animals,' said another minister. 'What happens when the dragon has eaten them all?'

'Then we must send ourselves,' said the king. 'We must write everyone's name on a piece of paper and put all the names in a box. Every day I shall draw one out, and that person must go to the dragon to be eaten. It's the only way to save the rest of the people in our city. We must hope that the dragon goes away before we have to resort to that plan.'

The dragon did not go away. It ate all the shepherd's sheep, then it accepted the other animals that the people sent. One animal each day.

At last the king had to explain to his people the plan of sending themselves to the dragon. Each person wrote his or her name on a piece of paper and dropped it into a box. Each day the king drew out a name and that person walked out of the city gates towards the lake, never to be seen again.

On the sixth day, the king drew out the name of his own daughter – the Princess Sabra. Everyone waited to see what the king would do, but he could do nothing. It would have been unfair if he changed the rules now, to save one of his own family.

Princess Sabra walked through the city gates. She heard them close behind her. She walked to the lake and as she approached it the waters rippled and splashed, then crashed into waves as the dragon emerged. It roared and lunged towards her. Suddenly, there was another sound, the drumming of horse's hooves on the ground, a shout, and a thrust of a spear. The dragon, taken unawares, had no time to draw its fiery breath. Princess Sabra watched in fear as the horseman thrust again and again with his spear. The dragon thrashed its huge tail in the shallow water at the edge of the lake, but the horseman dodged its cruel spikes and unsheathed his sword. With one mighty blow he cut off the dragon's head.

'Come,' said the horseman to the princess. 'Let us go and tell your father you are safe.'

'But who are you? How did you know?' asked Princess Sabra.

'My name is George of England,' said the man. 'And news of the dragon is known throughout the land. Come.' He lifted the princess on to the horse and rode back to the city.

'How can I thank you?' asked the king, when he heard what had happened. 'What can I give you to show you how grateful I am?'

'Give me nothing,' answered Saint George. 'But give thanks to God who gave me the strength and courage to kill the dragon.'

And the people sang a hymn of rejoicing for their salvation.

Saint Mark
25 April

Mark was an evangelist and the author of the Gospel bearing his name. There is no record of Mark's date of birth, but he is believed to have died c. 74, possibly in Alexandria. It is likely that Mark was the son of a woman named Mary, from Jerusalem, in whose house the Apostles used to meet. Mark at one time was the companion of both St Peter and St Paul, and was taken on the first missionary journey of St Paul and St Barnabas. However, Mark turned back at Perga and returned alone to Jerusalem. Paul then refused to take him on a second journey, but Mark travelled with Barnabas to preach in Cyprus. Later, Mark and Paul were reconciled and were together in Rome, where Mark reputedly wrote the Gospel.

Mark's name has been linked with Venice since the ninth century, when his relics were brought to the original church of San Marco. The present day basilica contains not only the relics, but also a series of mosaics dating from the twelfth to thirteenth centuries depicting Mark's life.

Mark is the patron saint of Venice and of glaziers.

Saint Mark and the great storm of Venice   *Trust/courage*

Venice is a beautiful city in the north of Italy. It is a city of light and reflections, because unlike other cities it is built on the waters of a lagoon.

The houses are built on wooden poles which have been driven into the mud at the bottom of the lagoon, and instead of streets, the city has canals; instead of travelling by road, everyone travels by water.

But many years ago – the story says it was on 25 February 1340 – a terrible storm threatened to destroy the lovely city of Venice. The wind howled and the rain beat down. The level of water in the lagoon rose higher and higher, and the buildings at the sides of the canals became flooded.

A fisherman who was out in his small boat in the central canal, decided to row to the side of the canal and waited for the storm to pass. The water-level was higher than he had ever seen it before, and the waves were getting bigger and rougher every minute. The canal, which earlier had been still and calm, was now like a racing river, sweeping everything it touched down into the open sea. The fisherman knew that if he stayed out on the canal he too would be swept away and would drown.

As the fisherman waited in the rain and the wind by the water's edge, another man came up to him.

'Will you take me to the other side of the canal in your boat?' he asked.

'I can't,' said the fisherman. 'The weather is too bad.'

'You are a skilled boatman,' said the stranger. 'You will be able to row your boat across. And God will protect you. Please take me across.'

Something in the stranger's calm and quiet manner made the fisherman say that he would, and together they climbed into the rocking boat and set off for the far side of the canal. To the fisherman's surprise, rowing across the canal was not as difficult as he thought it would be. The water seemed calmer, and even though the storm was still raging, they quickly and safely reached the other side.

'Wait there please,' said the stranger, and he disappeared inside a building. A few minutes later he came out again with another, younger man.

'Now, will you take us both across the lagoon to the island at the other side?' he said.

'I can't do that!' said the fisherman. 'Just look at the weather. The boat will capsize. We'll all drown. You'll have to wait until the storm has stopped.'

'No, we must go now,' said the stranger. 'It will be all right. Trust in God. Don't be afraid.'

Again the fisherman decided to do as the stranger asked, even though he knew that the water was too rough for his small boat. The three of them climbed in the small boat, and the fisherman began to row. To his surprise the journey was easy and they soon arrived at the other side of the lagoon.

'Wait here again,' said the stranger, as he and the young man went inside a building. A few minutes later they came out with a third man.

'Now, I want you to row us all out into the middle of the open sea,' said the stranger.

The fisherman looked at the waves on the sea. He looked up at the dark sky and the heavy swirling clouds. He looked at his tiny boat. He knew he should say no. No, no and again no. He knew it was foolish and unsafe, dangerous and unwise to set out to sea in this weather. But, 'I will take you,' he said, for he trusted this man, and knew there was something special about him.

All four men got into the boat and the fisherman began to row. It was hard work rowing against the wind and the waves, and the fisherman felt afraid.

Suddenly, the stranger said, 'Stop rowing. Stay still. Let the boat drift.'

'But it will capsize if I let it drift into the waves,' said the fisherman.

'Trust me,' said the man, and he held his hands high in the air in the shape of a cross.

Immediately the sea became calm. The wind died down, the rain stopped, the sky brightened, and the waves became as small as ripples on a village pond.

'Now, take us back the way we came,' said the stranger. 'You will find the journey easy. We will each get off the boat at the place where we got on, so you will need to take me back to the side of the canal where you first saw me.'

The fisherman did as he was asked, and soon all three men were back on land, where people were already beginning to sweep the last of the flood-water out of the buildings and to clean up the mud and debris that was left behind. The stranger began to walk away.

'Just a minute,' called the fisherman. 'You haven't paid me for taking you and your friends in my boat.'

The stranger looked at the fisherman. He was surprised that the fisherman should ask for money when he had just seen Venice saved from being destroyed by the storm and flood; when he had just seen a miracle happen. But he said, 'You are right. Go and see the Judge. Tell him what has happened and what you have seen. Tell him that I, Saint Mark, have saved the city that I love. Tell him that I am the protector of Venice. Go and tell him.'

'But what if he doesn't believe me?' asked the fisherman.

'Take him this,' said Saint Mark, pulling a beautiful ring from his finger. 'The Judge will recognise this, and he will know you are speaking the truth.'

And with that, Saint Mark walked away from the fisherman, who hurried to tell the Judge all that had happened.

At first the Judge was not sure that the fisherman was telling the truth, but as soon as he saw Saint Mark's ring, he knew that the story was true.

'Saint Mark has saved our city,' he said. 'We shall arrange a grand procession in honour of him, so that everyone will know he is the protector of Venice. And you,' he said to the fisherman, 'Will be given a reward. For without you, Saint Mark would not have been able to go out on to the sea to make the storm still. It is thanks to your bravery that our city is saved. And the ring,' said the Judge, holding it up so that it sparkled in the light, 'Will be placed amongst the treasures of the church. Today has been a special day for our city of Venice.'

Saint Zita

27 April

Zita, known as Sitha in Britain, was born in Lucca, Italy, in 1218. She went to work as a domestic servant in the home of Fatinelli, a wealthy weaver of Lucca, at the age of 12, and remained there until she died in 1278.

Zita was at first disliked by the servants because of her devotion, her hard work and her care and attention to detail; and by her employers because of her generosity: however, her patience, goodness, generosity and care for her fellow human beings eventually won their respect.

Zita is a little-known saint and has no churches dedicated to her name, although she has chapels at Ely and Palermo named in her honour. She is found in paintings, stained glass and other art work. She is the patron saint of servants.

Zita the servant   *Sharing/generosity/doing your best/setting an example*

Zita was twelve when she went to live in Mr Fatinelli's house in Italy. She was to work as a servant, and she was looking forward to making friends with the other girls who lived there.

Zita was a hardworking girl. She always tried to do her best even when she was asked to do something that she found difficult, but she soon found out that not everyone thought the same way as her.

'Don't bother doing that so carefully,' one of the girls said to her on her first day when she was cleaning the back step of the house. 'No-one's going to look at it, and anyway, you'll be cleaning it again tomorrow.'

'But I shall look at it,' said Zita. 'I shall know whether it's cleaned properly or not.'

'Well, please yourself,' said the girl, and she walked away.

Later that night Zita climbed the stairs to the bedroom she was to share with some of the others. She knelt down at the side of her bed to say her prayers as usual. 'Dear God,' she whispered. 'Please help me to be happy here. Please help me to do my best and to work hard. Please bless ...' But she got no further with her prayers because she heard giggling and laughter from the other girls. She opened her eyes. They were huddled together pointing at her, mocking, jeering, poking fun at her.

'Dear God please help me to work hard,' they mimicked in silly voices, then began to giggle again.

Zita felt unhappy, lonely and shut out from the people she wanted as her friends. She knew that if she stopped her prayers, and laughed with them, they might accept her. But Zita knew that not to say her prayers was not right for her. She closed her eyes again.

'God bless my family and all my friends. God bless my new friends here in this house. Amen.' And Zita climbed into bed. She noticed that the girls stopped laughing and got into their beds.

The next morning Zita was busy washing the back step again when a thin, ragged, dirty child came to the door.

'Can you give me something to eat please?' he asked.

'Get away with you,' shouted the cook, as she came to the door with a broom to sweep him away. 'I've told you before, we don't have beggars come knocking at our door. Go on. Away!'

'But he's hungry,' said Zita. 'He's probably got no home. We could spare him something. There's lots of food in this house.' And before the cook had time to say any more, Zita ran into the kitchen and came out with a handful of beans.'

'Here, take these,' she said.

The cook was horrified. 'Wait 'till I tell Mr Fatinelli. He'll not be pleased. Just you wait and see. You can't go giving away his food.'

'I'll have less to eat for *my* dinner,' said Zita. 'Then Mr Fatinelli will be no worse off.'

In fact, Mr Fatinelli was a lot worse off because Zita gave food to the beggars every day. She gave away bread and fruit, vegetables and meat, and even puddings left over from banquets that Mr Fatinelli used to give for his rich and influential friends. Zita knew she would be in terrible trouble as soon as Mr Fatinelli found out.

One evening, she met him at the gate as she was leaving the house to go to church.

'Ah, yes, it's Zita isn't it?' said Mr Fatinelli. 'Zita who gives my food away! Is that right?'

'I'm sorry Mr Fatinelli,' said Zita. 'But the beggars have nothing and you have a great deal. That's why I do it.'

'I ought to sack you, you know that don't you?' said Mr Fatinelli.

'Yes,' said Zita.

'Well, I won't,' said Mr Fatinelli with a twinkle in his eye. 'You might be small and only a servant, but you have taught us all to share what we have. We've learned a lot from you. Now, where are you going?'

'I'm going to church,' answered Zita.

'Then here, borrow my cloak,' said Mr Fatinelli. 'It'll keep you warm. But don't lose it, it's my best one.'

'Thank you,' said Zita, and she hurried off to church wrapped in the warm woollen cloak.

At the doorway to the church, Zita saw an old man sitting shivering. His clothes were wet, it had been raining a few minutes earlier. Without thinking, she took off the warm cloak and gave it to him, then went inside.

Mr Fatinelli was furious when she returned home without his cloak.

'You'd give away your last penny wouldn't you!' he shouted. Just then there was a knock at the door. An old man stood on the step with Mr Fatinelli's cloak in his hand.

'I've brought this back,' he said. 'Your servant lent it to me last night when I was waiting for my family outside the church. She's a very special girl that one. She's kind and good and generous. You're lucky to have a girl like that working in your house.'

Mr Fatinelli looked at Zita. Zita who had given away half his food. Zita who had annoyed the servants by always doing her very best work. Zita who said her prayers every night, even though the other girls laughed at her. Zita who had given away his best cloak to an old man who was cold.

'Yes,' said Mr Fatinelli. 'I know I'm lucky to have Zita in my house. She's a very special person.'

Zita stayed in the Fatinelli house for the rest of her life. She became very happy living there, and all the people she ever met felt better for having known her.

Rogation Sunday

5th Sunday after Easter

25 April (if Easter Day is at its earliest of 21 March)
to
30 May (if Easter Day is at its latest of 25 April)

The fifth Sunday after Easter (the Sunday before Ascension Day) is known as Rogation Sunday, and the Monday, Tuesday and Wednesday between it and Ascension Day are Rogation Days. On these days prayers are said to ask God's blessing on all that is planted, and on those who work on the land. The aspect of partnership between God and people is usually emphasised.

A partnership with God   *Working together*

Luc lived nearly 1,500 years ago, in a village near the mountains. It was his job to look after the land, and to try to grow food for the people of the village. Luc did his best, but he never managed to grow very much.

Whenever he remembered, he would plant a few cabbages, or carrots, or beans. Sometimes, he would plant a few grains of wheat, or he would put some potatoes in the ground. He used to say, 'God will do the rest. God will send the sun and the rain and he will make my plants grow.' And then Luc would sit back and wait for God to do his part of the work.

The trouble was though, that God did not seem to be doing his bit. The plants never seemed to grow properly. There was never enough food for the people of the village, certainly in the winter-time; and more often than not, the people went hungry.

'You'll have to do better than this,' they said to Luc. 'After all, it's your job to grow the food for our village.'

'I can't help it if God isn't doing his job properly, can I?' said Luc. 'It's not my fault,' and he went on just as before, planting a few things here and there, and waiting to see what would grow.

One day a wise man came walking through the village. He looked at Luc's straggly beans and struggling cabbages. He saw the few poor, thin, stalks of wheat and the potato plants choked with weeds.

'Why is your land in such a mess?' he asked. 'Why don't you look after it properly?'

'I do,' said Luc. 'It's God who doesn't do his job properly. I plant the seeds and wait for them to grow. But they never do. Well, not properly. It's God's fault.'

'I don't think it is,' said the stranger. 'I think you've forgotten that you need to work with God. You and He need to be partners. You can't just leave him to it.'

'What do you mean?' asked Luc.

'Well,' said the wise man, 'God will send the rain and the sun, but *you* have to do some work too. You have to dig the ground and clear away the stones. You have to get rid of the weeds and pick off the caterpillars and slugs.'

'It sounds like hard work to me,' said Luc.

'It is,' said the wise man. 'But then nearly everything that's worth doing is hard work. Would you like me to help you? We'll ask all the other villagers to help too.'

'Yes please,' said Luc.

That evening, the wise man asked all the people of the village to meet together in one of the fields. He told them that they must all help, if they were to grow enough food for the whole village. He said that they must remember to work with God, and that God and people need to be partners.

The people listened quietly. Then they asked what they should do.

'First we must dig the earth,' said the wise man. 'Then we must plant the seeds. When we've done that, we must ask God to bless our work. Then we must look after the plants as they grow; we can't just leave it up to God.'

'We'll help,' said the people.

They started work immediately. They cleared the land of stones and rubbish. Then they dug the rich dark soil. They planted wheat seeds, for their bread, and vegetables to make their soup. When they had finished, they stood in the middle of the land and asked God to bless the work they had done.

'Dear God, please bless our work. Please help these plants to grow, so that in time we can use them for our food,' they said.

That year, the plants grew well and the people had plenty of food for the winter-time.

Ascension Day

Forty days after Easter

29 April (if Easter Day is at its earliest of 21 March)
to
3 June (if Easter Day is at its latest of 25 April)

Ascension Day, one of the most important Holy Days of the Christian year after Easter and Christmas, is celebrated forty days after Easter, always on a Thursday, and commemorates the end of Christ's earthly work and his return to his Father in Heaven. It is a fundamental Christian belief that all followers will return to the Father in Heaven at the end of their earthly lives.

During the 40 Glorious Days between Easter and Ascension Day, Jesus appeared many times to his followers, confirming that he was indeed the Risen Lord.

The word 'ascension' means 'going up', and the day is so named because the cloud which hid Jesus from the disciples appeared to carry him up into heaven.

Ascension Day has been celebrated since at least the fourth century and is a holiday in many countries, although no longer in Britain. Well-known Ascension Day customs include Beating the Bounds (walking the parish boundaries), and Well Dressing (thanksgiving for the gift of water).

Jesus returns to his Father
adapted from Acts 1:6–12

Jesus had appeared to his disciples several times since Easter Day. Sometimes he had seemed different – a stranger – and his friends had had difficulty in recognising him. But at other times he seemed just as he always had been, and they knew straightaway who he was.

Forty days after Easter Sunday, Jesus met his friends in the upper room in Jerusalem; the same room where they had eaten their last meal together.

'I want to talk to you,' he said. 'It is almost time for me to go back to my Father in Heaven, but first I have things I need to say. Come with me. I want to talk to you outside.'

Jesus led the disciples out of the upper room and through the streets of Jerusalem. It was still early in the morning and few people were about.

They walked out through the city gates and down the hillside. They crossed the small stream in the bottom of the valley, and walked past the Garden of Gethsemane where Jesus had been taken prisoner on Good Friday. They climbed the hillside opposite and reached the Mount of Olives. From here they could look down on the white walls of the buildings in Jerusalem.

Jesus stopped at the top of a grassy hill, and the disciples gathered round him, wondering what he was going to say.

'I want you to know that I am not going to leave you alone,' he said. 'It is time for me to go back to my Father, but you are not to be afraid. I want you to go back to Jerusalem and wait there until I send the Holy Spirit to you. Then you will be strong enough to do my work. When this has happened, I want you to go out into the world, travel to every country, and tell everyone about me. Teach people the right way to live. The work will be hard, but I will always be with you even though you cannot see me.'

As Jesus finished speaking, a low early-morning cloud swirled round the hillside and hid Jesus from sight. The disciples could no longer see him. After a few minutes the cloud lifted, but Jesus had gone.

Then the disciples noticed two men, dressed in white, whom they had not seen before.

'What are you doing?' asked one of the strangers. 'Why are you all standing there looking up at the sky? Don't you know that Jesus is in Heaven now?' And the strangers disappeared.

The disciples went back to Jerusalem. Jesus was no longer with them, but they did not feel sad or unhappy. They knew he would keep his promise to be with them always. They knew he would send the Holy Spirit to make them strong enough to do his work.

They went back to Jerusalem to wait.

Whit Sunday (Pentecost)

Fifty days after Easter

9 May (if Easter Day is at its earliest of 21 March)
to
13 June (if Easter Day is at its latest of 25 April)

Whit Sunday, or Pentecost, is always 50 days after Easter Sunday, and is an ancient festival dating back to the third century, originally celebrated in the Eastern Church. The word 'Pentecost' means fiftieth day, and the Jewish feast of Pentecost (celebration of the harvest) is the fiftieth day after the Sabbath of the Passover. Thus it is also 50 days after Easter Sunday.

Whit Sunday celebrates the coming of the Holy Spirit to the disciples, giving them the courage, strength and ability to become missionaries for Christ. As soon as he received the Holy Spirit, Peter went out and preached to the people resulting in many being baptised to the faith. For this reason Pentecost is also celebrated as the 'birthday' of the Church.

The term 'Whit Sunday' originates from 'White Sunday' because of the white robes traditionally worn by those about to be baptised. (Easter and Pentecost were the traditional times for baptisms.)

The coming of the Holy Spirit
adapted from Acts 2:1–41

There were crowds of people in Jerusalem. They had come to celebrate the Feast of Pentecost; to thank God for the harvest. The temples were decorated with fruit and flowers, and people crowded to the special thanksgiving services.

Jesus's disciples; Peter, James, John and the others, were in Jerusalem for Pentecost. Early in the morning they were together in an upstairs room. They had been talking together, and praying, when suddenly a fierce wind blew through the room.

The weather outside was still and calm; the wind seemed to be inside the room itself. The friends were afraid. Then, as suddenly as the wind had started, it stopped, and there appeared above the head of each man, a beautiful, bright, flame of fire. The fire did not touch them or burn them; it hovered, still and quiet, above each one. And then they understood. God had sent this message to show them that his Holy Spirit would make them strong and brave. Strong and brave enough to go out and tell the world about Jesus.

Peter said, 'Let's go now. There are crowds of people here, let's go tell them what's happened.'

The friends agreed and together they went out of the upstairs room, on to a balcony. From here they could see the people in the street below. Peter went to the edge of the balcony and called down.

'Listen,' he said. A small group of people looked up and listened to what he had to say. Peter told them about Jesus. He told them that Jesus was a good man, but that he had been killed. He told them about Jesus being alive on Easter Day, and how some of the disciples had seen him. He told them about Jesus going back to his father in Heaven, and sending the Holy Spirit as he promised he would.

By now there was a huge gathering of people under the balcony, listening to Peter's words. A few days ago Peter would have felt afraid, speaking to such a large number of people, but now he felt no fear, only a determination to tell all these people about Jesus.

And the strange thing was, that even though many in the crowd were from different countries, and spoke different languages, every one of them could understand what Peter was saying.

'How is it that we can all understand what he says?' asked the people. 'This man is from Galilee; we are from Egypt and Rome, from Palestine and Libya, yet we can each hear him speaking in our own language. How can this be? What does it all mean?'

Some of the crowd believed that God was speaking to them through Peter, but others made fun of him and mocked him.

'Don't listen to him,' the disbelievers said to the others. 'Can't you see – he's drunk! He must be or how else could he talk in tongues, and with such confidence. No, he's not from God – he's drunk!'

But others in the crowd had been in Jerusalem on Good Friday when Jesus was killed. They remembered the things that had happened, and they felt ashamed of what the people had done. They listened carefully to what Peter said.

'Jesus is the son of God,' he told them.

'But we killed him,' said the people. 'What can we do now to put things right?'

'You must tell God that you are sorry,' said Peter. 'And come and be baptised, then you too will receive the gift of the Holy Spirit.'

Later that day Peter and the other disciples baptised almost three thousand people. Three thousand people who wanted to follow the way of Jesus. Three thousand people who wanted to say they were sorry to God for all the wrong things they had done. Three thousand people who wanted to promise to live good lives in the future.

And in the days after Pentecost, more and more people were taught by the disciples, and many of them, too, were baptised.

Trinity Sunday

Sunday after Pentecost

16 May (if Easter is at its earliest of 21 March)
to
20 June (if Easter is at its latest of 25 April)

Trinity Sunday is the Sunday after Pentecost, and is the day when Christians remember that God is three Persons in one; the Father who has always existed, the Son who came to earth to redeem humankind, and the Holy Spirit who gives strength and comfort. This philosophy of three in one, which sets Christianity apart from the other Judaic religions, is fundamental to Christian belief.

Three in one

Saint Patrick was in Ireland talking to the Druid king. At first Patrick and his friends had been afraid that the king might throw them out of the country, or take them prisoner, or even kill them, but they had quickly discovered that the Druid king was not as fierce as they had thought. He seemed interested in what they had to say.

'Tell me more about this man, Jesus,' he said one day. So Patrick told the Druid king how Jesus was born in a stable in Bethlehem. He told him about the shepherds and about the wise men. He told the king about Jesus being crucified on the cross on Good Friday and about him being alive again on Easter Day. He told him about Jesus going back to his Father in heaven, and about the Holy Spirit coming to make the disciples strong enough to go out into the world to do Jesus' work.

'But who sent this man Jesus in to the world?' asked the Druid king.

'God sent him,' said Patrick. 'Jesus is God's Son, and God sent him into the world to teach us how to live.'

'But you said that Jesus is God,' said the Druid king. 'How can God be two people at the same time?'

'God isn't two people at the same time,' said Patrick. 'God is three people. Three persons in one. He is God the Father of us all. He is Jesus, called God the Son. And he is God the Holy Spirit, who is in all of us and helps us to be strong enough to do what is right.'

'I still don't understand,' said the Druid king. 'I don't see how he can be three people all at the same time.'

Patrick wondered how he could explain it to the king. How could he make the king understand that God is three in one.

Suddenly Patrick noticed a patch of shamrock growing in the ground at their feet. Here was the answer. Here was a way of showing the king what he meant.

Patrick bent down and picked a shamrock leaf. He held it up carefully and asked the king to look at it.

'See how it is one leaf growing from one stem,' said Patrick.

'Yes,' said the Druid king. 'I can see that.'

'But see how the leaf is split into three sections,' said Patrick. It's not three separate leaves on three separate stalks; it's one stalk, and one leaf, but three parts to it.'

'Yes, I can see that, I can see it,' said the king. 'But what are you trying to tell me?'

'I'm trying to say that this shamrock leaf is a bit like God,' said Patrick. 'The leaf is one leaf, just as God is one God. But the leaf is in three parts, three sections, just as God is three persons. The three parts of the leaf all make up the whole leaf. They are all as important as each other. The three parts of God all make up one God, they are all as important as each other. The three parts of God are God the Father, God the Son, and God the Holy Spirit.'

'Now I think I see,' said the king. 'Now I think I understand.'

Patrick and the Druid king talked for a long time. Patrick helped him understand many things about the teaching of Jesus, and eventually the Druid king asked if he, too, could become a Christian. Patrick said that of course he could, if he wanted to.

Not only did the Druid king become a Christian, but he gave Patrick and his friends a piece of land so that they could build a church for everyone to come to and worship in.

Patrick never forgot how the shamrock had helped him explain the Trinity – the threeness of God – to the king, and the shamrock became Patrick's emblem.

Corpus Christi

Ten days after Pentecost

19 May (if Easter is at its earliest of 21 March)
to
23 June (if Easter is at its latest of 25 April)

The feast of Corpus Christi, celebrated since 1264, is little-known in Protestant countries but an important festival in the Roman Catholic Church. The name means 'the Body of Christ', and marks a day of thanksgiving for the gift of Holy Communion. The correct time for such a thanksgiving would be Maundy Thursday – the commemoration of Christ's Last Supper with the disciples – but since this is in the solemn season of Lent and close to Good Friday it precludes a celebratory festival. The feast of Corpus Christi, therefore, came to be celebrated ten days after Pentecost.

Corpus Christi is the last of the major festivals in the Christian year. In Italy it is celebrated as the 'Corpus Domini' (the Body of our Lord) and the 'Infiorata' (flower festival) processions. In England, it was customary to perform 'mystery' or 'miracle' plays for the festival. At a time of high illiteracy and little access to the Bible by ordinary people, the mystery plays were a means of teaching the people the stories of the Bible. It was usual for each guild to perform a story relating to its particular skills.

Juliana and the festival of Corpus Christi

Doing your best/perseverance/ patience/tolerance

When she was 16 years old, Juliana went to train to be a nun at the Convent of Mont-Cornillon in Belgium. Juliana worked hard, studied hard and always tried to do the best she could.

Juliana liked her life in the convent. She liked the way the year went round to a pattern, and then went round again, following the same festivals, always in the same order; Advent, then Christmas, Lent, then Easter, Ascension, then the feast of Pentecost. She liked to celebrate the special feast days of the Saints; Saint Stephen's Day in December, Saint Peter's Day in June. She liked the hymns they sang and the prayers they said on the special days of the year. But always Juliana felt that there was a day missing, a day that should be special but had somehow been overlooked at the time when special days were first decided.

Juliana had no idea which the missing special day might be, so she tried to treat every day as a special one. After all, every day was a new day, every day was a different day, every day was a special day in one way or another.

One day Juliana was in the small chapel, praying by herself. It was towards the end of day and she could see a patch of darkening sky through the tall, arched window near the altar. There was a single, pale star glimmering faintly, just visible beyond the clouds. Then the clouds parted and Juliana could see the moon. Tonight it was a full, round, clear, creamy-white moon. But as Juliana looked, it seemed that the moon had a mark near the edge of it, a dark spot, a stain, a blemish, which spoiled the smooth whiteness of its surface. The longer Juliana looked at the mark, the more noticeable it seemed to become. The mark worried her, it upset her, it seemed to be telling her that something was wrong, something was missing, something was incomplete.

Juliana continued to stare at the moon. She looked all round the circular edge of it, but the mark was stopping her eyes from travelling in a complete circle. It was like looking at a saucer with a piece broken out of it. It was like looking at a biscuit with a bite taken out. It was like looking at a whole year with a special day taken out.

Juliana looked away from the moon and at the altar. She saw the tall, golden cross in the middle, and she saw the special golden plate and cup which was used to hold the bread and wine for the communion service. Suddenly she knew what was missing. She understood the message of the moon. She knew what the missing day was that she had worried about for so long. There was not a special day in the whole of the year for celebrating the Body of Christ. There was no Corpus Christi.

When Juliana had finished her prayers she hurried off to speak to the convent Mother.

'There isn't a special day for Corpus Christi,' she said. 'Can we make a special day? Can we choose a day to celebrate Corpus Christi?'

'Most certainly not!' was the answer. 'We cannot choose new special days just because we feel like it,' said the convent mother. 'Let me hear no more of it.'

But Juliana could not let her idea disappear. She asked everyone she knew if they could help her make a special festival for Corpus Christi. At last the Bishop of Liege heard about her idea, and he declared that the feast of Corpus Christi should be celebrated in Liege.

Juliana was delighted, but the nuns in her convent were not.

'Who does she think she is, trying to change things,' they grumbled. 'She's no business altering anything. Things were best left as they were.'

Eventually, Juliana's life was made so miserable by the nuns who hated the change she had brought about, that Juliana had to leave her convent. She went to live by herself, many miles from Mont-Cornillon. She was sure that the Corpus Christi festival would no longer be celebrated in Liege.

But Juliana did not know that there was someone else who liked the idea of celebrating the festival of Corpus Christi. The Pope himself had heard news of what Juliana wanted to do. In September in the year 1264, Pope Urban IV declared that there should be a special day in the year when everyone would celebrate the festival of Corpus Christi.

The next time that Juliana looked at the moon, it seemed whole, complete, with no mark or stain or blemish or missing part. And at last she felt that the special days in the year were complete, with no missing days.

Saint Bede

25 May

The Venerable Bede has been described as the Father of English learning; first among English scholars, theologians and historians.

Bede was born near Sunderland in 673, orphaned at the age of seven and sent to the monastery at Wearmouth under the tuition of Abbot Benedict Biscop, who also founded Wearmouth's sister monastery at Jarrow in 682, where Bede later transferred. Benedict built up an extensive library containing a wealth of contemporary works from Europe, which enabled Bede to study as he did.

Bede became a monk and priest and was reputed to have spent his entire adult life at Jarrow, only occasionally travelling as far as Lindisfarne or York. He spent his days studying, writing, teaching and singing, but it is as an historian that he is best remembered. His 'Ecclesiastical History of the English People', *completed in 731, is acknowledged as his most significant work and as a world classic. It has been frequently translated throughout the centuries, including the twentieth.*

Bede died in 735, after completing a translation of St John's Gospel.

All is finished   *Perseverance/doing your best*

Bede was a monk who lived in the monastery at Jarrow. He had lived there for a long time, never leaving it, never travelling anywhere else.

'Why don't you go and see the world?' some of the younger monks used to ask. 'Why don't you travel to see other places, other cities, other countries?'

'I'm too busy to travel,' said Bede. 'I have too much to do. I have all these books to read in our library, and I have my own books to write. I'm too busy. Anyway, I'm happy here. Why should I want to go somewhere else.'

It was true. Bede was happy at Jarrow.

Every day he woke early and went to the chapel to pray and to sing hymns to God. Then he went into the library to read and to write. There were hundreds of books in the library. The first Abbot of Jarrow had travelled all over Europe and he brought books back with him. Bede was also busy writing books of his own. He had written books on music, astronomy, science, history and English. He was now working on a book called *The History of the English Church and*

People. It was about Saint Augustine bringing the news of Jesus to England, and about what happened during the next 150 years. Bede had done a great deal of research for this book.

Bede spent each morning working in the library. Then, in the afternoon, he worked as a teacher, helping the younger monks to study the Bible. In the evenings Bede went again to the chapel to sing, then he read until it was time to go to bed.

'No,' he used to say. 'I'm too busy to go travelling. I need to stay here to get on with my work.'

One day the monks went on a visit to York.

'Come with us,' they said to Bede. 'It would be better if we *all* went. Come with us.'

So, reluctantly, Bede went along. York was a lovely town and the minster was beautiful. It was built of stone so pale it was almost white. Bede enjoyed the singing in the minster most of all. He liked to sing. But he was unhappy away from Jarrow.

'I need to get back,' he said. 'I'm too busy to be here. I have my work to do.'

So Bede set off back to Jarrow monastery earlier than the rest of the monks. He had been away six days, but it was six days too long.

A few years later, the monks went to visit Lindisfarne Island, just off the coast, and again Bede was asked to join them. There was a monastery on Lindisfarne and the monks there welcomed the monks from Jarrow. But again Bede was unhappy about being away from Jarrow and his work.

'I must go back,' he said. 'I'm too busy to be here. I have my work to do.' Bede hurried back to Jarrow. This time he had been away eight days.

Bede had now started a new book. It was a translation of Saint John's Gospel from the Bible. But Bede by now was an old man. He was becoming ill and weak.

'He'll never finish this book,' the other monks said.

'I will finish it,' said Bede to himself. 'I'm too busy to be ill. I have my work to do.'

But Bede grew more and more frail. He was no longer able to sit at his desk and write, so he dictated the words to a young boy, and he wrote them down.

Then Bede became very ill and knew that he would soon die.

'It's time to stop working now,' said the doctors, but Bede would not give up.

'I can't die yet,' he said. 'I have my work to finish.'

Bede had just started the last chapter of his book, but he was now so weak he could only whisper the words to the boy.

'He'll not finish it,' said the monks sadly.

Bede struggled on, determined to finish his work.

'Write more quickly,' he whispered to the boy.

That evening, Bede knew he would live only a little longer.

'How much more is there to do?' he asked the boy.

'I am writing the last sentence,' he answered. Then, 'It is finished,' he said.

'Well said,' smiled Bede. 'All is finished now,' and Bede died, happy that his book was completed.

Saint Augustine of Canterbury
26 May

It is not known on what date Augustine was born, though he died in Canterbury c. 605. He is known as Augustine of Canterbury to distinguish him from Augustine who spent much time as a bishop in Africa and who became one of the four great Latin doctors of the Church.

Augustine of Canterbury was a missionary bishop, and was sent by Pope Gregory the Great in the year 596 to England to preach the gospel. Some 40 monks, led by Augustine, arrived in Kent in 597 and were welcomed by King Ethelbert, who later, together with a large number of his people, were baptised Christians.

Augustine established a church at Canterbury, and was made the first Archbishop of the English. He later founded bishoprics in London and Rochester, but was not accepted archbishop by the Christians in Wales and the south west. However, from the earliest times Augustine has been known as the evangeliser of England.

Saint Augustine and the children from England   *Perseverance*

A monk called Gregory was once walking through the market-place in Rome. He liked the market with its warmth and colour and lively atmosphere. He liked to walk past all the different stalls: the bread stall with its delicious smells, the fruit stall with its tumble of bright colours, the cloth stall with its gaudy lengths of fabric blowing in the wind like flags.

But he did not like to walk past the stall selling caged birds, or the stall where the children stood, waiting to be sold as slaves and servants to rich people.

On this particular day, Gregory saw a larger group of children than usual. He went across to see why, and was astonished to see some fair-skinned, fair-haired, blue-eyed children amongst the group of dark-haired, sun-burnt Roman children.

'Where are these children from?' he asked the stall holder. 'I've never seen such pale children before.'

'They're children from Britain,' said the man. 'They're called Angles, from

Angle-Land, and they're waiting to be sold as slaves.'

'They look more like angels than Angles, with that lovely golden hair,' said Gregory.

The man laughed. 'They won't know what angels are,' he said. 'They're heathens in Angle-Land. They don't know about God and angels.'

Gregory felt sad to think that a whole country of people did not know about God, or Jesus, or his love for the world. 'But they will soon,' he thought. 'For I shall travel to Angle-Land to tell them.' And he walked back to the monastery with his head full of plans of how he was going to travel to England, as it was called later, to tell the people there about God.

But his plans were not to be.

'Travel to England?' said the abbot of the monastery. 'I'm afraid you can't do that. There is important work for you to do here in Rome. You are soon to be made Pope. You cannot go to England. I'm sorry.'

But Gregory could not forget the children he had seen, and the people of England who did not know about God.

'If I cannot go to England,' said Gregory, 'then someone else shall go instead. I shall send Augustine.' Augustine was a monk from Gregory's old monastery.

'Will you go?' asked Gregory.

'Yes,' said Augustine. 'But I cannot go alone. I shall need people to travel with me.'

Augustine, with Gregory's help, made all the plans, and a group of 40 monks with Augustine in charge set off by ship for England.

It was a long and dangerous journey, but at last the ship arrived on the south east coast of England. The monks were taken to see the king.

'Be ready for a hostile meeting,' said Augustine. 'The king may not want to see us.' But King Ethelbert greeted the visitors warmly and wanted to know why they had come. The king listened carefully as Augustine and the other monks explained about God and about Jesus, his Son.

'You must tell all my people about this,' said the king, and he arranged for a great open-air meeting to take place at which Augustine and the monks could tell again the story of Jesus.

The day of the meeting came. Crowds of people packed into the open space to listen to Augustine. The crowd grew silent as Augustine started to speak.

'There is One True God, and he sent his Son, Jesus, to save us,' said Augustine. He went on to tell the people the stories of Jesus, and the crowd listened, spellbound. When Augustine finished speaking the people clapped and cheered and wanted to know if they, too, could become Christians. Augustine told them they could all be baptised if they wanted to follow Jesus.

Within a few months more than 10,000 people, including King Ethelbert, had been baptised Christians, and Augustine had begun to build a magnificent church at Canterbury, on land that the king gave him.

'You shall be archbishop here,' said the king. 'You will be the head of all the

Christians in England.

And so it was that Augustine became the first Archbishop of Canterbury, but he never forgot that it had been the sight of the English children in the market-place in Rome, that had inspired Pope Gregory to send him to England. So each time a child was christened, he or she was given a Christian name so that everyone would know that the news of Jesus had reached the children of England.

The visit of the Virgin Mary to Elizabeth

31 May

This day commemorates Mary's visit to her cousin Elizabeth in Ain Karim near Jerusalem. Some two months earlier Mary had been told by the angel Gabriel that she was to have a child by the Holy Spirit, who would be the Son of God.

Elizabeth was also carrying a child. Her husband Zechariah had been told by the angel Gabriel that their baby, to be called John, would in adulthood prepare the people for the coming of the Messiah.

When Mary arrived at Elizabeth's house, the Bible reports that Elizabeth was filled with the Holy Spirit and that her child moved within her. Mary then sang the song of praise we now know as the Magnificat.

Mary visits Elizabeth
adapted from Luke 1:39–56

Mary had been told by the angel Gabriel that she was going to have a baby, but she had mixed feelings about this news. She was happy and pleased that she had been chosen to be the mother of Jesus, but at the same time she was worried in case Joseph and her family did not understand.

She needed someone to talk to. Someone who would listen and not be angry with her. Someone who would understand.

'Elizabeth,' thought Mary. 'My cousin Elizabeth will listen to me, and she will understand how I feel. After all, she is soon to have a baby herself. I'll go and see her.'

Mary planned the visit. Elizabeth lived in the village of Ain Karim, nearly 80 miles from Mary's home in Nazareth. It would take several days to get there and Mary needed to make arrangements to stay with friends overnight on the way. She packed a few things to take with her, some clean clothes, a little food, some money. At last everything was ready. Mary said goodbye to Joseph, promised she would be back after her holiday, and set off.

The journey went well, and within a week Mary was walking up the hill towards Elizabeth's house. Elizabeth saw her and ran to meet her.

'Mary, you're here. I'm so pleased to see you. There's such a lot to tell you. I want to show you all the things I've got ready for the new baby. It won't be long now before it's born, only another three months. Come on, into the house, and then we can talk.'

Mary and Elizabeth went inside and Mary said, 'I have something to tell you, Elizabeth. I have some news, some wonderful news. I must tell you. I must talk to you about it.'

As soon as Mary started to speak, Elizabeth knew straight away what she was going to say. She felt pleased and happy, joyful and excited all at the same time. 'I am so glad for you,' she said. 'You are going to be the very special mother of a very special baby. Blessed are you among women, and blessed is your child.'

Then Elizabeth put her hands on her stomach, as though she was thinking of her own baby, due to be born soon.

'He's moving,' she laughed. 'I can feel him kicking. He's moving because even he knows that you're going to have a special baby.'

Mary smiled. She was relieved and happy to know that Elizabeth understood about her baby. She stopped feeling worried about what Joseph and the family might think. She knew now that everything would turn out all right. She felt so happy that she began to sing. She sang of her joy at being chosen to be the mother of Jesus. She sang of her happiness that Jesus was coming to help everyone. She sang of being glad that Jesus was going to be the Saviour that God had promised. She was so happy that the words she sang were as beautiful as poetry.

Mary stayed with Elizabeth for several weeks. They enjoyed their time together. They were good friends to each other, and talked and laughed and sometimes prayed together.

At last Mary knew it was time to go home again, time to go back to Nazareth, time to talk to Joseph about the future. She began to feel worried again. But there was no need. God had spoken to Joseph and told him what was going to happen, so that he, too, understood and was able to help Mary and look after her.

Saint Boniface

5 June

Boniface was born c. 680 in Devon, the eldest son of land-owning, Anglo-Saxon parents. Christened Winfrith, Boniface was educated at monasteries near Exeter and Winchester. He became a monk and teacher, and wrote the first Latin grammar in England.

Boniface left England and a promising career in the Church in 718, to become a missionary on the Continent. He worked initially in Germany, where he founded several monasteries before being made supreme bishop of all Germany. He then reformed the Church in France and at the end of his life returned to Holland, where he died a martyr in 754 still involved in missionary work.

Soon after his death, an English synod decided that there should be an annual celebration of the feast of Boniface, since he was regarded on a par with Gregory and Augustine. However, he is now better remembered in Germany and Holland than in England.

Because Boniface liaised closely with popes and with emperors, creating working partnerships, and because of the far-reaching influence of his monasteries, it is believed by some that Boniface had a greater overall influence on the history of Europe than any other Englishman.

Boniface is the patron saint of brewers and of tailors.

Boniface and the great oak tree

Perseverance/doing your best/ standing up for what you believe to be right

Boniface was a monk. He lived in England. He was a very clever man; he studied hard and learned a great deal about the Bible, so that he was able to become a teacher and teach other monks. Boniface could read and write Latin. He wrote a book about Latin to help the other monks learn it.

'You're a very intelligent man,' said the abbot of the monastery to Boniface one day. 'I'd like you to go and work with the Archbishop of Canterbury. You are very honoured to be asked to do this special job,' and the abbot smiled at Boniface, quite sure that he would be delighted to have been chosen for this job. So it was with some surprise that the abbot heard Boniface say, 'I'm sorry. I can't go. I don't want to work with the Archbishop of Canterbury. I know it's an honour to be asked, but it's not what I want to do. I've known for a long time that I really want to go to Germany and Holland and France to teach the people there about Jesus.'

The abbot was astonished. 'But there are no Christians in those countries,' he said.

'I know,' said Boniface. 'That's why I want to go. I want to help the people there to become Christians.'

The abbot could see that this was what Boniface really wanted to do, so arrangements were made for him to travel to the Continent.

With three friends, Boniface set sail for Holland and landed in a place called Friesland. He tried to speak to the king, but no-one would let him. He tried to speak to the people, but no-one would listen. In the end Boniface had no choice but to come home again.

'Don't worry,' said the abbot of his monastery. 'You can stay here and look after a monastery of your own. I've arranged for you to have one at ...'

'No!' said Boniface. 'I failed last time, but I'm not going to give up until I have helped those people to become Christians.'

'You're surely not going back?' said the abbot.

'Yes,' said Boniface. 'First I am going to Rome to ask the Pope for permission to teach Christanity in Holland and Germany. Then I am going back to Friesland and I am going to teach the people.'

Once again arrangements were made for Boniface to travel to Holland. Once again he arrived in Friesland, but this time armed with letters from the Pope giving him permission to teach.

Boniface travelled all around the area. He tried to talk to the people, but again they would not listen. They had their own Gods, they did not want to listen to Boniface talking about his.

One day Boniface was trying to talk to a group of people who were gathered round a large oak tree. He told them that he wanted to build a church where they could all come and worship God and learn about Jesus.

'We could cut down this tree,' he said, 'and use the wood to build the church.'

Suddenly there was a horrified silence. Then one man spoke.

'You must not damage this tree,' he said. 'This tree belongs to the great God Thor; Thor who is the God of Thunder, Thor the son of Odin who is the chief of all the Gods, Thor who is the son of mother earth herself. If you harm this tree, you will be killed immediately by a great flash of lightning. You must not damage this tree.'

'I will prove to you that my God is the one true God,' said Boniface. 'I will cut down this tree and you will see that nothing dreadful will happen to me. It is only an old oak tree. Give me an axe.'

Someone handed Boniface an axe, then all the people ran away to the edge of the clearing, so as to be out of harm's way when the great God Thor killed Boniface, as he surely would.

Boniface lifted the axe high into the air. For a split second the people held their breath as Boniface held the axe aloft. Then he swung it down, down, hard against the trunk of the tree. A chip of wood flew out of the trunk, as Boniface had expected, and he lifted the axe high in the air again ready for the second blow.

But before Boniface could bring the axe down again, there was a deep cracking, splintering, breaking noise and the tree split into four parts and crashed to the ground.

The people stared in astonishment. Boniface was standing there completely unharmed, but the tree, the great oak tree, the tree belonging to their God Thor, was lying broken, fragmented, destroyed, on the ground.

The people surged forward to see it. They stared again at the tree, then at Boniface. Then someone said, 'I think you are right. I think our Gods are not as strong as we thought, otherwise they would have killed you for destroying the tree. I think we would like you to tell us about your God.'

Boniface spent a long time telling them about God and about Jesus. The people listened, and soon many of them asked if they, too, could become Christians. Later, they all helped to build a new church out of the wood of the great oak tree.

Boniface spent the rest of his life working in Holland and Germany and France, and he was eventually made the Archbishop of All Germany.

Saint Columba

9 June

Columba was born in County Donegal in Ireland c. 521. He trained as a monk and spent 15 years preaching in Ireland and establishing monasteries at Derry, Durrow, and it is believed at Kells.

In 563 Columba left Ireland, possibly as an act of penance for his involvement in a battle between monasteries caused by a copied psalter. Columba and 12 monks sailed to Iona where he remained for the next 34 years until his death in 597, returning to Ireland only occasionally.

On Iona, Columba founded the monastery which became the heart of Celtic Christianity and which played such an important part in the Christian history of northern Britain. He preached among the Picts, converted King Brude to Christianity and made many missionary journeys to northern England and the Scottish mainland.

Columba was reputed to be the one who evangelised Scotland, but it is now evident that much further work was carried out by those who followed him. The biographer Adomnan described Columba as a man of strong build and powerful presence, an outspoken man unafraid of pursuing God's cause, yet also a scholar and poet, with a cheerful, loving personality

Columba sails to Iona   *repentance/doing your best/honesty/temptation*

Columba was a small boy when he was sent to the monastery near his home to learn to read and write. Not many children in those days, nearly 1,500 years ago, could read or write but Columba's parents knew that it was important.

On his first day at the monastery, Columba saw an elderly monk sitting at a tall desk. The monk was sitting very still and concentrating hard. Columba crept nearer to see what he was doing.

The monk was writing, very slowly, extremely carefully, very painstakingly on crisp, cream-coloured parchment, with a fine quill pen. At the top of the page was a large capital letter L, written in black ink but then decorated with a curling pattern of swirling, whirling leaves and flowers and animals. The pattern was painted in the most wonderful colours of red and blue and green and silver and gold. The capital letter shone and sparkled in the light above the smaller black lettering that the monk was now doing.

'What are you doing that for?' asked Columba.

'I'm copying this *Book of Psalms* to make a new book,' said the monk.

'Can I do some?' asked Columba.

'No,' laughed the monk. 'At least, not yet. First you must learn to read. Then to write. Then to write better. Then to write better still. Then, after a great deal of practice you'll be able to write like this. But you'll have to work hard. It's not easy. You'll have to do your best.'

Columba did his best and worked well at his lessons. He quickly learned to read and write, and was soon copying prayers and stories of his own. Columba knew that when he was grown up he wanted to be a monk and copy the beautiful prayer books and Bibles that he had seen the old monk working on.

Time passed and Columba became abbot of a monastery in Derry. He spent a great deal of time making books for the monastery by copying out other books that he had been given or lent.

One day the monastery borrowed a beautiful *Book of Psalms* from a monastery in a neighbouring kingdom.

'This is the most lovely book I've ever seen,' said Columba. 'Look at these wonderful illuminated letters. Look at the pictures and the colours. I wish we had a book like this.' And that gave Columba the idea of copying it. 'No-one will know,' he said. 'And even if they do, I don't suppose they'll mind.'

But Columba was wrong.

When the owners of the book found out that it had been copied, without permission, they were furious. They told their king, and before anyone had time to try to sort things out peacefully, a battle had begun between the two kingdoms.

Columba was desperately sorry to see that people were being killed, all because he had taken something that was not his to have.

'I must do something to show how sorry I am,' said Columba. 'People must know that I'm truly sorry. I will leave this place. I love it, but I'll leave it to show I'm sorry.'

Columba set off with 12 monks from his monastery, and they sailed away from the shores of Ireland. The sea was rough and wild, but they headed towards the rocky islands off the coast of Scotland. They landed on the island of Iona, where they were told they could stay.

Over the next few months, Columba and his friends built a church and made a farm. They cleared the land and sowed seeds. They planted vegetables and reared animals. They made a monastery on the island of Iona. And every day they said prayers to God to thank him for their lives and for their island.

'And now we must go and teach people on the mainland about Jesus,' said Columba.

'But we won't be allowed to,' said the monks. 'The king of Scotland is not a Christian, so he won't let us talk to his people about Christ.'

'Then I shall have to talk to him first, won't I,' said Columba.

He set off for the mainland and went to see King Brude, but as Columba approached the walls of the king's city, the gates were slammed shut in his face, and he could hear them being bolted against him from the inside.

'Let me in to speak to the king,' called Columba.

'You're not wanted here,' shouted a voice from inside the city walls. Go away!'

'But I come in the name of Jesus,' called Columba. Suddenly, at the name of Jesus, the locks and chains fell away from the gates and they swung open. Columba walked into the city.

King Brude allowed Columba to speak to him, and was interested in what he had to say. He invited him to stay for a while and talk to him some more. Columba stayed several weeks, preaching, teaching, talking about Jesus and his life on earth.

'I want to become a Christian too,' said King Brude one day.

Columba went back to Iona soon after that, glad that now he and his monks could travel throughout Scotland, teaching about Jesus, and building churches and monasteries. But always after their journeys they went back to the island of Iona, which they now thought of as their holy island, their home.

Saint Alban

22 June

Alban is known as the first British Christian martyr. He died at Verulamium, now St Albans c. 209. He is said to have died for giving shelter to a Christian priest.

Alban and the Christian

Alban was a rich man, living in a fine house near London in the days when the Romans ruled Britain. Alban was not a Christian; few people were in those days. He worshipped the heathen Gods, like most people of the time.

One day a man came knocking at Alban's door.

'Please help me,' gasped the man. 'The Roman soldiers are after me. They'll kill me if they catch me. Please help.'

'What makes you think I can help you?' asked Alban.

'I've heard you're a good man, a kind man. Please help me. Quickly. They're coming.'

Alban heard the sound of the soldiers' feet on the road. He heard their voices and knew they would show no mercy if they caught this man.

'Come in,' he said, pulling the man inside his house. 'And tell me what it is you've done that makes the soldiers want to kill you.'

The man was glad to be inside, safe for the time being. He closed the door firmly behind him.

'I've done nothing wrong,' he told Alban. 'I haven't stolen anything or murdered anyone. All I've done is to become a Christian, but I'll be killed if the Roman soldiers catch me. They kill any Christians they find.'

'It's true it's a dangerous time for the Christians,' said Alban. 'You must be very sure of your faith if you are prepared to put yourself in danger of death. So tell me about your God. Why is he so special?'

The man, who was a Christian priest, told Alban of God the Father, and of Jesus his Son. He told him of Jesus' love for everyone and of Jesus' wish that everyone should love one another. Alban was impressed by the man's belief in his god, and by his calmness and bravery.

For the next few days the man stayed in hiding in Alban's house. Each day he told Alban more about the life of Jesus, and Alban decided that he, too, would become a Christian.

Then, the soldiers came searching again. Alban saw them knocking at the door of every house on the street.

'It's no good,' said the man. 'They'll be here in a few minutes and they'll find me. But I'm not afraid to die now. Thank you for looking after me these past few days.'

'You're not going to die,' said Alban. 'Because they're not going to find you. Here, change clothes with me. You put on my cloak and go out through the back door. I'll deal with the soldiers.'

So Alban and the Christian priest exchanged clothes and the priest escaped through the back of the house, just as the soldiers came knocking at the front.

'Alban, let us in,' they shouted. 'We know you're hiding a priest in there. He's been seen. Come on, open up.'

The soldiers burst into the house and saw Alban standing there, dressed in the robes of the Christian priest.

'You've hidden him and allowed him to escape, haven't you?' said the soldiers. 'Why have you done this?'

'Because I, too, am a Christian,' said Alban.

'Then you, too, shall die,' said the soldiers, and they took Alban to Holywell Hill – the place of execution. A young Roman soldier was told to kill Alban with his sword.

'But he is a holy man,' said the soldier. 'I cannot kill a holy man of God.'

'Then you will die too, for disobeying instructions,' said the captain.

And so on that day, Alban and the young Roman soldier were put to death together on Holywell Hill.

The place where Alban died is now called St Albans, in memory of the first man in Britain known to have been killed because he was a Christian.

Saint Audrey (Etheldreda)

23 June

Audrey, also known as Ethelreda, was born c. 630 at Exning. She was one of five daughters (all honoured as saints) of King Anna of East Anglia.

Audrey's first marriage to a prince was believed not to have been consummated, and she was widowed after only three years. Her second marriage was to Egfrith, the 15 year old King of Northumbria, but they apparently had a platonic relationship which eventually led Egfrith to release his wife after 12 years.

Audrey became a nun and in 672 entered a convent in Coldingham. A year later she founded a double monastery at Ely on the site where the cathedral now stands, and remained there until she died in 679.

Bede wrote a lengthy hymn in praise of Audrey. She was certainly one of the most revered Anglo-Saxon women saints, and has a number of churches dedicated to her.

The word 'tawdry', derived from the now obsolete 'tawdry lace', is a corruption of 'St Audrey's lace' and referred to the cheap silk and lace fripperies to be found at the St Audrey's fair in Ely.

Audrey is the patron saint of Ely and of Cambridge University.

Audrey and the Isle of Ely   *perseverance/patience*

Audrey was a princess. When she was still a teenager she was married to a prince, but sadly he died soon after they were married and Audrey went to live in a place called the Isle of Ely, which had been given to her when she married. In those days Ely was a real island, surrounded by water and marshland where many eels lived, which is why it was called Ely.

Audrey decided to build a monastery on the island – a place where monks and nuns could work and pray and learn and serve God. She planned where the church would be built, where the houses would go, where the library and the dining hall and the gardens would be. But, before she had time to put any of her plans into action, her uncle told her she must get married again.

'We have found a suitable husband for you,' he said. 'His name is Egfrith and he is the new King of Northumbria. Just think Audrey, in a few months you will be queen.'

'But I don't want to be a queen,' said Audrey. 'I want to be a nun. I want to build a monastery at Ely and live there.'

'Don't be silly,' said her uncle. 'If you want to serve God, you can do it just as well from a palace as from a monastery. Anyway, it has all been decided. You will marry Egfrith soon.'

Audrey knew that she had no choice. In those days it was quite usual for marriage to be arranged between kings and princesses, so that two kingdoms could join together.

Audrey was taken to meet Egfrith.

'I will be your friend,' she said to him. 'But I cannot be a loving wife to you because I love God the most.' Egfrith felt sure that when they were married, Audrey would become a loving wife and that they would have children.

But he was wrong.

Living as a queen just made Audrey want more and more to live on the Isle of Ely and build her monastery, and although Audrey was very fond of Egfrith, she felt sure that she should never have married him.

'Please will you let me go back to Ely?' she begged time and time again. But each time she asked, Egfrith said no. Her place was with him as his queen.

Then one day, quite unexpectedly, Egfrith said yes. She could go. She could leave straight away if she wanted to.

Audrey set off immediately in case Egfrith changed his mind. And change his mind he did. Almost as soon as Audrey had gone, Egfrith wanted her back.

'Go and find her,' he said to his soldiers. 'Bring her back here where she belongs.' But the soldiers could not find Audrey. They searched in all the places they thought she might be. They went to Ely and looked there. But Audrey was nowhere to be found. They went back to tell Egfrith she was lost.

'Lost!' shouted Egfrith. 'Then find her! Call out more soldiers. Call out the army. I'll even come myself. But find her!'

Egfrith and the soldiers discovered that Audrey had visited her aunt at her convent in Coldingham, but she had already left, and her aunt would not say where she had gone. Then a neighbour said he had seen Audrey, going towards Coldeburgh Head, and he pointed out the way.

Egfrith took the road he had been shown. He saw Audrey ahead, hurrying. He called to her but she ran further on, scrambling over to a huge rock that jutted out into the sea.

Egfrith followed her. He was catching up with her now. A few more strides and he would be able to reach out and touch her. He knew she could not escape from him because there was nowhere else for her to go; the sea was all around.

Egfrith stretched forward to catch Audrey's hand, but the sea swirled between them and separated them. With each wave the sea between them grew deeper, rougher. Audrey was safe on the rock, but Egfrith could not reach her.

Egfrith waited for the tide to go down. 'It won't be long,' he thought. But although he waited and waited, the tide stayed high. He waited all the next day and night, but the sea still separated him from Audrey. Egfrith waited a week, but the sea still swirled between them.

At last Egfrith decided that this was a sign from heaven that God wanted Audrey to go to Ely and live her life the way she wanted to.

'All right,' he said. 'I will release you from our marriage. I can see that it is right for you to go to Ely and build your monastery. I shall not stop you,' and Egfrith left Audrey on the rock and went back home.

As soon as Egfrith had gone, the sea grew calmer, smoother, shallower. The tide went down and Audrey was able to leave the rock.

She travelled to Ely as quickly as she could, and the very next day began making plans again for the monastery. It took a long time to build, but there has been a cathedral on the site ever since.

The birth of St John the Baptist

24 June

Through the Old Testament Prophets, God had promised to send a redeemer, a saviour for his people, but the way had to be paved for the Messiah, the people had to be prepared. God chose Zechariah and Elizabeth to be the parents of John, the man who would later tell the people that the Messiah was coming, and who would ask them to change their ways, follow the will of God, and be ready to accept the saviour.

John, later known as John the Baptist, lived in the desert until the time came for him to begin God's work. When he knew that the time was right, John went to live near the River Jordan, where he spoke to people about the coming of the Messiah, asked people to repent of their sins, and symbolically cleansed them of sin by baptising them in the waters of the Jordan.

John one day baptised Jesus, and as the baptism took place, a dove flew from heaven as the voice of God said, 'This is my beloved son in whom I am well pleased.' Jesus then knew it was time to begin his ministry on earth.

John the baptist is patron saint of farriers, tailors and motorways.

The birth of John the Baptist
adapted from Luke 1:5–23 & 57–66

Zechariah and Elizabeth had been married for many years, and lived in the village of Ain Karim near Jerusalem. They were kind people, well liked by their friends and neighbours, happy mostly, except that they had no children, and now it seemed that they would never have a child because they were getting old.

Zechariah was a priest in the temple at Jerusalem, and one day there was great excitement in the village because he had been chosen out of all the priests to be on duty in the holiest part of the temple. This was a very special job that every priest looked forward to being asked to do. It was such a special task that a priest could only be expected to do it once in a lifetime, and now Zechariah had been chosen for it.

Zechariah walked into the coolness of the temple. The other priests, together with Elizabeth and some more people who had come to pray, had to stay in the outer part of the temple but Zechariah went in to the holiest part, alone. He walked towards the golden altar.

Suddenly Zechariah became aware of someone else standing by the altar, someone else in this holiest part of the temple. Zechariah felt afraid.

'Don't be afraid,' said the stranger. 'I come from God to tell you that you and Elizabeth are going to have a baby. You are going to have a son. You are to call him John. When he grows up he will have a special job to do. You see, God is to send his own Son into the world soon. John's job is to tell the people to get ready for him, to prepare for him, to be ready to listen to him when he comes. John is to be a special person, and you and Elizabeth have been chosen to be his mother and father.'

'But I can't believe this,' said Zechariah. 'We are too old now to have a child. I can't believe what you're saying to me.'

'You cannot believe the word of God?' said the stranger. 'I am the angel Gabriel who has brought you this good news from God, but you cannot believe it? Well, since you do not believe me, you will be silent until after the baby is born. Then you will see that I have told you the truth.'

Zechariah stood by the altar not knowing what to believe. In the meantime, the people outside were wondering why Zechariah was taking so long. Surely he should have finished his job by now. Why was he such a long time. What was he doing.

Eventually Zechariah came out of the inner temple, and straight away Elizabeth and the others knew something had happened. Zechariah could not speak.

That evening Zechariah wrote down what had happened in the temple so that Elizabeth could understand. And a short time later, neither Zechariah nor Elizabeth were surprised to find out that Elizabeth was pregnant. She would soon have the baby she had wanted for such a long time.

At last the baby was born. A beautiful baby boy.

When the child was eight days old, Zechariah and Elizabeth had a naming service, followed by a party for all their friends and relatives.

'He's a lovely baby,' everyone said. 'You must be very proud of him. He's beautiful.'

'You'll be naming him Zechariah after his father, won't you?' they all said. 'After all, it's the thing to do, to name a first born son after his dad. Baby Zechariah!' they all said.

'No!' said Elizabeth. 'Our baby won't be called Zechariah. He's going to be called John.'

'But no-one in the family is called John,' someone said. 'You must call him Zechariah.'

'No!' said Elizabeth again. 'He will be called John.'

Someone turned to Zechariah and asked him what he thought. They gave him something to write with because they knew he could not speak. Zechariah wrote 'John', and then to everyone's surprise he said, quite clearly, 'Our baby will be called John.'

At that moment, when Zechariah could speak again, he knew that the angel Gabriel had spoken the truth. He knew that John would be a special baby with special work to do for God when he was older.

And having found his voice again, Zechariah wasted no time in telling everyone the story of the angel in the temple and of the special work that John would do when he was grown up.

'He is a very special baby,' everyone said. And Elizabeth smiled at her son, because she knew he was.

Saint Peter
29 June

Peter, together with his brother Andrew, were fishermen of Bethsaida, on the Sea of Galilee, when Jesus called them to follow him. Peter's original name was Simon, but Jesus gave him the title of 'Kephas', meaning rock, and said, 'upon his rock I will build my Church'. Peter is the English equivalent of the name.

Peter was the leader of the Apostles, loved Jesus and acknowledged him as the Son of God, yet denied Jesus on three separate occasions at the time leading up to the crucifixion. He was the first Apostle to whom Jesus appeared after the resurrection and was the one Christ asked to 'feed my lambs'. Peter was also the leader of the Christian community, the one who spoke to the crowd at Pentecost, and was the first Apostle to perform a miracle.

Peter was martyred in Rome c. 64. He is the patron saint of fishermen.

Peter heals a lame man
adapted from the Acts of the Apostles 3, 4 & 5

Courage/standing up for what you believe to be right

It was three o'clock in the afternoon and time for prayer. Peter and John were walking towards the temple with many other people who were also going to pray. When they reached the Beautiful Gate – the entrance to the temple courtyard – Peter noticed a lame man, sitting at the side of the road, begging for money.

The man had been lame all his life, and every day his friends brought him here to the gate so that he could ask the people going into the temple for money to buy food. When the man saw Peter and John, he asked if they would give him something.

Peter looked at the man and said 'Look at us.' The lame man looked up and held out his hands, expecting to be given one gold coin at least from these two kind men. But Peter said 'I have no money to give you, but I give you what I can; in the name of Jesus Christ of Nazareth, stand up and walk.'

'I can't walk … ' began the man, but Peter took him by his right hand and pulled him up from the ground. Straight away the man's feet, ankles and legs became strong. He put one foot in front of the other. He could walk. He hopped and jumped and leapt and ran.

'I can walk!' he shouted. 'After all these years I can walk! Look everyone,' and he ran on ahead, through the Beautiful Gate and into the temple, telling everyone he saw what had happened. The people crowded round him, amazed to see that he really was the lame beggar who had sat at the gate of the temple for more than 40 years.

'How did you do it?' they asked Peter. 'How did you get him to walk again?' Peter told them about Jesus and about him being the Son of God. He told them of Jesus' life on earth, and of how he had been killed. He was just about to tell them that Jesus rose from the dead on Easter Day, when some soldiers came pushing through the crowd.

'You're not allowed to preach here,' they said. 'It's against the law. Come with us,' and they arrested Peter and John and took them away to prison.

'What are we going to do with them?' said the men in charge of the prison, and the councillors, and the high priests. 'Everyone knows that they have cured a lame man. The people have seen it with their own eyes. But we don't want these two men spreading the word of Jesus around the place. They must be made to keep quiet. They must not tell anyone else about Jesus.'

So Peter and John were called in front of the rulers and high priests. They were warned that they could go, on condition that they did not talk about Jesus any more.

'But we have to speak of what we have seen and heard,' said Peter. The rulers and priests told them once again that they must not talk of Jesus, and Peter and John were released.

When they got out of prison, they found even bigger crowds waiting for them outside. By now many more people had heard of the miracle of the lame man who could walk again, and they wanted to see Peter for themselves. Some people believed that catching sight of Peter would cure them of anything that was wrong with them. Many, many people asked if they, too, could become Christians and follow Jesus.

As soon as the rulers and high priests saw the crowds speaking to Peter, and heard that lots more people were wanting to become Christians, they were even more angry than before.

'Arrest them again!' said the chief priest, and so once more, Peter and John were thrown into jail.

But that night, an angel unlocked the prison gates and said to Peter and John 'Go and stand in the temple and tell the people again about Jesus.' Peter and John did as they had been asked.

In the morning the high priests had a meeting to decide what to do.

'Bring the prisoners here,' they said to the prison guard. He went to the gates and unlocked them, but was astonished to find neither Peter nor John inside. He hurried back to the meeting. 'They're not there,' he said. 'Yet the gates were locked and barred. They can't have escaped.'

'Then where are they?' asked the chief priest.

Just then an old man came into the meeting room.

'The men you are looking for are in the temple,' he said. 'They are teaching the people there.'

'Bring them to me!' ordered the chief priest. 'I will kill them.'

Again Peter and John were brought before the rulers and high priests. But one man spoke up for them.

'If they really are working for God, then nothing we do is going to stop them,' he said. 'I think we should let them go.'

So Peter and John were released. They continued to go out among the people every day, telling them the good news about Jesus and of the Christian way of life.

Saint Swithin

15 July

Swithin was born in Wessex c. 800 and educated at Winchester, its capital. He was chaplain to Egbert, King of Wessex, and tutor to his son, Ethelwulf, who succeeded to the throne in 839. In 852 Swithin was appointed Bishop of Winchester where he stayed until his death in 862. During those ten years Wessex became the most important kingdom in England.

Little else is known of Swithin yet his name is familiar; there are almost 60 English churches dedicated to his name, and few have not heard the saying:

'St. Swithin's day, if you do rain,
For forty days it will remain.
St. Swithin's day, if you be fine,
For forty days the sun will shine.'

The story behind this legend appears to come from the removal of St Swithin's remains from the cemetery outside the door of the old minster to within the cathedral itself. The task was completed on 15 July 971 when there was a heavy rainfall. This was believed to be an illustration of St. Swithin's power.

Saint Swithin's request   *Keeping your word/humility*

Saint Swithin was Bishop of Winchester over a thousand years ago. He was a good man and spent his life trying to help poor people. It was his wish, that when he died, he should be buried outside the church, with the ordinary people.

'I don't want a special place inside the cathedral,' he said. 'I want to be buried outside the door, by the path where the ordinary people come and go. That way, I shall feel that I am still with my people.'

'But that's not the way things are done,' said his friends. 'Important people like you should have a special place inside the cathedral. It's only right. It's a mark of respect for your important position, and an acknowledgement of all the work you have done in Winchester.'

'But it's not what I want,' repeated Bishop Swithin. 'Please promise me that when I die, you will bury me outside the doors where the ordinary people are.'

Some years later when Bishop Swithin died, his friends remembered what he had said. And because they respected his wishes, they arranged for him to be buried outside the church.

But the new Bishop of Winchester was outraged.

'It is not right that the body of such an important man should be laid to rest outside the church, surrounded by the graves of the poor,' he said. 'He should have a place of honour here, inside the church.

'But it's what he wanted,' said his friends. 'He specifically asked that he might be buried outside the door, by the path where the people come and go. He said it would make him feel as though he were still with the people he loved.'

'No. It is not right,' said the new bishop. 'He must be moved, and given a place of honour within the cathedral.'

So arrangements were made for Bishop Swithin's body to be moved inside the church.

But, on the day on which the move was to take place, it rained.

'We'll wait until tomorrow,' said the workmen.

The next day it rained even harder. Heavy rain. Soaking-to-the-skin rain. Storm-force rain. Rain which stopped all work of every kind.

'Tomorrow,' said the men. 'We'll do the work tomorrow when it's stopped.'

But there was rain and then more rain.

'Tomorrow. We'll do it tomorrow,' said the men.

And still the rain continued.

Someone was keeping count of the rain days.

36, 37, 38, 39 days.

'Will it never stop?' the people asked.

'It will stop when we stop the plans to move Bishop Swithin,' said someone.

'You're right,' said someone else. 'All this rain is because we want to move him. We're no longer doing what he wanted. He wanted to rest in peace outside the church.'

'Perhaps you're right,' said the new bishop. 'Maybe we should stop our plans.'

'Yes,' said the people.

'Then it shall be so,' said the new bishop. 'He shall rest in peace where he is.'

The workmen hurried home, dodging the raindrops as they went.

The next day, the fortieth day, the rain stopped and the sun shone, watery at first, then stronger, brighter.

'It was because we wanted to move his body against his wishes,' said the people. 'But now Bishop Swithin is where he wanted to be. Outside the church, by the path where all the people come and go. He will feel at home there. Let him rest in peace.'

Saint Christopher
25 July

Little is known of Saint Christopher except that he died a martyr in Palestine or Syria at some time in the third century.

Saint Christopher is the patron saint of all travellers and now also of motorists. The legend of Saint Christopher is often depicted on medallions worn as talismen by travellers, although the story as it is known in the West differs from the Greek version.

Christopher is patron saint of all travellers but especially sailors and motorists.

The legend of Saint Christopher   *Courage/perseverance*

There was once a man called Offero who was as tall and as strong as a giant. He could lift up a horse with one hand, or sit six children on his shoulders, or pull up a tree as easily as you or I would pick a flower. But for all his strength and size, Offero was gentle and would never hurt anything or anyone.

One day Offero decided that he wanted to go and work for the greatest king in the world, so he set off to find out who it was. He had not travelled far when he met a mighty army.

'I'm looking for the greatest king in the world,' said Offero. 'Where will I find him?'

'He's up there,' said the soldiers. 'Our king is the greatest in the world.'

Offero went to speak to the king.

'I've heard you are the greatest king. Can I come and work for you?'

'Yes,' said the king.

But Offero soon noticed that the king became frightened every time anyone mentioned the Evil One.

'Who is the Evil One,' asked Offero. 'And why are you afraid of him?'

'He is the most evil being in the world,' said the king. 'I am afraid of him because he is so strong and powerful.'

'Then I must go and work for him,' said Offero. 'You see, I want to work for the greatest king in the world, and the Evil One must be greater than you since you are afraid of him.'

So Offero left the king and went in search of the Evil One. He found him eventually in the depths of a dark mountain.

'I have heard that you are the greatest king in the world,' said Offero. 'Can I come and work for you?'

'Oh yes,' said the Evil One. 'I have many jobs you can do for me. Come.'

But Offero soon noticed that whenever the Evil One rode past a cross built on the top of the mountain, he shivered with fear.

'Why are you frightened of a cross made of stones and wood,' asked Offero.

'It is not the cross I fear,' answered the Evil One, 'but Christ, whom the cross represents.'

'Then I must go and work for him,' said Offero. 'You see, I want to work for the greatest king in the world, and Christ must be greater than you, since you are afraid of him.'

Offero left the Evil One and went to find Christ. But although he searched far and wide, he could not find him.

At last he came to the banks of a great, wide, fast-flowing river, and here he met a man praying to God.

'Please tell me where I can find the king of the cross,' said Offero to the man.

'He is everywhere,' said the man. 'You will find him if you pray.'

'I don't know how to do that,' said Offero. 'The only thing I know how to do is work.'

'Then work here,' said the man. 'There are many people wanting to cross the river here, but there is no bridge or ford or ferry. With your strength you could carry the people safely across to the other side.'

'I'll do it,' said Offero.

He lived in a hut by the side of the river, and every day he carried people backwards and forward across the water.

Then one night there was a terrible storm. The rain beat down and the swollen river gushed and surged more fiercely than ever.

'No-one will want to travel on a night like this,' said Offero, as he closed his windows and door against the weather.

But no sooner was he warmly inside his hut than he heard the cry of a child.

'Please carry me across the river.'

Offero took a stick and a lantern and went out again into the dark night. There, at the water's edge stood a tiny child.

'It will be no problem to carry you across,' said Offero, and he gently lifted the child high on to his shoulders, and waded into the swirling water.

But, the further into the river Offero waded, the deeper the water grew, the more fiercely the wind blew, and the heavier the child became. Offero struggled, using every bit of his strength, but fearing that both he and the child would be swept away and drowned.

At last he staggered to the far side of the river and set the child down on the ground.

'Who are you, child?' he asked. 'If I'd been carrying the whole world on my shoulders it couldn't have been any heavier than you! Yet you are such a tiny child.'

'You have carried the whole world on your shoulders,' said the child. 'For I am Christ, and I carry the sorrows of the world. But you have carried me and my burdens bravely, and for this I shall give you a new name. I shall call you Christopher, which means Christ-bearer.'

'Then you are Christ,' said Christopher. 'You are the great king I have been looking for. Now I have found you and I want to work for you for the rest of my life.

The Christ-child continued on his journey, and Christopher spent the rest of his days carrying people across the river, working for the greatest king in the world.

Saint James the Great

25 July

James was the son of Zebedee, the fisherman, and the brother of John the Evangelist. He is known as James the Great to distinguish him from the other Apostle of the same name. James and John were called 'Boanerges' – sons of thunder – by Christ because of their fiery temperament and impetuous nature. They were called to be disciples of Christ on the same day as Andrew and Peter. James, John and Peter were held in special esteem by Jesus, and were witnesses of the Transfiguration and of the agony in the Garden of Gethsemane. James was the first of the Apostles to be martyred, being put to the sword by King Herod Agrippa in Jerusalem in the year 44.

In Spain, where James is patron saint, he is known as St Jago or Santiago. Spanish tradition claims that James preached in that country and that his body was returned there after the martyrdom. However, evidence would now refute this and the belief is not held outside Spain. Nevertheless, the shrine at Santiago de Compostela, once one of the great centres of Christian pilgrimage, is still visited by pilgrims today. James is the patron saint of pilgrims and of labourers.

There are many legends concerning St James of which the following is but one.

Saint James and the evil magician

Courage/trust/forgiveness/ friendship

Saint James was away travelling, and while he was away, a wicked magician moved into Judea.

The magician was called Hermogenes. He was an expert in evil. He hated anything good or beautiful. He hated people who were kind or gentle or considerate to others. He liked people who were cruel and nasty, vicious and mean and spiteful.

Hermogenes had heard of Saint James. He had heard people speak well of him. He knew that Saint James was well-liked because he tried to be kind and understanding, and because he told the people about Jesus who stood for everything that was good. Hermogenes hated Saint James, and Jesus, and anyone who tried to be good.

Hermogenes had an accomplice called Philetus, who worked with him and helped him with his evil magic. One day Hermogenes heard the news that James was back in Judea.

'We must get rid of him,' he said to Philetus. 'Go and see him. Do some of your magic in front of him and challenge him to perform one of his miracles! Make sure there are plenty of people around when you do your magic. Make sure plenty of people see you. James will not be able to equal your magic and he'll look foolish in front of the crowds. He'll look so silly and weak, he'll have to leave Judea and we can have it all to ourselves. Go!'

So Philetus went to see James, and Hermogenes waited for him to come back, sure that his evil magic would drive James away.

Several days went by and Philetus did not return. A week went by and there was still no sign of him. A month passed and still Philetus did not come. Then, after five weeks, Philetus came and knocked at Hermogenes' door.

'I'm sorry,' he said to Hermogenes. 'I have only come to tell you I'm leaving. I cannot work for you anymore. I went, as you said, to see James. I tried to work the evil magic on him, but I couldn't. You see, he is not afraid of evil. He is not frightened of the evil spells or of the magic potions or of anything that you or I can do. He has good on his side. He has God on his side. He has told me about Jesus and I have decided to become a Christian.'

'You stupid fool!' shouted Hermogenes. 'I sent you to get rid of him, not to join him. How dare you disobey my orders. How dare you not do as I say. But I'll teach you never to do such a thing again. I'll make sure you never do anything again. I'll make sure you never move again.' And Hermogenes worked his magic so that Philetus lay on the ground paralysed; unable to move his hands or feet or back or head or any part of himself.

'Now let's see if your precious master can save you,' said Hermogenes, venomously. 'I think he will not, for no-one is as powerful as me.'

Philetus lay still on the ground, but did not feel afraid. He called to a passer-by, 'Please go and get James. He'll know what to do. He'll help me.'

The woman hurried to find James, sure that he would come straight away to help Philetus. But James merely said, 'Take my cloak to him. Cover him with it.'

'Aren't you going to come and see him?' said the woman.

'There is no need,' said James.

The woman hurried back to Philetus and covered him gently with the cloak, but no sooner did the cloak touch Philetus that the spell was broken and he could move again. Philetus jumped to his foot and ran to find James to thank him.

But Hermogenes was watching. Once again he felt anger against James and against Philetus, whom he felt had betrayed him. Once again he worked his evil magic. He sent demons to sieze James and Philetus. But angels came to the rescue and released them. Then the angels brought Hermogenes in front of James. It was the first time the two men had met.

The crowd who had gathered round called out to James, 'Now it's your turn to get your revenge. You can do what you like with him now. You can kill him or beat him up. You can stone him to death or throw him on a bonfire. You can tie him up and leave him to die or you can chase him out of Judea. What are you going to do. We don't blame you whatever it is you decide. We think you should kill him. Go on. Kill him. Kill him.'

Saint James stood and looked at the crowd. He listened to their wild shouts. He turned to look at Hermogenes and saw fear in the man's eyes. He turned back to the crowd.

'You should be ashamed of yourselves,' he said. 'Don't you know it's wrong to kill? Jesus taught us to forgive, and that's what I shall do.'

James turned to look again at Hermogenes. 'Go in peace,' he said.

'Aren't you going to kill me?' said Hermogenes, quietly.

'No,' said Saint James. 'I shall not kill you. I shall not do anything to you, for I know that your evil will not beat the goodness that I represent. I know that good will always win over evil. Therefore, I know I have nothing to fear if I let you go. But I also know that you have a great deal to fear if you continue your evil ways. So I say again, go in peace.'

'I'm sorry,' said Hermogenes. 'I know now that there is room enough in the world for us both. And I know that there is much that you can teach me about goodness. Will you help me to learn to turn away from the evil I have been used to?'

'I will,' said Saint James.

From that day forward, Hermogenes became one of Saint James's most faithful followers, and turned his back on the evil he had known all his life.

Anne, Mother of the Virgin Mary

26 July

There are no known historical details of the grandparents of Christ, but tradition has given them the names of Joachim and Anne (sometimes Ann, Anna or Hannah). A second century apocryphal document – the Protevangelium of James *– describes events surrounding Mary's birth, and suggests that Anne and Joachim were childless until Anne was visited by an angel who told her she would bear a child. Anne promised to dedicate the child to God. The story closely resembles the biblical story of the child born to Samuel and Hannah (I Samuel 1). Joachim was* *believed to have died soon after the Presentation of his grandchild to the temple in Jerusalem.*

Anne's feast day was observed in England as early as the twelfth century, and it became an obligatory feast in 1382. Despite much opposition, particularly by Luther, to the observance of the feast because of its lack of historical evidence, it was extended to the Universal Church in 1584.

Anne is the patron saint of miners.

Joachim and Anne   *patience/keeping your word*

Joachim and Anne lived in Nazareth and had known each other since they were children. Now they were grown up and planning to get married. The wedding ceremony and the wedding feast was all arranged; their new house was ready and waiting for them.

'I wish we were getting married tomorrow,' said Anne. 'I can't wait.'

'You'll have to wait,' laughed Joachim. 'But only another week. It's not long now.'

'When we're married I want us to have lots of children,' said Anne.

'Lots of children take lots of looking after,' said Joachim. 'Lots of children mean lots of hard work!'

'I don't mind hard work,' said Anne. 'And I'm looking forward to looking after you and our family.'

'Be patient,' smiled Joachim. 'There's plenty of time to think about having a family of children.'

As it happened, Joachim and Anne needed to be patient for longer than they ever expected.

Years went by and they remained childless. Oh, they were happy together, but Joachim and Anne knew that they would be even happier with a child.

Sometimes one or other of them would hear one of their friends or neighbours saying, 'Isn't it sad? All these years married and poor Joachim and Anne have never had a child. And they would make such good parents.'

Or sometimes Anne would see her best friend or her cousin with their children and she would say, 'I wish Joachim and I could have a child. I used to want lots and lots of children, but now I would be so happy if we could have just one. Just one child to love and to care for.'

One day when Anne was almost 40, almost too old to have a child, Joachim said to her, 'I am going to go away for a few days. I want to be alone so that I can pray to God. I am going to ask God one last time to send us a child.'

'But where will you go?' asked Anne.

'I shall go into the desert,' said Joachim. 'There will be nothing there to distract me. I shall be able to concentrate on my conversation with God.'

So Joachim set off with a small bundle of food and a blanket on his back.

The next day, Anne was sitting underneath the laurel tree in her garden when she decided that she, too, would pray to God.

'Perhaps if Joachim and I are both praying at the same time God will listen to us and answer our prayer,' she thought.

As Anne knelt down to pray, an angel came quietly into the garden and said, 'Anne? Listen to me. God has heard your prayers. You and Joachim will have a child, who, in times to come, will be praised throughout the whole world.'

'I should be so happy if I could have a child,' said Anne. 'And whether it's a boy or a girl, I shall bring the child up to serve God and to love him.'

Later when Joachim returned home from his prayers in the desert, Anne told him of the angel's visit.

'Do you think it's true?' she asked. 'Do you think we will have a child after all this time.'

'We must be patient,' said Joachim. 'We must wait and see what happens.'

In a few weeks' time Anne and Joachim knew that they would soon have a child, and a few months later a baby girl was born.

'We'll call her Mary,' they said.

Joachim, Anne and Mary lived happily in the small house in Nazareth. Anne, just as she had promised, taught her daughter to love and to serve God. Mary was a good child, she was honest and kind, obedient and caring. She was helpful to her parents and concerned that they should be happy. Her parents loved her very much and she loved them.

Years went by and Mary grew up, until she, too, was old enough to get married. A wedding was arranged between Mary and a young man called Joseph, who was a carpenter, also from Nazareth.

Then one day, Mary came to see her mother to tell her some wonderful news.

'I am going to have a baby,' she said. 'But my baby is going to be special. My baby is going to be the son of God. An angel has spoken to me and told me that I am to call him Jesus.'

'An angel once spoke to me,' said her mother. 'An angel once told me that I would have a child, and that in time to come, she would be praised throughout the whole world. You are my child, Mary. And when you have your child, your special baby, you will be praised as his mother.'

Then Anne knelt down to say thank you to God for Mary her child, and for Jesus her grandchild who was not yet born, but who would be special and would help the world.

Saint Ignatius of Loyola
31 July

Ignatius was born in 1491, the youngest child of a Basque nobleman of Loyola. Originally a soldier, Ignatius became a Christian on reading about Jesus while convalescing after being wounded during the Battle of Pamplona in 1521.

Ignatius then spent a year in retreat in Catalonia where he began work on his book Spiritial Exercises, *which was to have a profound influence on Christianity over the next four centuries, before going on pilgrimage to Jerusalem. Ignatius returned to Europe and studied in various Spanish universities and in Paris, where he inspired a group of six students to take vows of poverty and chastity and to engage in missionary work in Palestine. However, they were unable to reach the Holy Land because of war, and in 1537 went to Rome to offer themselves to Pope Paul III for him to use as he chose. They were ordained priests, took additional vows of obedience and of being at the Pope's disposal at any time and anywhere, then founded a new religious order called the Society of Jesus (Jesuits).*

Until he died on 31 July 1556, Ignatius remained in Rome, overseeing the Jesuit Order as it grew from ten members to one thousand and spread across nine countries. The Order reached Britain in 1542. The Jesuits were involved in missionary work and in providing education in schools and universities.

Ignatius was known as a man of prayer, a man with great spiritual insight, and a man who offered friendship and loyalty.

Ignatius the soldier

*Friendship/loyalty/
setting an example/working together*

Ignatius was a young man and a soldier. He had always wanted to be a soldier and now, at last, he was in a real war, a real battle, a real fight. But things did not turn out quite as Ignatius had imagined they would. On only the second day of the battle, he was injured. He was shot in the leg and unable to walk or stand. He was in dreadful pain, and would have bled to death had it not been for a friend risking his own life to get Ignatius to the field doctor.

He was sent to hospital where his shattered leg was set, then broken and set again. Ignatius knew he would never be able to walk properly again.

'You'll have to stay in hospital a long time,' said the doctor. 'It's going to take several months before you're right again.'

'Then send me lots of books to read, won't you?' said Ignatius. 'Otherwise I'll die of boredom! Send me some really good adventure stories.'

They sent some books to Ignatius, but he was disappointed to see that they were not what he had asked for. They were stories about a man called Jesus.

'Still, I've nothing else to read, so they'll have to do,' he said, as he opened the first one.

Ignatius quickly discovered that the books were very good. He became more and more interested in Jesus, and asked for more books about him. Soon Ignatius decided that he would like to become a Christian.

'I will be a soldier of Jesus', he said, 'Instead of a soldier for men.'

When Ignatius was well enough to leave hospital, he went on a journey to Palestine.

'I want to see for myself where Jesus lived,' he said.

He stayed in Palestine for almost a year, then travelled to Spain and to France, where he went to university to learn more about God and the Bible.

When he was in Paris he met six men who all became very good friends. Ignatius told them about how he had become a soldier of Jesus after his stay in hospital, and the six friends decided that they, too, would become soldiers of Jesus.

'We'll travel and tell everyone about Jesus,' they said. 'We'll promise each other that we'll stay together, and look after each other. We'll stay poor, just like Jesus was, and we'll go around teaching, just like he did.'

The friends decided to go to Palestine and begin their teaching there, but they were unable to do so because of a war which had just broken out.

'We'll go to Rome and see the Pope instead,' said Ignatius. 'We'll tell him that we are soldiers of Jesus and we'll do whatever he wants us to do.'

In Rome, Pope Paul said, 'But what do you want to do?'

'We want to teach people about Jesus,' said Ignatius. 'We want to show people how to be soldiers for Jesus. We want people to fight for what is right and fight against things that are wrong.'

'Then do it,' said the Pope. 'You can start a new group of people who will work as teachers and missionaries. You could call it the Society of Jesus.'

'May we do that?' asked Ignatius.

'Of course,' said Pope Paul.

So Ignatius and his friends set to work. They planned the rules of the Society. Everyone would have to promise to be obedient, and to stay poor, and to belong only to the group and not to any other groups or families. They would all have to promise to do anything the Pope wanted them to do. Ignatius wrote a book which would help new members of the group know what to do and how to do it. He wrote prayers to help the soldiers of Jesus. One of them said:

'Teach us, Good Lord,
To serve Thee as Thou deservest;
To give and not to count the cost;
To fight and not to heed the wounds;
To labour and not to ask for any reward,
Save that of knowing that we do Thy will.'

Ignatius stayed in Rome and helped the Society of Jesus to grow and grow, as more and more people wanted to join. The Jesuits, as they came to be known, sent teachers and missionaries all over the world, to tell everyone about Jesus. They worked in tiny villages and huge cities. They worked in small schools and big universities. Within just a few years the group of seven friends had grown into a group of thousands of people – all wanting to serve God and live as Jesus wanted them to.

Lammas Day

1 August

Lammas is now largely forgotten, but was once observed as harvest festival. The name is derived from 'hlafmasse' (an old English word meaning loaf-mass); the festival of the loaf on which loaves baked from the first-cut corn of the harvest, were used in the Holy Communion service. Lammas Day celebrates the harvest in general and 'first fruits' in particular.

The festival had Celtic origins; the first of August was the Celtic quarter day of Lugnasad when praise was given to the God Lugh for producing another harvest although originally the festival was associated with the summer round-up of sheep and cattle prior to their exchange at local fairs.

Lammas is now celebrated in only a few churches, and harvest festivals are mostly held at the end of the harvest instead of at the beginning. It has also become customary to include any 'fruits' of the earth, including items such as fish and coal, in thanksgiving services.

In America, Thanksgiving Day, commemorating the first harvest of the European pilgrims, is held on the fourth Thursday in November. Thanksgiving Day in Canada is held on the second Monday in October.

The Lammas Day loaf

Honesty/responsibility/temptation/ doing your best/working together

It was almost harvest time and the farmers were anxiously watching the weather.

'Corn's ready. We ought to cut it now,' said Callum.

'No. Wait another day,' said Ben. 'Let's do it tomorrow.'

'Wait another day and it might rain!' said George. 'If the corn gets wet it'll be ruined. I say cut it now.'

George and Callum knew the importance of starting the harvest at just the right time. The corn must be perfectly ripe, but it must also be perfectly dry.

They could not risk it raining before the harvest was all in.

They looked at the sky again. Blue, clear, bright. But there was no telling how long it would stay like that.

Callum decided. 'We start now,' he said.

The others hurried to tell their wives, families, children. Everyone helps get the harvest in. Everyone.

They began. The first job was to cut down the tall golden stalks of corn, and the first stalks to be cut were the most important. The corn from these stalks would be ground into flour and used to make the first loaf of bread of the harvest.

'Ben!' shouted Callum. 'You cut the first stalks. It's your turn this year to cut the first corn and make it into the first loaf.' It was an honour to be given this job, but Callum had made a mistake in giving it to Ben.

Some boys standing nearby started to giggle and whisper.

'It's no good giving the job to Ben. It'll never get done. Everyone knows how lazy Ben is. He's useless when it comes to hard work.' They waited to see what would happen next.

Ben said, 'Aye. I'm coming. I'll see to it. I'll cut the first corn and bake the first bread. Leave it to me.'

'Bet you he doesn't!' the boys whispered to themselves.

But they were surprised to see Ben set to work and cut the first stalks. The tradition was that as soon as the first cutter had cut the first corn, the rest of the workers could start.

Soon everyone was joining in with the harvest. The work was hard. No-one had time to stop and rest. Everyone had a job to do, and they were each so busy with their own work that no-one noticed Ben had stopped.

'Why should I bother?' he said. 'There's plenty of people working without me having to bother,' and with that he settled down behind the hayrick for a long sleep.

But the boys noticed Ben's disappearance, and they decided to get up to some mischief of their own.

'Let's pinch it,' one of them said.

'You mean steal it?' said another.

'Yea. Let's filch it. Let's take the first-cut corn. Let's make our own bread with it, and eat it.'

'Yes!' they all said, and they sidled across to the golden stalks and ears of corn lying on the ground. No-one saw them. No-one looked. No-one noticed. Within a couple of minutes, dozens of ears of corn were stuffed into pockets and the boys were running, fast as the wind, across the corn field and away.

They went to one of their houses. They stripped the grains of corn from the husks and began to grind them into a sort of flour between two flat stones. They mixed the flour with water. They made a kind of dough and put it into a loaf tin and baked it in the oven for a long time.

Meanwhile the harvesters were still hard at work in the fields. When the corn was cut it was turned with forks so that it would dry in the sun. Then the stalks were tied together in bundles, called sheaves. The sheaves were loaded on to carts and taken into the barns. Not until the last sheaf was safely inside the barn could the workers relax.

Then, when the work was done, they could celebrate. A huge harvest home supper was made and everyone was invited. They ate and drank, danced and sang, cheered and shouted and clapped.

'The boughs do shake and the bells do ring,
Merrily comes our harvest in,
We've ploughed, we've sowed,
We've reaped, we've mowed,
We've brought our harvest in.'

Suddenly, in the middle of all the merry-making, Callum looked round.

'Where's Ben?' he asked.

Everyone looked around, but of Ben there was no sign. He was missing.

'What about the first-cut corn?' said Callum. 'What's he done with it? Where is he?'

A search began, and eventually Ben was found skulking round the back of the barn.

'Well?' boomed Callum, when Ben was dragged in front of him. 'Where is it? Where is the first-cut corn?'

'I don't know,' blubbed Ben. 'I fell asleep. I don't know where that corn is. I suppose it must have got mixed up with all the other corn.'

'But what about the Lammas loaf? What about our loaf of bread from the first corn? What will we take to church with us on Lammas Day? You'd better find that first corn or it will be the worst for you,' shouted all the harvesters.

It quickly became apparent that the happy feeling of the harvest-home supper was disappearing. The harvesters were ready to kill Ben because he had not done his job.

The boys looked at each other.

'Do you think we ought to tell?' they asked each other. They all knew the answer to that.

'We know something about the first corn,' the eldest boy said.

'We're sorry, but we stole it,' said the youngest boy.

'We didn't mean any harm,' they all said.

'What did you do with the first-cut corn?' asked Callum.

'We took it home and made a loaf with it.'

'Where is the loaf now?'

'It's still at home,' they said. 'We tasted it but it's not very nice. It's sort of flat. Not like a loaf should be.'

'Never mind,' said Callum. 'At least it's a loaf and it's baked from the first corn. It'll have to do. Go and get it. Bring it here. We'll have to use it for the service tomorrow. We have no choice.'

And so it was, that that year's Lammas loaf was made from stolen corn by children who did not know how to make bread. It was a flat, sorry-looking loaf, with a piece missing from the end where the boys had tasted it, but nevertheless it was a Lammas loaf and it was used in the church service of thanksgiving.

Ben learned his lesson about laziness, for it was a long time before the villagers trusted him again. And as for the boys, well, their parents had something to say about stealing, even though everything did turn out for the best in the end.

Saint Keneth (Cenydd)

1 August

Little is known of Keneth (Welsh name Cenydd), but according to Welsh tradition he was born in the sixth century, the son of Saint Gildas – a Welsh abbot and writer. Keneth became a monk and founded a monastery on the Gower Peninsular. Keneth is later believed to have travelled to Brittany. His feast is celebrated in Wales, Brittany and England.

Keneth undoubtedly existed, his mention in early calendars and in place names testifies to this, but the colourful legend of his being reared by gulls is purely fictitious.

Keneth and the gulls   *Caring/kindness/friendship*

Once upon a time a prince from France sailed over the sea to Wales. He settled with his wife and servants in a place called Gower, and there his little son was born. The child was lovely, but unfortunately he had something wrong with his leg, and his father could not bear to look at him.

'He'll never be able to run and play with the other children,' the prince said to his wife. 'He'll never be able to be a soldier like me, so he must die.'

The princess pleaded with her husband to spare the child, but the prince would not listen. He ordered his servants to take the baby and kill him.

But when the servants saw the child, they could not do what the prince asked. So they made a tiny coracle – a boat made of out of twigs and leather – and they lined it with a blue wool blanket, then they carefully put the child inside and set it on the sea.

'Someone will find him and will care for him,' they said. Then they went back to tell the prince that they had killed the baby.

The tiny boat bobbed and skipped over the waves until it came to a rocky island, and there it stopped, abruptly, washed up on the shore by the tide.

Watching the progress of the tiny boat was a flock a seagulls, high overheard, hovering, waiting to see what it would do. When the coracle stopped on the beach, the gulls flew down in a great swirling cloud, they took hold of the boat with their beaks and their claws and lifted it high in the sky. They carried it over the foaming sea to the top of a high cliff, and there they gently set it down.

Then the birds plucked soft feathers from their bodies and lined the boat like a nest. They tucked the baby into his bright woollen blanket, then spread their wings, tip to tip, over him to keep him dry and warm in the night.

In the morning, at the first finger of light, the baby woke, crying from hunger and thirst. He waved his arms, and the gulls noticed for the first time that his hand held a tiny golden bell. It rang with a silvery, shivery sound as the baby moved, and at its sound a mother deer came running from a nearby wood. The deer went close up to the cradle-boat. She sniffed the baby, then licked him with her rough tongue and fed him with her milk.

And so the pattern of the days began. The human baby was cared for and protected at the top of the tall cliff by the seagulls, and he was fed and washed each day by the mother deer.

Then, one day, a man walked by; a shepherd who was out checking on his sheep and lambs.

'What's this then?' he said as he saw the coracle-crib lined with feathers, and the baby curled up contentedly in his bright blue woollen blanket in the middle.

'A baby!' he said, as he picked up the cradle-boat and hurried home with it to his wife; his wife who loved children but had none of her own. But at every step of the way, the baby cried and screamed and howled for his friends.

They heard. The gulls and the deer heard the baby's cries and followed him. No sooner had the shepherd taken the cradle-boat child into the house to show his wife, than the gulls swooped and screamed, into the house after him. They picked up the corners and sides of the bright blue woollen blanket, with the now smiling, gurgling baby inside it, and whirled out of the house back to the place on the top of the cliff.

Once there, the seagulls made the baby a new feather-bed nest in a hollow in the cliff, tucked him up in his blue woollen blanket and told him to go to sleep.

Weeks and months passed. The gulls protected the child and the deer fed him milk. The shepherd and his wife brought food and clothes for him. Years went by. The baby grew into a child, a young man, an adult. By now he was looking after himself and living in a home-made wooden house on the top of the cliff. He taught himself to read and write, and he learned about God and the stories in the Bible. He became friends with the other people who lived round about. They gave him a name – Keneth, and they taught him how to get along with people as well as with the animals.

Keneth decided that he wanted to continue living alone in his house on the cliff top. He wanted to live a quiet and a holy life. He tried for a time living in a town, with people crowding round about him, but he did not like it and soon went back home to his gulls and his deer. He sometimes went travelling, and everywhere he went he told people to care for and protect wild animals and birds, 'For they once cared for me,' he said. 'They once protected me.' And he told everyone the story of the baby in the cradle-boat who was brought up by the gulls and the deer.

'God sent them to help me,' he said. 'They were my mother and father, my brothers and sisters, my aunts and my uncles, my family,' he said. 'And now I want to ask everyone to care for the animals in return.'

The Transfiguration

6 August

The Transfiguration celebrates the manifestation of Christ's glory to the three disciples, Peter, James and John.

The disciples saw Jesus standing in a dazzling light, that blinded them at first but afterwards helped them to realise that Jesus was the Son of God. They did not, however, fully understand the Saviour, as God himself, redeeming humankind through suffering, until after the Resurrection.

Three disciples begin to understand
adapted from Mark 9:2–13

Peter, James and John were hot and tired. They had been working hard, helping Jesus as he went around talking to the people and teaching them how to lead good lives. But now they were tired and the day seemed to be getting hotter and hotter.

'Can we rest soon?' James asked.

Jesus looked at the friends and saw how tired they were.

'Yes,' he said. 'We'll walk a little way up the mountain, it'll be cooler there. Come on.'

They started to climb the path that led up the side of the mountain. Mount Hermon was the highest mountain in the whole of Palestine and James looked up and saw snow on its summit.

'Are we going right to the top?' he asked.

'No,' said Jesus, smiling. 'We'll stop there,' and he pointed to a level, grassy area a little further along the path.

When they reached it, Peter, James and John sank down on to the grass, leaning against a large moss-covered boulder, and within a few minutes all three friends were asleep.

Jesus walked a little further on, away from the rock and towards the middle of the grass. It was beautiful here. You could almost taste the fresh, cool, clean air. You could smell the scent of wild flowers growing in the crevices in the rocks. You could hear the song of birds being carried on the wind. You could feel the springiness of the grass beneath your feet. And you could see for miles and miles.

Jesus stood in the middle of this beautiful place and began to pray.

Suddenly, something woke all three disciples at the same time. They looked, and saw in front of them a brilliant, shining, dazzling, white light. At first the light was so bright it blinded them and they could not see what it was or where it was coming from. Then they saw that Jesus was in the centre of the light. It was as though the light was coming from him, making everything around him shimmer with brilliance. Standing close to Jesus were two men, one was Moses and the other Elijah. Both men had once lived on earth.

The picture that the three disciples could see in front of them was so beautiful that Peter wished it could stay there forever. But it began to disappear as a mist swirled around Jesus.

Now the disciples began to feel afraid. What was it? What was happening? What did it mean? They hid their eyes from the sight. It was then that they heard the voice of God,

'This is my Son,' said God. 'Listen to him.'

The disciples felt even more afraid. Peter hid himself in his cloak. James and John crouched behind the rock.

God did not speak again, and the mist and the bright light faded. But Peter, James and John dared not look. Then Jesus walked across to them and touched them on the shoulder.

'Don't be frightened,' he said. 'There's nothing to be afraid of.

And the disciples suddenly understood that Jesus was very special, that Jesus was indeed the Son of God. But they did not yet know how special.

Jesus said to them, 'Don't tell anyone what you have just seen. At least, don't tell anyone until after the Son of God has risen again from the dead.'

But the disciples did not know what he meant. They did not know that Jesus would die, and that he would rise again from the dead.

Saint Oswald

9 August

Oswald was born c. 605, one of three sons of Ethelfrith the King of Northumbria. On the death of their father, the sons fled to Scotland where they were baptised Christians on Iona. In 633 Oswald defeated King Cadwalla and recovered Northumbria. He sent to Iona for a bishop to establish Christianity in Northumbria, and met Saint Aidan who was to become a good friend. Oswald frequently travelled the realm with Aidan and acted as his translator.

Oswald united both parts of Northumbria – Bernicia and Deira – and was established as overlord by the other Anglo-Saxon kings.

After a reign of only eight years Oswald was killed in 642 by the pagan King Penda of Mercia. Oswald is remembered for his bravery, generosity and godliness, as an Anglo-Saxon hero and a Christian saint.

He is well-known in Germany, Austria and Switzerland, as well as in Britain where over 70 churches are known to be dedicated to him, several of which are in Yorkshire.

Oswald and the silver dishes   *Caring/sharing/generosity*

Oswald was King of Northumbria. A few years earlier Northumbria had been taken away from Oswald's family in a terrible battle, but now he had won back the kingdom. Oswald was king.

The first thing he did as king was to send to the monastery on Iona in Scotland for a monk.

'I need someone to teach my people about Jesus,' he said. 'The monks on Iona are the people to help. They taught me about Jesus; now I'd like them to teach my people.'

A monk called Aidan was eventually sent to Northumbria, and he and Oswald became good friends. They travelled round the Northumbrian countryside together, talking to people, with King Oswald often translating because Aidan did not speak English very well.

Aidan not only taught the Northumbrians about Jesus, but he also taught King Oswald about caring and sharing and looking after people. One day there was an incident which made Aidan realise that the king had understood.

King Oswald had organised a banquet. It was to be held at his castle at Bamburgh and people from far and wide had been invited. Aidan was to go as well, of course.

The day of the banquet came. The guests started to arrive. They were looking forward to the meal. King Oswald always had good food and drink, and the castle was always comfortable and welcoming.

The guests sat down to dine. The long tables were set with silver knives and silver dishes, glittering under the light of hundreds of candles. This was going to be a meal to remember.

The servants came in then, one after another, each carrying a huge silver dish piled high with meat or bread, fish or vegetables. Steam rose into the air from the hot food and the guests' nostrils smelled the aroma of rich gravy, newly baked bread, herbs, ale and mulled wine. Mouths watered and fingers waited impatiently for the food to be served.

Then another servant came in, hurrying, worrying, agitated about something, and asked to speak to the king.

'What is it?' asked Oswald. 'What's the matter?'

'There are lots of people at the gate, sir,' said the servant. 'Poor people. They're asking for food. They say they have none. What shall I do? They won't go away.'

Oswald looked at Aidan, who merely nodded his head, as if to say, 'Yes. Go on.'

Oswald then looked at the line of servants carrying food, just about to serve it to his guests.

'Stop!' he cried.

The dining hall fell silent. Everyone was still.

'Stop,' said Oswald again. 'We all ate food yesterday. We shall eat food tomorrow. It will do us no harm to go without food today. These people outside have nothing. They shall have our dinner.' And without waiting to hear what his guests would say, without waiting to see what the reaction would be, King Oswald ordered his servants to turn around and march out of the dining room, out of the castle, out of the gates, and share the food with the people waiting there.

'They need money, as well as food,' added Oswald. 'They shall have silver,' and he picked up the great silver dish in front of him and broke it into pieces. 'Give them all a piece of silver to spend,' he said to another servant. 'It will buy them food for tomorrow.'

Then Oswald ordered the rest of the silver dishes on the table to be gathered together, broken up, and given to the poor.

The guests sat in astonishment and amazement at Oswald's actions. They sat selfishly disappointed that they were not to have the dinner they had waited for. But Oswald did not care what they thought. His guests were all wealthy people, except for Aidan, who always gave away everything he was given anyway. His guests could well do without dinner for once.

Aidan was the first of the guests to move. He stood up and approached the king.

'Thank you,' he said. 'Thank you for generously helping those who have less than you. Thank you for helping your people. God bless you.'

And the guests, who had all learned a very valuable lesson that night, also said, 'Thank you. It was a brave and good thing to do.'

Saint Helen

18 August

Helen, sometimes known as Helena, was born c. 255 in Drepanum – later Helenopolis – in Asia Minor, the daughter of an innkeeper. She married the Roman general, Constantius Chlorus and bore him a son, Constantine, in 274. In 292 her husband was made Emperor, whereupon he divorced Helen in a politically advantageous move and married the Emperor Maximian's step-daughter.

When Constantius died in York in 306, Constantine was immediately proclaimed Emperor in his place. He gave his mother the title Augusta and demanded the respect due to her as mother of the emperor.

Helen converted to Christianity when she was about 60, and she and Constantine promoted Christianity following the Edict of Milan in 312, which ended the persecution of Christians. In 324 Constantine became the first Christian emperor of the entire Roman Empire, both East and West, and moved his capital to Constantinople.

Now elderly, Helen set off on a pilgrimage to the Holy Land where she assisted the poor and helped found churches on various sacred sites. Legend (probably apocryphal) states that she discovered the True Cross while in the Holy Land. She died in Nicodemia in 330.

There are some 130 churches dedicated to Saint Helen in England, many of which are in the north east, possibly because of Constantine's connection with York. The St Helens in the Isle of Wight and Lancashire are believed to have been towns which developed around a church named after the saint, while the island of St Helena in the South Atlantic was believed to have been discovered by Spanish sailors on her feast day.

Saint Helen and the True Cross   *Keeping your word/perseverance/thinking*

The Emperor Constantine had not always been a Christian. He had once believed in the old Gods and Goddesses of the Romans. But Christianity was getting stronger and stronger, and Constantine had heard about Jesus and his life.

Constantine had just been proclaimed emperor by the Roman army in York, but even so, there were many people in other parts of the Roman Empire, and in Rome itself, who would not accept that he was in charge, and so he had to fight to prove he was emperor.

Constantine was just about to go into battle again. This battle would decide everything. But Constantine was feeling nervous. Then he had a vision, a kind of dream, in which he saw a golden cross high in the sky. The glittering cross seemed to be telling him to follow it. He could not get the image of it out of his mind, and he decided that if he won this battle, he would become a Christian.

The battle was fought and Constantine won. He remembered the promise he had made to himself and he became a Christian. He asked the people in his family to think about becoming Christians too. Helen, his mother, was one of the first to be baptised. One day when she was thinking about Jesus, she wondered what had happened to the cross on which he had died.

'I shall find it,' she said to herself. 'I shall go to Palestine and I shall find it.'

'You can't do that,' said her son. 'It's three hundred years since Jesus died, that cross could be anywhere.'

'I feel that God wants me to go and search for it,' said Helen. 'I must go.'

'But you are too old to go travelling,' said Constantine.

'I am nearly 80,' said his mother. 'I am old enough to do what I think is best for me.'

And so Helen went to the Holy Land in search of the True Cross.

The place where Jesus had been crucified was built over. The Emperor Hadrian had built a long terrace on which was a statue of the Roman God Jupiter and a temple to the Goddess Venus.

'The True Cross could be hidden under the terrace,' said Helen, and she ordered workmen to dig it up so that they could search underneath.

The digging took a long time. There was a lot of earth to move. The foundations of the terrace and the temple were deep. But Helen was determined that they should keep on looking. At last the workmen dug to a layer of rocks.

'I'm sure the cross will be near here,' said Helen.

They dug further, and at last, three wooden crosses were unearthed. They were old and dirty and all looked the same.

'Well,' said one of the workmen. 'I don't know how you're going to tell if one of these is the cross you're looking for.'

'The True Cross will be special,' said Helen. 'In some way it will be special.'

Later that day Helen heard of a man who was very ill.

'He will die soon,' said his family. 'He is very weak.'

Helen went to see the man.

'Can I say a prayer with you?' she asked.

The man said she could, but was surprised to hear what she said to God.

'Please make this man well again if he is laid on the True Cross,' she said. 'Please cure him if he touches it.'

They carried the man gently to where the excavated crosses were. They laid him carefully, so as not to hurt him, on the first cross. Nothing happened.

They moved him gently, so as not to cause him any discomfort, to the second cross. Nothing happened.

They carried him to the third cross, and laid him carefully, gently, on it. The man was cured. He was well again. His pain and illness had gone.

'This is the True Cross,' said Helen, and she made arrangements for a great church to be built where the True Cross could be kept. Then she took a small piece of the wood of the cross and took it to Rome, together with two nails she had found in the ground near the cross.

For hundreds of years pilgrims went from all over the world to Jerusalem to see the True Cross, until it was destroyed when Jerusalem was captured.

Saint Aidan

31 August

Aidan was an Irishman who played an important role in evangelising northern England. He was a monk living on Iona, in 635, when King Oswald regained Northumbria from the heathen King Penda of Mercia. Oswald, a Christian, sent to Iona for a monk to preach the gospel to his people.

Aidan was given Lindisfarne Island where he established a monastery and became its first bishop. Here, with monks from Iona, he educated English boys and trained them to work as missionaries on the mainland. Aidan lived in poverty and allowed no wealth to accumulate in the monastery; any surplus was given to the poor or sick.

After the death of Oswald, Aidan was befriended and supported by his successor, King Oswin. After Oswin's death in 651, Aidan lived only another two weeks, reputedly dying of grief. He was buried on Lindisfarne.

Aidan in Northumbria   *Caring/sharing/generosity/patience/friendship*

Aidan was a monk living on the island of Iona, in Scotland, when the message came that King Oswald of Northumbria wanted a monk to go and live on the mainland to help him teach the people there about Jesus.

'Who shall we send?' the monks asked. 'The people in the north of England are very wild and uncivilised. We must send someone who is strong and forthright.'

They chose a monk called Eldric to go and help King Oswald.

'Take care,' the monks said as he set off. 'God be with you.'

Eldric did his best to teach the English about Jesus, but things did not go well, and after a few weeks he came back to the monastery of Iona.

'Why are you back?' the monks asked. 'What happened? Why didn't you stay?'

'It was impossible,' answered Eldric. 'No-one could teach those people anything. I did my best, truly I did, but they are unteachable. The English across there on the mainland are stupid and obstinate and wild and uncivilised. They wouldn't listen to me. They wouldn't learn.'

'Was it they who wouldn't learn, or you who couldn't teach?' asked Aidan. 'Was it their fault or was it yours? Perhaps you were too tough with them. Perhaps you were not gentle enough.'

'Gentle!' exclaimed Eldric. 'They were not gentle with me!'

'Aidan, perhaps you should go to the mainland instead of Eldric,' said the abbot of the monastery.

'Yes,' said the monks. 'Aidan is clearly the man to go. Send him to teach the people of Northumbria.'

So Aidan was sent to the mainland. He quickly became good friends with King Oswald who gave him an island on which to build a monastery.

'The island of Lindisfarne is just off the coast,' said King Oswald. 'It's a good place for a monastery. At low tide people can walk across the sands to visit you, but at high tide the island is cut off by the water, so you will have privacy then to pray and study your books.'

Aidan sent for some of the monks from Iona to come and join him, and together they began to build the new monastery. Soon it began to take shape.

In the meantime, Aidan and King Oswald walked all round the kingdom of Northumbria, talking to the people they met, teaching them about the life of Jesus. Aidan talked calmly, quietly, gently, patiently, to the people, explaining again anything they did not understand. Slowly the people began to know him, to trust him, to respect him. He showed the people how to live a good life by his own example. He gave away everything he had to help people who were poor or in need. He showed peple how to share what they had with others.

One day Aidan was having dinner with King Oswald and many of his friends in Oswald's manor house, when a servant came into the dining hall.

'There are people at the gate asking for food,' he said. 'We have given them the food from the kitchen, but we have nothing else left to give them. What shall we do?'

Aidan looked at King Oswald to see what he would do.

'Give the people the food from our table,' said Oswald. 'We are not hungry. We all ate yesterday and we will all eat again tomorrow. Give them today's food.'

King Oswald gave away all the food from the table. Then he gave away the silver dishes as well, so that the poor might have money to buy food.

'Thank you,' said Aidan. 'Thank you for sharing what you had.'

Soon after that dinner, King Oswald was killed in battle, when his enemy, King Penda of Mercia again invaded Northumbria.

Aidan was deeply upset when he heard his friend had died.

'No other king could be as good as Oswald,' he said. But Aidan was soon to meet the new King of Northumbria. His name was King Oswin, and he also became Aidan's friend.

Oswin gave Aidan a beautiful and valuable horse as a gift one day.

'You walk everywhere,' said Oswin. 'With this horse you'll be able to travel further, to meet new people. It'll help you in your work as well as making life easier for you.'

But Oswin became very angry when, only two days later, he heard that Aidan had given the horse away to a man who was lame.

'How could you!' shouted King Oswin angrily. 'How could you give away my gift!'

'I gave it away because someone needed it more than I,' answered Aidan. 'You shouldn't be angry because I wanted to help someone. Jesus taught us to give. He gave his life for us. I have only given away a horse.'

'I'm sorry,' said King Oswin. 'You are right. The gift was yours to do with as you wanted. You are helping me to understand how to share what I have with others.'

After that incident, King Oswin shared his riches with the people of Northumbria, until he too, was killed in battle.

Aidan was so sad to have lost two good friends, that he went back to the monastery on Lindisfarne, and died only a short time later, some said of a broken heart.

But the message of caring and sharing stayed with the people of Northumbria, and they were better people for having known Saint Aidan.

Saint Gregory the Great

3 September

Gregory was born in Rome c. 540, and became the first and greatest of 16 Popes of the same name. For a number of years he was chief magistrate of Rome. He became a monk at the age of 35, after donating some of his inherited wealth to found a monastery in Rome and others in Sicily. From 579 to 585 Gregory is known to have been papal agent at Constantinople, and five years after his return he became the first monk to be elected Pope. Gregory died in 604.

Gregory's achievements while Pope included the reformation of the administration of church estates, the strengthening of the Roman Church's power in the East and its position in Italy, France and Spain, and the setting up of charities to assist those suffering the effects of war, famine and poverty. He also sent missionaries to England after seeing and freeing British captives about to be sold as slaves on the streets of Rome. (See also Saint Augustine.)

Gregory is one of the four great Latin doctors of the Church whose ideals were the inspiration for the clergy of the Western Church. Gregory chose for his title 'the servant of the servants of God', a title used by Popes ever since.

Gregory is the patron saint of teachers, students, singers, musicians and masons.

Saint Gregory and the angel

Sharing/caring/ consideration for others

One day, when Gregory was a monk living alone in a small hut in the woods, a beggar came to his door.

'I have nothing,' said the beggar. 'Please will you give me something to eat?'

'Well, I haven't much,' said Gregory, 'but you're welcome to share what I have. Come in.'

The beggar went inside and sat at the plain wooden table. Gregory went to a cupboard and took out two plates, two beakers, a loaf of bread and a jug of milk. He gave half of everything to the beggar. They talked as they ate, and then the beggar thanked Gregory for his kindness, and left.

The next day he came back. 'I'm hungry again,' he said. 'Will you give me something to eat?'

'Come in,' said Gregory. 'You're welcome to share my meal, but there's even less than yesterday. You see I only have what people give me. Today I have only an orange, a few grapes and a jug of water. But here, take half,' and Gregory gave half of the food to the beggar. Once again they talked for a while, and then the beggar left.

The next day the beggar came again. 'Can I share your meal with you please?' he asked.

'I'm sorry,' said Gregory. 'You're welcome to come in and rest, but today I have no food at all. I have nothing to share with you. Not even a crumb.'

'But I'm hungry,' said the beggar.

'I'm sorry,' said Gregory. 'Look! My cupboard is bare,' and he opened the cupboard doors to show the beggar that he had no food.

But there, on the top shelf was a silver bowl.

'Wait a minute,' said Gregory. 'There is something you can have. My mother brought me some soup in this bowl last week. I was waiting until she called again to give it back to her, but she won't mind if I give it to you. Here. Take it. You can sell it. It should fetch a good price, then you can buy yourself some food.'

The beggar took the silver bowl, said thank you, and left.

He never came back to Gregory's hut in the forest, and Gregory never expected to see him again.

Years passed, and Gregory became Pope. He left his tiny hut and went to live in the Pope's palace, but he never forgot the poor people. Every evening he insisted that 12 homeless people be invited to the palace to share his evening meal. Every evening he sat with the 12 people, ate with them and talked with them.

One evening, 13 people sat around the table with Gregory. He called to his steward. 'I gave instructions that 12 should be invited to the meal. Why are there 13 here?' he asked.

'Surely there are only 12,' said the steward, and he counted the visitors again. He counted 12, and Gregory realised that only he could see the thirteenth guest.

The meal was brought in and everyone was served. When the supper was over, Gregory went to speak to the extra visitor.

'Who are you?' he asked.

The stranger smiled and said, 'A long time ago I came to your door and asked for food. You shared all you had with me. In the future it will be written: "Remember to welcome strangers into your homes. There were some who did that and welcomed angels without knowing it." Now do you know who I am?'

'Yes,' answered Gregory, for he knew that the stranger was an angel sent from God.

Saint Lambert

17 September

Lambert was born c. 635 in Maastricht, to a wealthy and influential family, and was educated by the Bishop of Maastricht, Theodard, whom he succeeded in 670. Lambert worked as a missionary bishop for some 30 years, during which time he spent seven years in exile in a monastery at Stavelot because of the political jealousies of his rivals. He was murdered at Liege and venerated as a martyr because of the violence of his death.

Lambert, although little known in England, is revered particularly in Belgium, where many churches are dedicated to his name.

Lambert does as he is told   *Obedience/humility*

Lambert was an important man. He was the Bishop of Maastricht, in Belgium.

When Lambert was young, everyone said, 'Lambert will go far. He is hardworking and intelligent. He always does his best. He always tries his hardest. He wants to learn. Yes, Lambert will do well in life,' they said.

And they were right. Lambert worked hard at every job he was given, until eventually he was appointed Bishop of Maastricht – a very important job indeed.

The people of Maastricht liked having Lambert as their bishop. Even though he was very busy, as important people usually are, he always found time to talk to them, he was never too busy to answer their questions or help them with their problems. He was always kind and understanding, and when he tried to sort out arguments or difficulties, he always tried to be fair, to listen to each side of the story. Yes, the people felt they were lucky having a man like Lambert as the bishop of their city.

For a while all went well. Then, one winter, there was a problem when a new lord mayor was chosen. Some of the people in the city objected to the new mayor, and wanted a different man to be chosen. People took sides and started arguing about whose side they were on. The arguments became heated and angry, and more and more people became involved. People started lying about what other people had said. Some people accused Bishop Lambert of lying, even though he had not. Then someone threatened to kill him.

'You ought to go away somewhere and hide,' said one of Lambert's friends. 'This situation is getting dangerous. It's getting out of hand.'

'But I don't want to run away and hide,' said Lambert. 'I have done nothing wrong. I have nothing to be ashamed of.'

'We know,' said his friends. 'But it really would be better for the time being, if you went into hiding.'

Lambert's friends arranged for him to go and spend some time in a small monastery just outside Maastricht. They took him to the abbot.

'Can he stay here with you?' they asked.

'Of course,' said the abbot. 'We are pleased to be able to help. But we've never had such an important person to stay with us before. We've never had the Bishop of Maastricht to visit us before.'

Lambert was shown to his room and soon settled in. But later that night he could not sleep. Lambert decided to get up and go to the chapel to pray. He crept out of bed so as not to wake anyone. He pulled on a thin woollen robe and picked up his wooden sandals. He tiptoed to the door in his bare feet so as not to make any noise. But as he was opening the door, one of his sandals fell to the floor with a dreadful clatter.

'Who's making all that noise?' said the voice of the abbot from his room down corridor. 'We will not have that noise in the night. Go and stand by the cross outside the front door. Stand there as punishment for making such a noise.'

Now Bishop Lambert could have explained to the abbot what had happened. He could have said that it was just an accident; the abbot would have surely let him off if he had known it was Bishop Lambert making the noise. He could have said sorry and got back into bed. He could have simply ignored the abbot and carried on walking to the chapel.

But Bishop Lambert did none of those things. He did as he was told because he knew that the abbot was in charge of the monastery, and that everyone should do as the abbot said. So Bishop Lambert went and stood by the cross outside the front door. He said his prayers there, instead of in the chapel.

In the morning when the monks were all up and awake and warming themselves by the dining room fire, the abbot asked if everyone was there.

'We're all here except the one who's standing outside by the cross,' someone said.

'Is he still outside?' asked the abbot. 'The one who was making all the noise in the middle of the night? Is he still there? Bring him in. He must be frozen.'

Someone went to get the monk who was outside. He was brought in, cold, shivering, covered in snow, almost frozen to death.

'It's you? Bishop Lambert?' said the abbot in surprise when he saw Lambert. 'I'm so sorry – I didn't know it was you – I didn't realise – I wouldn't have said if I'd known it was you – please forgive me. This is no way to treat an important guest. I am so sorry.'

'You have no need to apologise to me,' said Lambert. 'I am staying in your monastery and I'd like you to treat me the same as everyone else. I don't want you to treat me differently from the rest of the monks. It has done me no harm to stand outside and say my prayers.'

Bishop Lambert did not want to be treated as an important person; he wanted to be treated the same as everyone else in the monastery. He was not conceited or big-headed. He was happy to obey the abbot who was in charge.

Lambert stayed seven years in the monastery near Maastricht, then at last it was safe for him to go back to the city and become bishop again. But he never forgot the time he spent as an ordinary monk in the monastery.

Saint Matthew

21 September

Matthew, an Apostle and evangelist, lived in the first century. He was a collector of taxes for the Roman Government at Capernaum, to the north of the Sea of Galilee.

The first Gospel is said to have been written by Matthew, and it is believed that he was eventually martyred, possibly in Ethiopia or Persia, but little else is known of his life.

Matthew is patron saint of accountants and bookkeepers, tax collectors and customs officers.

Matthew is called to follow Jesus   *Trust/repentance/forgiveness*
adapted from Luke 5:27–31

Levi was a tax collector near his home town of Capernaum at the time when Jesus was alive. Levi worked for the Roman Government and it was his job to collect taxes from the merchants as they carried their goods into Capernaum to sell. No-one was allowed to enter the city without paying a tax first.

The people disliked and distrusted the tax collectors. They disliked having to pay to enter the city in the first place, and they distrusted the tax collectors because they often charged more than they should, then kept the extra money for themselves.

One day, Jesus travelled to Capernaum and he stood at the roadside watching the people queuing up to pay their tax. He saw traders from the towns and villages nearby, he saw salesmen and dealers from Damascus and Caesarea, and he saw businessmen from as far away as Persia and Arabia. He saw Levi, the tax collector, taking their money and putting it into bags on the table in front of him.

But Jesus saw something else when he looked at Levi. He saw a man who could be kind and understanding; a man who, given a chance, could be a loyal and faithful friend; a man who could be a disciple.

Jesus walked up to the tax collector's table, and Levi held out his hand expecting this to be another man paying to enter Capernaum. But Jesus held out no money. Instead he looked at Levi and said 'Follow me.'

Without hesitation, Levi left his table of money, his job, his security and his riches, and followed Jesus, happy to have been asked to do so.

Later, Levi organised a great feast at his house, to honour Jesus and to show him how happy he was that Jesus had chosen him to be a disciple. He invited all his friends along to meet Jesus; his friends who were tax collectors like himself; his friends who had not always been honest and good.

But some Pharisees and important men who were teachers of the law, saw who had been invited, and could not understand it.

'Why should Jesus want to eat with them?' they asked. 'They are tax collectors and thieves and robbers. They are sinners. Why does he mix with bad people like that? Why doesn't he eat with good people who are honest and trustworthy?'

Jesus overheard what they were saying, and he replied, 'If you are well you do not need a doctor, you only go to a doctor if you are sick. I do not come to ask good people to repent; I ask those who have something to be sorry for, to admit they were wrong and say they were sorry.'

Levi was sorry for all the wrong he had done in the past. He asked to be forgiven. From then on, he changed his name to Matthew, which means 'gift of God', and he stayed with Jesus for the rest of his time on earth, happy to be one of the chosen disciples and to have a new way of life.

Saint Cadoc

25 September

Cadoc was born c. 522 and was one of the outstanding Welsh saints, founding a monastery at Llancarfan near Cardiff, where the monks were well-known for working the land in addition to studying.

Cadoc was reputed to have been a great traveller and spent some time in Scotland, Cornwall and Brittany. It is believed he also visited Rome and Jerusalem.

It is not known when Cadoc died, but the story goes that he was carried in a cloud from Llancarfan to Benevento in Italy where he was made bishop, but that he died while celebrating mass.

Saint Cadoc and the mouse   *Sharing/patience/being observant*

Once upon a time a rich man built a beautiful house in a green valley among the mountains of Wales. The house was strong and sturdy, built of stone, with a fine slate roof, polished wooden floors and a safe, cool, dry, storage cellar.

The man had many corn fields, and every year he stored his spare corn in the cellar, against the day when he and his family might need it. But harvests were good and crops were plenty, so the man never needed to use his corn store. It stayed, safe and dry in the cellar.

Then one year, fighting broke out in the valley. People were killed and homes were destroyed. The beautiful stone house was burned to the ground and all that remained was a heap of stones and broken slates.

Time went by and the ruins of the house became covered in wild grass and moss and ivy. It was now hard to tell that a house had ever stood there.

Years passed and the wild flowers and grasses grew stronger and taller. Bushes and trees began to grow between the fallen stones, and no-one who did not already know that a house had once stood there could have guessed that it had.

And then, slowly and gradually, people came back to live in the valley. But these people were not like the rich man who built the fine stone house. These were poor people, who built little houses out of rough stone and wood. They ploughed little fields in which to grow their corn and vegetables. They had little harvests, but they shared what they had with each other.

Until the year that the crops failed.

It had been a year of heavy rain but little sunshine. The corn did not ripen, and the people had no stored corn from the previous year to see them through.

They went to see the holy man who lived near their village.

'Ask God to help us,' they said. 'Ask God to send us some food or we will all starve.'

'We will pray together,' said the holy man. And they did. They asked God to send them food to see them through the winter.

A few days later, a young boy called Cadoc came down from his home in the hills to see the holy man.

'I want to learn to be like you,' he said. 'Please can I live here with you, and be your servant? You don't need to pay me. Just teach me about God.'

'I'm sorry boy,' said the man. I would gladly teach you all I know, but you can surely see how it is. There isn't enough food for the villagers who already live here. We can't invite anyone else to stay. I'm sorry. Go to another village where they have food in plenty. You'll find someone else to teach you about God.'

Cadoc was disappointed. He'd travelled a long way to come to this village. He felt this was where he ought to be. But he understood the situation and knew there was not enough food to go round. Cadoc walked away sadly, wondering what to do. He came to a grassy mound a little way outside the village, and sat down to think.

He sat very still, for a long time, and as he sat he watched a mouse scuttling through the grass.

'Lucky you,' thought Cadoc. 'You know where you're going. Look at you. So busy. Hurrying. Scurrying. And look at me. I don't know what to do.'

Cadoc watched the mouse disappear into a tiny crack at the side of a grass-covered stone. Two minutes later it re-appeared with a grain of corn in its mouth.

'Lucky you again,' thought Cadoc. 'You know where to find food as well. You're certainly better off than me.'

Cadoc continued to watch the mouse and saw it eat the corn then disappear into the crack again, only to re-emerge with another grain, then another and another and another.

'Where are you getting it?' said Cadoc out loud. But at the sound of a voice, the mouse whisked away, frightened.

Cadoc dug with his fingers at the tiny gap next to the stone. He widened the gap and loosened the stone. He wiggled the stone from side to side until he was able to pull it away from the grass and soil. Below was a big flat stone, like a trap door, but it was cracked and Cadoc put his eye to the crack.

Corn!

Piles and piles of golden corn. He was sure that's what he could see, down there, under the ground. But how? Why?

He ran as fast as he could, back to the village.

'Come quickly. Come and see. It's enough food for the whole village for winter. Come on.'

The villagers came running. They pulled aside the grass covered stone and the big flat trap door. They found the cellar, hidden for all those years, but still safely guarding its golden treasure of corn.

'It's the answer to our prayers,' said the people. 'God has heard us and sent us food.'

'Thank you boy, for finding it,' said the holy man. 'God has provided for us and surely intended for you to live here with us.'

Later, the people dug out the fallen stones of the old house and built a fine church on the place where it had stood. They carved a picture of Cadoc and the mouse to remind everyone of the time they prayed for food and had their prayers answered.

Cadoc stayed many years with the holy man, and then he left, to travel to other valleys to help their people and to teach them about God.

Saint Wenceslas

28 September

Wenceslas (907–929) was born a Bohemian prince and educated by his grandmother Ludmilla, a Christian. Ludmilla's influence over her grandson angered a section of the pagan nobility, resulting in her murder. When Wenceslas became king he worked to promote Christianity and to improve his people's education, but met with opposition from his brother Boleslav. Eventually Wenceslas died at the hands of Boleslav's followers.

Although the deaths of Wenceslas and his grandmother were not wholly concerned with religious matters, both people were acclaimed martyrs and Wenceslas became the patron saint of Bohemia, later Czechoslovakia. (Ludmilla's feast day is observed on 16 September.)

J.M. Neale's carol, 'Good King Wenceslas' made the saint's name a household word, but the lyrics are not based on any known incident in the life of Wenceslas.

Wenceslas is the patron saint of Czechoslovakia and of brewers.

King Wenceslas   *Greed/envy/kindness/loyalty*

Ludmilla had two grandsons, Wenceslas and Boleslav. Wenceslas was the older of the two, and was kind and thoughtful, as well as being good at thinking things out. Boleslav was the younger. He was lazy, he did not like things to change, and he was not as good at thinking for himself as his brother.

When the boys were small, their grandmother Ludmilla was their teacher. Wenceslas tried hard to remember all he was told. He wanted to learn, to be able to read and write, to know about the world. But Boleslav could not be bothered. He did not see why he should even try to work hard. Soon he stopped coming to his lessons, and Wenceslas and Ludmilla carried on without him.

Eventually the boys grew up and Wenceslas became king. Boleslav did not like this, and began to plan how to get rid of him.

'You don't need to get rid of him,' said Drahmira, their mother. 'The people will do it for you. Wenceslas will be useless as a king. The people will soon get tired of him, then they'll throw him out. All you have to do is wait. He'll go, just you wait and see, and then you'll be king instead. You'll make a much better job of it.'

But their mother, Drahmira was wrong. The people did not want to get rid of Wenceslas as their king. They liked him. He was fair and just. He was honest and truthful. He treated everyone with respect. He was a good king.

'Don't worry, he won't stay king for long,' said Drahmira. 'I've heard that King Radislav from Germany is about to pay Wenceslas a visit. Everyone knows how strong he is. There'll be a fight, Radislav will win, and that'll be the end of Wenceslas. Just you wait and see!'

But once again Drahmira was wrong.

King Radislav came to visit Wenceslas. He came with an army of soldiers. He came to fight Wenceslas, he intended beating him and winning the kingdom.

'There is no point in all your soldiers fighting all my soldiers,' said Wenceslas. 'People will get hurt. Soldiers will die. No, it will be much better if you and I settle this between ourselves. We are responsible for our people, so we should settle our differences between the two of us.'

'That's all right by me,' said King Radislav. 'You and I will fight. We'll see who is the stronger and we'll see who wins.'

'Let's talk about it first,' said Wenceslas. The two kings sat down together to talk. After a few minutes they realised they had no need to fight. They realised they could sort out their differences peacefully, by talking, not by fighting. The two kings became the best of friends.

'This is ridiculous,' grumbled Boleslav to his mother. 'I'm going to be waiting forever if I have to wait for someone else to get rid of Wenceslas. There's nothing for it, I shall have to do it myself. I shall have to kill him.'

So Boleslav and Drahmira planned how they were going to kill Wenceslas.

'We'll invite him to a party,' Boleslav said. 'We'll have a party in the castle to celebrate my son's birthday. He'll be one year old tomorrow. There couldn't be a better reason for a party.'

The arrangements were made. The castle was decorated with ribbons and flowers and the cook baked a cake.

Wenceslas arrived for the party. Everything went well and everyone enjoyed themselves. The party tea was delicious and everyone joined in the games. It was fun.

After tea Wenceslas went out into the garden for a walk. And it was there that someone jumped on him from behind and stabbed him. Afterwards no-one was able to say exactly what had happened. No-one knew who had killed Wenceslas. People had their own ideas of course, their own thoughts, but no-one dared say anything.

Boleslav and his mother smiled at each other, quietly, secretly. Now their problems were over.

'Now you will be king and everything will be all right,' said Drahmira.

But once again she was wrong.

Boleslav was a bad king. He was unfair and unjust. He was dishonest. He treated everyone as though they were unimportant. He showed no respect to anyone, and he listened to no-one except himself.

And despite the fact he was now king, Boleslav was not happy. He knew he was a bad king. He knew he could not compare with Wenceslas. And he could not live with his conscience. Boleslav knew he had done wrong in killing his brother and he could not put it out of his mind. He began to imagine he could see Wenceslas everywhere he went. He began to think that people were whispering about him, and that everyone knew he had murdered a man.

He arranged for Wenceslas to be buried in the big cathedral in Prague.

'Everyone will forget about Wenceslas after the funeral,' said Drahmira. But once again she was wrong. The people never forgot that Wenceslas had been a good and kind king. And Boleslav never forgot that he had killed one of the few really good people he had ever known in his life. He had his conscience to live with for the rest of time, and was never happy again.

Saint Michael and All Angels

29 September

Michaelmas is the feast of the Archangel Michael; the guardian of God's chosen people, the captain of the heavenly host and the vanquisher of the devil. The formal cult of Michael seems to have begun in the East, but there were churches dedicated to him in Britain since early times. By the end of the Middle Ages there were almost 700 English churches dedicated to him.

St Michael's Mount in Cornwall was believed to commemorate an eighth century vision of him. The most famous dedication is undoubtledly Le Mont-Saint-Michel in Normandy, a tenth-century Benedictine Abbey which was also believed to have been built to commemorate an apparition of Saint Michael.

Since 1969 the Roman calendar has commemorated the Archangels Gabriel and Raphael along with Michael on the shared feast day of 29 September.

Michaelmas, occurring at the time of the autumn equinox, at the end of the agricultural year and at the culmination of the harvest, is one of the traditional quarter days (the others being Lady Day – 25 May, Midsummer – 24 June and Christmas – 25 December), and an important time for paying rents, dating farming tenancies and terminating hiring agreements. Thus began the custom of

Michaelmas Fairs, sometimes called Hiring Fairs or Mop Fairs, where, in addition to the usual sale of animals, workers hired themselves out to new establishments. Goose Fairs were also traditionally held at Michaelmas. Goose was thought to be at its best at this time of year.

'Whoever eats goose on Michaelmas Day
Will never lack money his debts for to pay.'

Michael is patron saint of Brussels and of the sick.

Michael and the dragon
loosely adapted from Revelation 12:7–9

Standing up for what you believe to be right/temptation/ appearances can be deceptive

The Evil One was angry. He did not want there to be any good in the world. He did not want any good in the universe. He wanted everything everywhere to be evil, wicked, sinful, mean, ugly, foul, vile, bad. And he intended to make sure he got what he wanted.

'There are people trying to be good,' he grumbled. 'There are people following God!' he said. 'So if I am to conquer goodness; if I am to get rid of everything that is honest or right or true or good – then I must get rid of God himself.'

The Evil One made his plan. He would somehow get into heaven, then he would be able to confront God. The Evil One knew that God was strong, but he was sure that when it came to a fight, he, the Evil One, would win because he was powerful as well, and he knew he could lie or cheat if he needed to. He was bound to win. There would be no problem once he got into heaven, he thought.

The Evil One turned himself into a dragon; a huge dark blood-red dragon with seven heads each bearing a golden crown, and ten horns each as sharp as a scimitar and flashing silver light. He had feet as big as a bear and a roar like a lion. He jumped into the sky and swept a third of the stars aside with his tail, then he watched as they cascaded, shimmering, shining, down to earth. He chased the sun and the moon and the remaining stars across the darkening sky, and shouted, 'Where is he? Where is God. Come out and fight. Let me see how big and brave and strong you really are. Let me see you beat me.' And he rattled and shook his scales until the noise was like thunder.

It was not God who came to meet the Evil One, but the Archangel Michael, with other angels to help. They looked small and insignificant compared to the mighty Evil One. He laughed when he saw them.

'You?' he shouted. 'He's sent you to fight me! I don't believe it!' But in the few seconds it took the Evil One to look, then laugh, then speak, Michael and the others had attacked. The Evil One cursed and swore, he insulted God with every word, but the sound was drowned by the songs of praise sung by Michael and the angels.

In a very short time the dragon was defeated. The Evil One was beaten. Evil was conquered by good.

'Leave!' said Michael. 'You are not wanted here. There is no place for you where there is goodness. You can only go where there is evil.'

'Don't you think you're really going to win!' shouted the Evil One. 'Don't you think you've seen the last of me. I'll be back. I'll win in the end. You'll see.'

'I don't think so,' said Michael, and he pushed the Evil One so hard he fell backwards, down, down, through the dark sky, until he landed with a bump on the earth.

'Well! If I can't beat God in heaven, I'll beat him on earth,' said the Evil One. 'I'll make all the people follow me, instead of God. When he sees that he has no followers he'll give in to me. He'll know then that I am the stronger. He'll concede victory.'

The Evil One changed himself from the dragon-shape to a man-shape, and he started his work.

He visited every person on earth. He changed his shape often. He could become anything he wanted to., He could become anything he thought the next person would be tempted by. He tricked and cheated and deceived the people he met. He lied to them and was dishonest and untruthful. He told people to do things that they knew were wrong. Sometimes people followed him. Sometimes people were taken in by his smooth talk and clever ways. But more often people saw through his tricks and told him to go away, to leave them alone.

Gradually the Evil One realised that he was not going to beat God; that God and goodness were too strong even against the power of evil. He knew that his brave words about going back to fight God in Heaven were foolish, empty words. He knew that Michael and the Archangels would always be too strong for him.

But the Evil One did not give up. He stayed on earth, working against God by working against the people. He watched and waited, always ready to pounce on someone in a moment of weakness; always ready to tempt someone to do something they should not do. Sometimes he managed to get someone on his side. But mostly he failed. Mostly people knew the difference between right and wrong and stayed on the side of good. Mostly peoples' consciences told them whether to do right or wrong.

'But I'll never give up,' said the Evil One. 'I'll always stay on earth ready for people if they want to follow me.'

Saint Jerome

30 September

Jerome was born in Dalmatia, now Croatia, c. 342. He was well educated and, as a young man, travelled extensively in France and Italy. He was a fluent linguist, able to read and write Hebrew, Latin and Greek among others.

Between 382 and 385 he served as secretary to Pope Damascus in Rome, but was disliked by many because of his sharp tongue and controversial ideas.

Eventually, in 386, Jerome settled in Bethlehem with a group of his disciples, and by c. 404 he had completed his opus magnum – a translation of the Bible into Latin, for which he became famous.

Jerome died in Bethlehem in 420. His emblem is a lion, and he is known as one of the four great Latin doctors of the Church, the others being Saint Ambrose, Saint Augustine and Saint Gregory the Great.

Jerome is the patron saint of librarians.

Saint Jerome and the lion   *Caring/friendship/doing your best*

The lion came limping out of the shadows one summer evening in Bethlehem.

The monks, who had been sitting quietly, talking, leapt to their feet and ran inside without waiting to ask any questions. Only Jerome stayed where he was and watched.

He saw the lion struggle to walk without putting one of its front paws on the ground. He saw the paw held high, its pad red and swollen and bleeding. He saw the look of pain on the lion's face. He saw the lion stagger towards him, then fall, exhausted, to the ground.

Jerome quietly walked towards the lion. He gently touched the swollen paw, and saw that there was a large thorn embedded in the pad. The lion made no move to attack Jerome, but lay there and let him examine his paw. Jerome called to the other monks to come and help; to bring water and healing herbs and bandages. Carefully he pulled out the thorn, cleaned the festering wound and bandaged the paw. Then he fed the lion.

After a few days the lion's paw was fully healed and Jerome said 'Time now for you to go. Back from where you came. Off you go now,' and he led the lion to the monastery gate and left him there. But the lion showed no signs of leaving, but just sat there, forlornly, looking back at Jerome.

'You can't stay here,' said Jerome. 'Lions don't live in monasteries.' The lion continued to look at him, sadly.

'I mean, if you stayed what could you do? Everyone in the monastery has to work,' Jerome said.

Just then a boy came past, leading a donkey whose back was piled high with firewood. The lion jumped to his feet, took the donkey's reins in his mouth, and walked with it all the way back to the monastery.

'Well, that's it!' said Jerome. 'The perfect job for a lion. He can lead the donkey to the woods each day. The woodcutter will load him up with firewood as usual, and the lion can lead the donkey back again. No harm will come to the donkey while the lion is guarding him, and the boy will be free to work in the fields.'

And so it was that the lion came to live at the monastery and to have the job of looking after the donkey each day as it went for the firewood.

All went well for several weeks. The monks became used to having a lion about the place, and the lion worked well, until one hot day when he fell asleep as the donkey was waiting for his first load of wood.

When he woke up, much later, there was no sign of the donkey. The lion searched the forest, but it was no good. The smell of strangers and the footprints of men told him that the donkey had been captured by robbers.

The lion trudged back to the monastery, ashamed that he had failed to do his job. The monks were angry.

'He'll have to go,' they said. 'It was a stupid idea to let him stay. He'll have to go.'

'No,' said Jerome. 'He allowed the donkey to be stolen; he must stay and do the donkey's work. We need an animal to carry the firewood.' So from that day on, the lion carried wood on his back, just like a donkey.

One day, as he was standing having the last few sticks piled on his back, he saw a long line of merchants on the road below the forest. The merchants were using camels to carry their goods, and all the camels were tied together, one behind the other. The merchants were walking alongside the camels and at the head of the line was a donkey. The lion threw back his head and sniffed the air. It was! It was his donkey.

The lion let out an enormous roar. The camel train stopped as the merchants looked warily around. Then the lion leapt into action, scattering logs and sticks as he went. He roared down the hillside and the merchants dived for cover. The camels stamped and struggled against their ropes, dropping parcels and packages over the road. Only the donkey stood still, waiting to greet the lion.

The lion took the donkey's reins in his mouth and walked with him all the way back to the monastery.

The monks could hardly believe their eyes as the lion and a donkey, followed by a lumbering line of camels, scattering parcels and chased by a group of angrily shouting merchants, came straggling into their courtyard. The noise was indescribable.

'Whatever's going on?'

'What's happening?'

'Get that lion under control. It's stolen our donkey.'

'We've lost half our goods.'

'Is this lion yours?'

'You'll pay for this.'

Only Jerome understood what had happened. He went to speak to the head merchant.

'This donkey,' he said, 'where did you get it?'

'We found it in the forest,' said the merchant.

'I thought so,' said Jerome. 'This is our donkey and our lion recognised it. Now, you give us back what is ours, and we'll give you back what is yours, then go in peace.'

Soon, order was restored in the courtyard. The camel train set off on its journey, the monks returned to their work and the lion and the donkey went to the forest to collect firewood.

And not surprisingly, the lion never went to sleep again when he was working.

Saint Theresa of Lisieux

1 October

Marie-Françoise-Thérèse was born in Alençon in 1873, the youngest daughter of Louis Martin, a watchmaker, and his wife Azelie-Marie Guerin. When the child was four, her mother died and the family moved to Lisieux where the children were cared for by an aunt, and then educated by Benedictine nuns.

Thérèse, aged only 15, followed her sisters into a Carmelite monastery, and took the name Theresa of the Infant Jesus. She remained in the convent for the next nine years, until she died of tuberculosis of 1897, leading a quiet, ordinary, uneventful, simple life of obedience to the order.

Theresa might well have been forgotten had it not been that she had written, under obedience, her spiritual biography. This was published after her death, entitled Histoire d'une âme (Story of a Soul), *and met with instant acclaim. The book was translated into many languages which led to the widespread veneration of the young nun from Lisieux. Theresa of the Infant Jesus had become the most popular saint of modern times.*

Theresa believed, and proved, that one does not need to be great or to achieve great accomplishments in order to become a saint. She achieved sainthood by being ordinary, by doing her best and by being obedient.

Theresa is joint patron saint of France with Jeanne d'Arc. She is also patron saint of missions with Francis Xavier, and of florists.

Saint Theresa of Lisieux   *Humility/obedience/cheerfulness*

Theresa was only 15 when she decided she wanted to become a nun like her older sisters.

'You can't go. You're too young,' said her father. 'Wait until you're older before you decide what to do.'

'But I know what I want to do,' said Theresa. I've known it for a long time. I want to be a nun, then one day I want to become a saint.'

'Don't be silly,' said her father. 'You have to be an important person, a great person, or you have to do something really special, to become a saint. You are just an ordinary girl; ordinary people don't become saints.'

'I think an ordinary person could become a saint,' said Theresa quietly, and she asked her father again if he would let her go to the convent to become a nun.

At last Theresa's father could see that this was what his daughter really wanted to do, so he agreed that she could go, even though she was the youngest girl ever to have entered the convent.

Theresa was really happy at the convent. She worked hard and did her best in everything she was asked to do. She always did as she was told, and always worked cheerfully, even when she was doing unpleasant jobs like cleaning the toilets, scrubbing the floors, or peeling potatoes. She had a great sense of fun, and she liked to laugh.

But Theresa was not outstandingly good at anything in particular, except being cheerful, working hard, and doing as she was told. She was not a brilliant scholar, she was not even very good at reading and writing. She was not a wonderful mathematician, or a marvellous painter, or brilliant at history, or expert at sewing. She was just an ordinary girl.

Sometimes the other young nuns would tease her and poke fun.

'She wants to be a saint!' they'd say. 'What's so special about her that she should be a saint. She's so ordinary. Everyone knows you have to be someone really special to be a saint.' And they would laugh and giggle behind her back. But Theresa took no notice. She carried on doing her best, believing that she was serving God by doing her ordinary every day jobs as well as she could.

Theresa lived at the convent in Lisieux for nine years, then, sadly, she became ill and died. She was only 24 years old. She would probably have been forgotten, but someone found a little book that she had written just two years before she died.

'It's the story of her life,' said the girl who found it. 'Look, it's all about when she was a child and how she wanted to be a nun. What shall we do with it?'

'We should take it to the Mother Superior,' said another nun.

The book, which Theresa had called *The Story of a Soul*, was shown to Mother Agnes.

'Yes. I remember,' she said. 'I remember that I asked Theresa to write a story about why she wanted to be a nun. She always did what I asked her to do. She was a very good girl. I'll read it.'

Mother Agnes read Theresa's story and decided it ought to be published. But first she asked two of Theresa's sisters to edit the story – to reword it and get rid of all the mistakes and prepare it for publication. The two sisters also added a chapter on to the story about Theresa's life during the two years before she died. Then they gave it a new title; they called it *The Autobiography of a Saint*.

Theresa's book was published and it went on sale. It was a huge and instant success. Everyone wanted to read the story of the ordinary girl who became a nun. The book was translated into other languages, and people from other countries read about the nun from Lisieux. 'She was a saint,' everyone said.

Theresa; the girl who was not a brilliant scholar, or a wonderful mathematician, or a marvellous painter, or brilliant at history, or expert at sewing; the girl who was not particularly good at anything except being cheerful, working hard, and doing the best she could; the ordinary girl who knew she was serving God in the ordinary things she did every day; had become the most popular saint of her time.

Saint Francis

4 October

Francis was born in Assisi c. 1181, the son of a wealthy cloth merchant. His early life was one of adventure and extravagance, but Francis changed this to one of simplicity, lowliness and poverty after having a vision of Christ. In response to his son giving away money and possessions, Francis' father disowned and disinherited him.

Francis founded the Franciscan Order and spent much time travelling and preaching to the people. He suffered much ill-health throughout his life and died aged 45 in 1226.

Francis is known particularly for his unassuming nature, his gentleness, his concerns for others and his love of all animals. Francis is patron saint of merchants and animals, and in 1979 he was declared patron saint of ecologists.

Saint Francis tames a wolf   *Trust/kindness/friendship*

One day Saint Francis was travelling in northern Italy, when he came to a small walled city. It was mid-morning but there was no-one about. No-one was working in the fields, no-one was out walking or gossiping, children were not playing. What a strange desolate sort of place, thought Saint Francis.

Suddenly he heard a sound; a long low growl of a sound that made Francis stop in his tracks to listen. The sound came again; a deep, fierce, frightening, spine-chilling growl. Francis stood quite still and looked around. Nothing. Then the bushes at the side of the path parted and out sprang a great grey, wild wolf, its teeth bared and its eyes white and angry.

In that moment Francis knew why there were no people to be seen, no children playing out. He knew that the people were safely behind their city walls, afraid to venture out in case they were attacked and killed by this beast. He knew that any second now the wolf could leap on him and sink its teeth into his flesh. Francis knew he would have little chance of surviving such an attack.

Francis continued to stand quite still. Then he spoke in a calm, quiet voice.

'Brother wolf. Why would you wish to harm me? I am not going to hurt you. We are both creatures made by God, we are brothers in his eyes, and there is room enough in this world for us both. Let us be friends, as brothers should. Let us go together into the city and I will find you food. I know you are fierce and angry because you are hungry. Hunger can make beasts of us all.'

It is unlikely that the wolf could understand the words of Saint Francis, but he understood the kind and gentle manner with which he spoke. He understood that this man was not about to beat him with sticks and clubs, as other men had done. He understood that this man showed no fear of him. The wolf stood with his head on one side and his ears pricked, listening to the man.

Saint Francis went on, 'The people of the city are afraid of you because you are fierce and because you kill for food. If I ask them to feed you, will you promise not to attack them?'

The wolf, of course, said nothing. But he came and lay at Francis' feet. Francis touched his head and stroked his fur. The wolf lay on its back and looked up at Saint Francis.

Together they walked, like a man and his dog, to the gates of the city. Francis knocked. 'Let me in please,' he said. 'I have come to stay in your city for a while.'

'You can't come in here with that beast,' said a man behind the gate. We know that animal. It's wild and fierce and not to be trusted. It attacks anyone it sees. Kill it first, and then you can come in.'

'Why should I kill one of God's creatures?' asked Saint Francis.'They have as much right to life as you or I. This animal only attacked out of hunger. Feed it and it will be as docile as a pet. Let us in and I'll show you.'

Cautiously the man opened the gate. Francis and the wolf walked through, and all the people stepped back out of the way. Francis led the wolf to the market-place, where he bought it a dish of meat and some water. He put the food on the ground and the wolf ate hungrily.

Francis called to a small child. 'Come and stroke him,' he said. The child and its mother came and touched the great grey wolf. It gently licked the child's hand and the child smiled.

'Now do you see?' asked Francis. 'All creatures, including people, belong to God's family.'

The people of the city adopted the grey wolf as their pet. They fed it and cared for it and loved it, and in return the great grey wolf gave them his loyalty and his friendship for the rest of his life.

Saint Luke

18 October

All the information we have about Luke is from the New Testament. He was possibly born at Antioch in Syria, and was a Gentile. He is known to have travelled with Saint Paul on his second and third missionary journeys, and was with Paul on the voyage to Italy when they were shipwrecked off the coast of Malta. After Paul's death, Luke is believed to have returned to Antioch where he led a Christian community and remained until his own death, possibly around 80 years of age.

Luke wrote the third Gospel and the Acts of the Apostles. *He was an accurate observer, a careful historian, a skilled and empathetic storyteller; an artist in words. He refers to events in secular history as well as to biblical events, and recent archaeological findings have supported his historical accounts.*

Of all the Gospels, Luke's stresses the compassion of Christ. He tells of Christ's love of society's underdogs; the sick, the disabled, the poor. He speaks of women more than the other Gospel writers and tells of the birth of Christ very much more from Mary's point of view, compared with Matthew who emphasises Joseph's. Luke's writing is aimed at a Gentile audience, unlike Matthew's which presents Christ as the Jewish Messiah.

Luke's feast has been celebrated in England since early times, and 28 ancient churches were dedicated to his name.

Luke is the patron saint of doctors, surgeons and artists.

Luke the writer   *Caring/consideration for others/thinking*
adapted from Luke 17:11–19

Luke was thinking. He was trying to remember everything he could about Jesus – his life, the special things he did, the stories he told, the things he said – so that he would write it all down. Luke knew it was important that everything was written down so that people in the future would know about Jesus.

Luke was good at writing. He was good at noticing detail, good at writing exactly what happened, good at knowing how people felt about things.

Luke sat and thought.

He remembered the day they had walked from Galilee, through Samaria, on their way to Jerusalem. He remembered that they had just crossed the border from Galilee into Samaria when they saw the group of men.

At first Luke thought the men were travelling, like themselves, but then he realised they were lepers. Luke knew about lepers because he was a doctor. Leprosy was a dreadful disease which affected people's skin and hands and feet. When people had leprosy they were sent away to live apart from other people. They had to leave their homes and families and friends and jobs. They became outcasts. No-one wanted to be near them because they were frightened that they, too, would catch the disease. Lepers had to live wherever they could. They had to beg for their food, but they were not allowed to go near people to ask for some, so they had to ring a bell when they came near a village and call out 'unclean' so that the villagers had chance to put down some food if they wanted to, but then get away before the lepers came near.

Yes, Luke knew all about these poor people with leprosy.

As the lepers saw Jesus and his friends approach, they called out 'Have pity on us. Please give us some food.' Then they waited, expecting the strangers to hurry away from them as strangers usually did. But to their surprise Jesus came nearer. He looked at them. He did not seem afraid of them or of their disease.

There were ten men altogether; all in different stages of the disease. Some had been ill for a long time. Others for only a few months, but all of them had damage to their skin, their hands, their feet, and their faces.

'Come here,' said Jesus gently.

The men shuffled nearer.

Jesus looked at them again.

'Go to your village and let the priests there examine you,' he said.

'But we're not allowed,' began one of the men.

'Go,' said Jesus.

The ten men set off towards their village, and on the way something wonderful happened. Each man became well again. Every sign of the disease disappeared.

'Look!' they said, showing each other their hands and feet and skin. 'Look. We're well again. We can go home. We can live with our families again.'

The men hurried now, anxious to get back, anxious to tell everyone the wonderful thing that had happened to them. But one man waited. He turned back to look for Jesus. He saw him walking on the road to Jerusalem with his friends. The man ran to catch up with Jesus.

'Thank you,' he said. 'It isn't enough I know, but I don't know what else to say. Thank you for making me well again.'

'Where are the other nine men?' asked Jesus.

'They have gone already. Gone to tell their family and friends that they are well again,' said the man.

Jesus turned to his friends. 'Only one of them could find time to say thank you,' he said sadly. 'Only one out of ten could come and say thank you to God.'

Jesus turned back to the man, 'Go now,' he said. 'Go home. Your faith has made you well.'

Luke remembered the incident very clearly. He remembered that the man who had come back to say thank you was a Samaritan, a foreigner really to Jesus and the other nine men, yet he had been the only one who had thanked Jesus. Luke remembered how sad Jesus had been that the other men had not bothered thank God for being made well again. And he remembered how Jesus was kind and caring to everyone, no matter where they were from, or what was wrong with them.

Luke gathered together his writing things and began to write down the story, while it was still fresh in his memory.

Saints Crispin and Crispinian

25 October

Crispin and Crispinian were probably martyred in Rome c. 285, but their cult has centred on Soissons in France since the sixth century. Legend has it that the two men were brothers who travelled to France as missionaries, and earned their living as shoemakers. They were supposedly tortured and had attempts made on their lives, but when the perpetrator was unable to kill them he committed suicide by drowning. The story goes that they were then executed at the order of the Emperor Maximian.

Another legend says that the brothers fled to Faversham in England during the Roman persecutions, and that they worked as shoemakers in a house that stood on the site of the present Swan Inn in Preston Street. This tradition probably accounts for the reference to the feast of Saint Crispin in Shakespeare's Henry V *(Act 4, Scene 3) on the eve of the Battle of Agincourt.*

The reality is more likely that they were martyred in Rome and that their remains were translated to Soissons where their shrine was later rebuilt by Saint Eloi.

Crispin and Crispinian are the patron saints of leather workers, shoemakers and cobblers.

Crispin and Crispinian

*Courage/forgiveness/standing up
for what you believe to be right*

Crispin and Crispinian were brothers who lived in Rome. They had heard about Jesus, his life and his work, and they decided that they, too, wanted to become Christians. But it was a dangerous time for people who wanted to follow Jesus. The Romans persecuted the Christians. They hunted them out and threw them in prison. They tortured them and even killed them.

Crispin and Crispinian tried to hide from the Romans, but it was becoming more and more difficult to find somewhere safe.

'It's no good, we'll have to leave Rome,' said Crispin one day.

'But our home is here. Our house and furniture and all our friends and relatives are here,' said Crispinian. 'If we go we'll have to leave everything behind.'

'If we don't go we'll be killed,' said Crispin. 'We have no choice.'

So the two brothers packed a few things in a bag and left Rome that night. They travelled north through Italy and into France. In France they thought they would be safe and they stopped in a place called Noviodunum, which is now called Soissons.

'But what are we going to do here?' asked Crispinian. 'How are we going to live? There's no-one here to help us, we've left everyone behind.'

'We'll earn our living by doing what we know how to do,' said Crispin.

'But I can't do anything except mend shoes,' wailed Crispinian.

'Then we'll mend shoes!' said Crispin.

So the two brothers rented a house and set up as shoemakers and cobblers. They were good workers and soon built up a good business. The people in Noviodunum soon learned that the new shoemakers gave value for money, that they were honest and hardworking and that they were kind and helpful. They also learned the Crispin and Crispinian were Christians.

'Tell us about Jesus,' they said.

So Crispin and Crispinian talked to their customers about Jesus. They explained about his life and they told some of the stories Jesus told. Many of the people of Noviodunum decided that they wanted to become Christians too.

Crispin and Crispinian lived quietly, happily, contentedly in Noviodunum for many years. But then the Emperor Maximian visited Noviodunum, and the trouble began.

One of Crispin and Crispinian's neighbours told the emperor that the brothers were Christians.

'And they're turning the townspeople into Christians too,' he grumbled. 'They ought to be stopped. We don't want things changed around here.' The emperor left instructions for a Roman general, called Rictiusvarus, to sort out the problem.

Now Rictiusvarus was a very cruel man. He set about persecuting Crispin and Crispinian in the most terrible way. He had them followed by spies. He burned down their house and destroyed all their leather and tools. He told lies about them and prevented them from renting another house or setting up in business again. Then he captured them both and threw them into prison. He tortured the brothers to try to make them say they hated Jesus.

But Crispin and Crispinian were true Christians. They refused to say anything against Jesus, and no matter what Rictiusvarus did to them, they remained calm and quiet and dignified. This made Rictiusvarus so angry that he threw himself into the river and drowned.

The Emperor Maximian heard what had been happening in Noviodunum.

'Crispin and Crispianian must be dealt with,' he said to his soldiers. 'Bring them here.'

So the brothers were brought from their prison and made to stand in front of the emperor.

'We have had enough of this nonsense,' said the emperor. 'You either give up all this talk of Jesus and you start worshipping the Roman Gods again, or I shall have you killed. What do you say?'

'We say we can only stand by what we believe is right,' said Crispin.

'We say we believe in Jesus,' said Crispinian.

'Then you must die,' said Maximian. 'Take them away to the place of execution,' he said to his soldiers.

Crispin and Crispinian were taken away. Just before they were killed, Maximian asked them again if they would deny Jesus.

'No,' said the brothers. 'But we forgive you for not understanding. We forgive you for what you are going to do.'

They were killed then, but the Emperor Maximian never forgot their bravery and their quiet, calm dignity.

All Saints

1 November

All Saints' Day, sometimes known as All Hallows (Hallow being an archaic word meaning Saint or Holy Person), is a feast day for all forgotten, unknown or unrecognised saints, who do not have a special feast day of their own.

The feast actually starts the previous evening, the Eve of All Hallows or Hallowe'en, which has its origins in the Celtic feast of Samhain, the beginning of winter on 1 November, when people carried out various activities to frighten away the evil spirits which were thought to accompany the long hours of winter darkness. Christians adopted the festival believing that good always conquers evil, and that Jesus, the Light of the World, defeats all the fears of darkness.

All Saints' Day, together with All Souls' Day are known collectively as Hallowtide.

Saint Unknown and the goat

forgiveness/temptation/kindness/ tolerance/generosity

The story goes that a saint lived in a monastery in France. But the story is so old, and people's memories so dim, that the saint's name and the names of the other people in the story have been quite lost and forgotten. The only one that is remembered is Daisy, and she was the goat. Of that everyone is certain.

Daisy lived in the monastery with the monks and the abbot – he was the saint – and since he needs a name we will call him Saint Unknown.

Life was quiet and ordered and simple and ordinary. It went on day after day, week after week, following the same pattern of sleep and prayers and work and meals and a little leisure time. The people in the village next to the monastery could set their clocks by the times that the monks did their work, or ate their dinner, or said their prayers. Life was peaceful and organised and straightforward and without surprises. Until the day that Daisy led the dance.

The day began as usual. The monks rose early, said their prayers, ate their breakfast and began their work. Daisy had been milked, her milk was already in the dairy, cooling, waiting to be made into cheese to be sold at market at the first opportunity, and she was back in the orchard by herself, sunbathing, snoozing, nibbling a little grass, as goats do when they are idling their time away.

She heard footsteps and turned to see who was there. Strangers. Daisy backed away a little. She didn't know these people. The men unlatched the gate to the orchard. They came in, noisily, roughly, brandishing sticks.

'This one'll do,' one of them said. 'We'll take this one.'

The hair on Daisy's back bristled with fear. She was not used to rough talk, rough handling. One of the men threw a sack over her head. Then they grabbed her round her middle and half-dragged, half-carried her through the orchard gate.

They thought they would steal her easily. After all, she was not a very big goat. She was not a strong billy goat with tough, sharp horns. She was small even for a nanny goat. But she was big on bravery, and on feeling indignant. She had never been treated like this before, and she was certainly not going to put up with it now.

She tossed her head and shook off the old smelly sack. She bleated as loudly as she could and at the same time kicked out her back legs, striking one of the men in the stomach. He let go of her and fell to the ground. She trod on him for good measure. Then she put down her head and butted him as he struggled to get up. One of his companions started to laugh at him, which helped Daisy because the two men started fighting and gave her time to skip away.

'Grab her, stupid,' shouted a third robber. 'Don't let her go now we've got this far.'

The other two men, now arguing fiercely with each other, did as they were told and ran to catch Daisy. But she was nimble and quick and sure on her feet. She skipped and danced in front of them, always just a few feet ahead. They huffed and panted and shouted and raved and grabbed and lunged to try and catch her, but every time they failed. Every time she danced just out of reach. The men grew redder and hotter and madder, they could almost see her smiling at them, teasing them, leading them a fine dance.

'Let her go for goodness sake!' gasped one of the men. 'I've no breath left for chasing a goat.'

'We're not giving up now,' shouted the one in charge. 'Keep after her. She'll get tired soon, then we'll have her. Go on! Get her!' And the dance began again.

Now, anyone with half an eye could see that Daisy was not going to tire as easily as the robbers. And anyone with half a brain could see where she was leading them. But the robbers were using neither their eyes nor their brains, and they did not realise that the dance had led them in a full circle back from whence they came. Back to the orchard.

Daisy skipped in through the orchard gate, straight into the arms of Saint Unknown, who had come to gather a basket of apples.

'Well! Well! Well!' he said, as three robbers came tumbling in behind Daisy, gasping and panting and red in the face. But their faces quickly became the colour of the daisies on the grass. White! They realised they were caught. For stealing animals in those days, was punishable by death. They stood and waited for Saint Unknown to call the sheriff.

Saint Unknown looked at the ragged, wretched, trembling robbers, cowering in front of him. And he understood their temptation. He understood that they had seen Daisy and thought they could get away with stealing her. But Saint Unknown also understood a joke when he saw one. So he said, 'Thank you so much. You are all so kind to bring back our little goat. We were getting quite frantic with worry about her. We just couldn't think where she could be. Now it's quite clear that she escaped through the orchard gate and you found her and brought her back. And I can see that it has not been an easy job catching her. You all look quite worn out, so come with me and I will get you something to eat and drink, and a small reward I think, for bringing our own Daisy safely home again. Then, when you have eaten you shall go on your way, we don't want to delay you. Come!'

The robbers were so surprised that they were not being taken immediately to prison to have their heads parted from their bodies; they were so surprised that this man was forgiving them and actually letting them go free, that they fell on their knees and promised Saint Unknown they would lead good lives in the future. And the curious thing was, they did.

As for life at the monastery, it resumed its normal pattern again of sleep and prayers and work and meals and a little leisure time, but the story of Daisy's dance with the robbers was never quite forgotten, even if everyone did forget the names of the people in it. All except Daisy, of course.

All Souls

2 November

All Souls' Day is also known as the Day of the Dead, and is a day for remembering everyone who has died, regardless of whether they have led exemplary lives or not. The day is not however intended as an unhappy occasion, but rather a celebration of lives lived and of happy times remembered, and an opportunity for the living to pray that the souls of the departed are now at peace.

Like Hallowe'en, All Souls has Celtic origins and was a time when people lit candles and bonfires to light the souls' way to the afterlife. Later, it became the custom for poorer Christians to offer prayers for the dead, in return for money or food (soul cakes) from their wealthier neighbours. People would go 'souling' – rather like carol singing – requesting alms or soul cakes:

'A soul, a soul, a soul cake,
Please to give us a soul cake,
One for Peter, two for Paul,
Have mercy on us Christians all.'

The hermit of all souls
Caring/consideration for others/friendship/
kindness/patience/sharing

There was once a man called John, who set off on a journey to France. He was travelling to the monastery at Cluny, in Burgundy, to see the abbot there. John knew he had a long journey ahead of him, but when he set off, he did not realise just how long it would be.

John set out from his home in England and travelled on foot to the south coast. From here he would travel by boat across the sea to France, then he would have to walk several hundred miles before he reached Cluny. But things did not turn out quite as he planned.

The walk to the south coast of England was no problem. And there was no problem at first with the boat. Oh, it was small, and looked as though it needed a coat of paint to smarten it up, but John did not mind what it looked like as long as it took him safely across the sea. When the boat set off, it was early morning and the weather was good, but as the boat sailed further from land, the weather worsened. The wind whipped the sea into frothing white caps, which soon turned to dark grey heaving waves. The clouds gathered low in the sky, dark and heavy and filled with rain.

The boat rode the waves bravely at first, but the captain and crew were finding it harder and harder to control. They had no powerful engine, like the ships of today have. They had no radio contact with land. They had only sails for the wind, and men pulling oars. But in this storm the sails were no use, the wind was too strong. And the men were not strong enough to row against the mountainous sea.

'Let her ride out the storm,' ordered the captain. And the crew held on tight to the rigging and waited for the storm to blow over, hoping that the boat would not capsize in the waves.

But the sea was too strong, and the boat far too small. A wave pushed against the side of the boat as another crashed over its bows. The mast snapped in two. The deck split apart. The men were sucked into the sea.

Some drowned straight away. Others stayed alive a little while, clinging on to bits of floating wood. John was lucky. He spent a number of hours in the sea, more dead than alive, but then, as the first fingers of light appeared in the sky the next morning, he was washed up on the beach of a small island just off the north coast of France.

He was too weak to walk. Too weak to move. Too weak to do anything but lie there and hope that he would be found.

Later that morning, when the sun was high in the sky, a man came walking along the beach and found him. The man carried John to his hut in the hills, and there he cared for John until he was well and strong again.

'Thank you,' said John. 'If it were not for you I wouldn't be alive. But where am I? Where is this place? And in all the days I've been here I've seen only you. Who else lives here and where are they?'

'This place is called Hermit Island,' said the man. 'It has that name because no-one lives here but me. I am a hermit and I choose to live here alone so that I can concentrate on my prayers.'

'You live here all by yourself?' said John. 'But what do you do all day?'

'I pray,' said the hermit. 'I pray for all the people who have died. You see, many people who die have no family, no friends, no-one to remember them, no-one to pray for them. So I pray for them. I remember them. I ask God to look after them in heaven.'

'But why?' asked John.

'So that they are not forgotten,' said the hermit.

John was impressed by this quiet, good, kind, caring man, who had given up an ordinary life so that he could spend every day praying for people who had died, so that they would not be forgotten.

John stayed with the hermit on his island for nearly a month, and the two men became good friends, but John knew that he could not stay there forever. He knew that this lonely life was not for him, and he knew that the hermit wanted to have his island to himself again. It was time for the two friends to part. They knew they would not forget each other, and they knew they had learned a lot from each other, even though they were very different people.

John began to spend every day looking for a ship to take him to the mainland so that he could carry on his journey. He saw several, but they were all too far away to contact. Then, one day, a boat came in to land and John was able to get on board. He said goodbye to the hermit, and both friends knew they would never see each other again.

The boat took John to a busy port on the western side of France, and from there John set out on the long walk to Cluny. He was so many weeks behind schedule, but at last he arrived at the monastery and went to find the abbot.

'Where on earth have you been?' asked the abbot. 'We'd given you up for lost.'

'I very nearly was lost,' said John. 'But listen to what happened to me.' And he told the abbot the full story of the shipwreck and his encounter with the hermit of Hermit Island. The abbot listened with interest and said, 'This man obviously cares very much about people to have given up his whole life to pray for those who have died, and to have looked after you when you were washed up half-drowned from the sea. But he has given me an idea. We should have a special day in the year when we remember everyone who has died. We will pray for them as well as your hermit friend. But we will make sure it is a happy day, not a sad one. Let it be a day when we remember all the joyful times, all the happy times, all the good times. Let it be a day when we celebrate the lives of all the people we have known but that are no longer here on this earth.'

The abbot looked at his calendar and marked 2 November as the special day for remembering everyone who had died, for saying prayers for them, and for remembering all the happy times in their lives.

Saint Martin

11 November

Martin was born the son of a soldier in what is now Hungary c. 315. He was brought up in Italy, but served in the Roman army in France. The story of Martin giving up his cloak to a beggar is said to have taken place at Amiens and to have precipitated Martin's conversion to Christianity.

In 360 he is believed to have founded the first monastery in France and was made Bishop of Tours in 370. He died c. 400. Martin was an active missionary

and became known as the evangeliser of rural France. His influence is widespread, ranging from Ireland to Africa, and in England there are many churches dedicated to his name, perhaps the best known of which is St-Martin-in-the-Fields in London.
    Martin is patron saint of soldiers, beggars and innkeepers.

Saint Martin and the beggar

Consideration for others/caring/
kindness/sharing/courage/
standing up for what you believe to be right

Martin was the son of a Roman soldier, and when he was 15 years old he also became a soldier in the Roman army.

One winter's day Martin was riding through a town called Amiens in France with other soldiers, when he saw a beggar standing in the roadway.

'Get out of the way!' shouted the soldiers, as they galloped their horses past the man. 'Move! Or you'll be killed.'

The beggar jumped aside and fell into the mud at the edge of the road.

'Serves him right,' shouted the soldiers. 'He shouldn't have been in the road.' And they rode on, not caring what happened to the man.

Martin stopped.

'Are you all right?' he asked the beggar. 'Are you hurt?'

'No,' said the man. 'Just hungry. Can you spare me a coin or two to buy food?'

'I'm sorry,' said Martin. 'I have no money to give you. I have nothing to give you. I just stopped to make sure you were not hurt.'

'No,' said the man again. 'I'm not hurt.'

Martin looked at him and saw his muddy, tattered clothes. He saw how thin the man was, and how he shivered with the cold. He wished he had something to give him.

Then Martin had an idea. He was wearing a warm, red, woollen cloak. It was so big that it wrapped round Martin twice. He took it off and drew his sword. The man cowered in fear, afraid that Martin was going to kill him.

'No, I'm not going to hurt you,' said Martin. 'Here!' And he ripped the cloak in two with his sword and gave half to the beggar. 'That should keep you a bit warmer,' he said as he mounted his horse and rode off.

'Thank you,' called the man.

That night, Martin had a strange dream. He saw the man the Christians called Jesus in his dream. He saw him walking along a muddy road, but the strange thing was, Jesus was wearing half a cloak. Half a warm, red woollen cloak. Half of Martin's cloak.

The dream was so vivid that Martin woke up and could remember it clearly. He was sure that the beggar he had seen in Amiens was Jesus and that the dream was a message telling him to become a Christian.

'I will,' he said. 'I will be a Christian and follow the way of Jesus.'

During the next few weeks, Martin found out all he could about Jesus, and was baptised into the Christian faith.

'Now I want to leave the army,' he said. 'If I am to do God's work it is wrong for me to fight in the Roman army. I must go out into the world and fight evil. I must tell the people of France about Jesus.'

So Martin asked the Roman general if he could leave the Roman army.

'Certainly not!' shouted the general. 'Only cowards want to leave. Are you a coward?'

'No,' said Martin. 'I want to leave because I think I have more important work to do; I have God's work to do. I want to leave because I want to tell the people of France about Jesus.'

'You are a coward' said the general. 'Otherwise you would stay and fight in the Roman army.'

'I'm not a coward,' said Martin.

'Then prove it!' said the General.

'I will,' answered Martin. 'In the next battle I will stand between the front line of soldiers and the enemy. When the fighting starts perhaps I will be killed, or perhaps I won't. If I am killed, it is clearly God's will that it should happen. But if I am not killed, then it is God's will that I should go and teach the people of France about Jesus.'

'If you are prepared to be killed for your God, then you are not a coward,' said the general. 'So you may leave the army, and may your God be with you.'

So Martin was allowed to be discharged from the Roman army. He went to live alone for a while, to pray to God and to ask for strength to do God's work. Then he built a monastery – the first in France – where others could come and serve God. Later, Martin travelled all over France, telling the people about the life of Jesus, and baptising all those who wanted to become Christians.

Saint Hilda

17 November

Hilda was born in Northumbria in 614. She was christened in York when she was 13 by Saint Paulinus, but did not decide to become a nun until some twenty years later.

She was made abbess of a convent in Hartlepool in 649 by Saint Aidan, and eight years later founded the community at Whitby where she remained until she died in 680.

Hilda enjoyed much personal prestige in her position as abbess. She attained influence and authority without, of course, being ordained. Kings, rulers and commoners sought her advice. The community, a double monastery where men and women lived in adjoining quarters, became famous as a place of learning, and as a place of preparation for the priesthood. The monastery was also the site of the famous Synod of Whitby in 664 at which decisions were made concerning Celtic and Roman ecclesiastical customs. Hilda supported the Celtic party in the discussion about the date of Easter, but accepted the decision in favour of Rome with utmost loyalty.

Hilda's following was particularly strong in the north of England where 13 churches are dedicated to her, 11 in Yorkshire and two in Durham.

Hilda, Abbess of Whitby

Caring/tolerance/loyalty/
doing your best/responsibility

Hilda was born a princess in Northumbria, but when she was grown up she decided that being a princess was not for her. She wanted to be a nun.

She went to see a monk called Aidan, to ask his advice.

'I want to be a nun,' she explained. 'I have thought about it for a long time, but I don't know what to do.'

'I am building a new convent near here, at Hartlepool,' answered Aidan. 'Why don't you go and live with the nuns there? They will teach you.'

Hilda went to the new convent, and before long became its abbess – the person in charge. She quickly became known as a kind and caring person, someone who was always ready to help those in need; someone who always gave good advice, but someone who also listened to the ideas and opinions and thoughts of other people.

She discovered that some monks wished there was somewhere in Northumbria where they could train to be priests. She heard that the nuns wished they had a library with lots of books. She found out that the local people wished there was a place where the children could go to learn to read and write.

We need a new monastery, thought Hilda. We need a monastery where people can come to learn – all people, men, women and children. We need a new community, a new abbey. As she spoke, Hilda imagined a wonderful church, built high on a hill where everyone would see it. She pictured the monastery built alongside, and people coming, going, singing, learning, talking, meeting, working, all day long.

Hilda spoke to Aidan about her dream for a new community.

'There's a piece of land at Whitby,' he said. 'You could have that, then you could build your own abbey, your own community.'

Hilda went to see the land. It was high on a windswept cliff looking out over the wild and stormy North Sea. There was a tiny bay, bitten out of the cliff face by the weather, and a river running down from the hills, through a dip in the cliffs, down to the bay and the sea. It was a perfect place for an abbey.

Work began. The abbey soared to the sky and a double monastery was built, half for the monks and half for the nuns. A library was built where they could study. People came from far and near to see the abbey and to meet Hilda. Kings and rulers and ordinary people all came to visit, to offer a prayer to God. And everyone called Hilda 'Mother Hilda' because she was the caring 'mother' of the community on the cliffs at Whitby.

One day it was decided that an important meeting of the church, called a Synod, should be held at Whitby. Mother Hilda and her community of monks and nuns were to organise it. The meeting was to be held to decide on a number of matters which were causing concern, one of which was the date the church should celebrate Easter.

The meeting started. Hilda thought they should keep to the old Celtic date for celebrating Easter, but many other people thought the Roman date was better. It would have been easy for Hilda to persuade her community to vote the way she wanted, but she knew that would not be fair, or honest, or right.

The vote was held, and the majority of people wanted to celebrate Easter on the Roman date. The vote had not gone the way Hilda wanted, but she accepted the decision because she knew that was what the majority wanted. Hilda was loyal enough to accept the decision, even though it was not her choice.

Hilda continued to be the Mother Abbess at Whitby, always having her own opinions, but always ready to listen to the opinions of others.

Saint Hugh

17 November

Hugh was born in Burgundy in 1135, and had been a Carthusian monk in France for 17 years when Henry II of England sent for him to take charge of a newly-founded monastery in Somerset. Later, he was made Bishop of Lincoln.

Hugh was a plain-speaking man, unafraid to support the common people against unfairness and injustice, and unafraid to speak up against noblemen and even kings. On two occasions he is said to have stood alone against rioting anti-semitic mobs. He had an affinity with children and the sick, and had a sense of humour that enabled him on more than one occasion to calm the king's rages. Hugh was responsible for the start of the rebuilding of Lincoln Cathedral.

Hugh died in London in 1200, after 14 years as a bishop. He has been described as one of the most attractive characters of medieval England.

There are several legends about Saint Hugh, perhaps the most famous one being the one concerning his pet swan, which eventually became his emblem.

Hugh is the patron saint of sick children.

Saint Hugh and the wild swan

Sharing/courage/kindness/
friendship/trust

The lake near Bishop Hugh's palace was beautiful. It was wide and deep, edged with trees and wild flowers, and home to lots of birds and animals.

Although the lake was inside the palace grounds, Hugh used to let people come and enjoy it if they wanted to. Children used to play near it and adults would walk round it when they wanted a few minutes peace and quiet.

One day a great white swan flew to the lake and made its home there. It was a wild and angry creature; friendless, fierce and bad-tempered, as though it had fallen out with the world and everyone in it.

At first people said 'It'll calm down. When it realises that no-one is going to hurt it, it'll be quieter and more friendly.' But the great wild swan did not become quieter. It became more aggressive. It angrily attacked anyone or anything that came near it. It snapped its beak and hissed and snorted. It beat its huge white wings and rushed out of the water at every creature it saw.

The first to leave the lake were the smallest creatures; the mice and voles, the hedgehogs and water rats.

'It's just too scary to stay here,' they said. 'That great wild swan is too fierce for us. We're off to find new homes.'

The ducks and geese, some herons and two tame swans were next to leave.

'It's just not the place it was,' they said. 'That great wild swan had taken all the pleasure out of living here. We're leaving.'

The larger animals left next.

'That great wild swan attacks us every time we go to the water to drink,' said the rabbits and hares, the badgers and deer. 'It's no good, we can't go on like this.'

Even the people stopped coming to the lake.

'It doesn't matter which bit of the lake you go to,' they said, 'It's there – snapping and biting and flapping its wings.'

The children were the last to leave.

'Ya ha, you don't scare us,' they shouted. But their shrieks of laughter turned to tears when the snapping beak of the swan bit one of the girls and its beating wings broke one of the boys' arms.

At last, news of the swan's behaviour reached Bishop Hugh.

'It won't let anyone near it,' said the monks. 'It's nasty and vicious and everyone's afraid of it.'

'Everyone?' said Hugh, and he set off towards the lake.

As soon as the wild white swan saw him, it attacked; snapping and flapping. Hugh stood still. The swan rushed closer and Hugh could feel the beating of its enormous wings. Yet he stood still. The swan hissed and spat, snarled and snapped. Hugh stood still.

The swan backed off, unsure what to do against this man who seemed unafraid. It watched Hugh hold out something in his hand. Bread! It cautiously waddled towards Hugh, grabbed the hunk of bread and gobbled it down.

'So, you like bread, eh?' said Hugh. 'Then here's another piece,' and he held out his hand again to the swan. 'I think you'd like a friend as well,' he said gently.

Hugh fed the swan more pieces of bread, quietly talking to it all the time. The swan, of course, could not understand Hugh's words, but there was no mistaking his kind and gentle voice.

In the days that followed, Hugh and the wild swan began to know and trust each other. The swan learned to wait by the water's edge at the time he knew Hugh usually came. Hugh never let his friend down; he came every day with food.

Then the swan began to meet Hugh along the path to the lake, and soon began following him part-way home after he had been fed. One day he followed Hugh as far as the palace door and Hugh said, 'Come along then. Come in. Come and see where I live. Come and sit with me in my study.' And to everyone's amazement, the swan did!

From that day on it followed Hugh everywhere and became as faithful as a dog. Only when Hugh had to go away on business did the swan return to live on the lake, but somehow it always knew when Hugh was due home, and was always waiting at the door to meet him.

Saint Clement

23 November

Little is known of Clement's life, but he is believed to have been the third Pope after Saint Peter, and is venerated as a martyr.

It is known that he sent a letter to the Corinthians, possibly in the year 95, which was of note since it was the first example of a Bishop of Rome intervening in the affairs of another Church. In Corinth, then the capital of the Roman province of Achaia, Christian leaders had been overthrown and Christian beliefs were being mocked. Clement wrote asking for peace and suggesting that there was room for Christianity in the city. The letter also contained valuable historical references to Peter and Paul at Rome. There are other writings bearing Clement's name, but these are now thought unlikely to be his.

Legend has it that Clement was exiled to hard labour in the Crimea because of the extent of his missionary work in Rome, and that there he continued preaching but was eventually killed, probably in the year 100, by being thrown into the sea with an anchor tied round his neck.

Clement is the patron saint of those responsible for lighthouses and lightships, i.e. Trinity House, London. There are 43 churches dedicated to him in England, the most famous of which is St Clement Danes in London.

Clement prays for peace

Courage/standing up for what you believe to be right/caring

Clement was Bishop of Rome not long after Jesus was alive. There were many people in Rome who were Christians at the time, but there were also many people who were not. Clement lived in the days when Christians were often persecuted by the Romans; Christians were often thrown into prison or killed for believing in Jesus.

Clement had many friends in Rome, but many enemies too, who were looking for a chance to get rid of him. At last their chance came. Clement had just baptised twenty people. Twenty new Christians.

'That's it!' shouted the Romans. 'He's gone too far. He's converting too many people. Out with him.' And without any more ado, they bundled Clement into a cart and drove him out of the city.

Clement expected that they would set him down somewhere outside Rome to find his own way back, but no, his enemies transported him across Italy, over the sea, then over a thousand miles of mountainous countryside to the Crimea.

'There!' they said. 'You can live here in this place. See how your Christianity helps you here.' And they left him.

Clement found himself in a sort of prison camp where everyone was made to do hard manual work. They had to dig boulders out of the hillside with their bare hands. They had to cut the stones with hammers and chisels, and carry the huge blocks down to the edge of the sea. They were given hardly any food. Many people died.

Clement found the work hard, but he did his best and rarely complained or grumbled.

'How do you stay so calm?' some of the other prisoners asked him.

'I pray, and I think of the suffering of Jesus,' answered Clement. And he told them about Jesus and his life on earth. Each evening when their work was finished Clement told the workers stories of Jesus. None of them had heard of Jesus before, and many said they wanted to follow Jesus, too.

One day Clement managed to get hold of some things to write with. He began to write letters. He had no idea whether anyone would ever receive his letters, but it seemed important to him to write them.

'We should live in a world of peace,' he wrote. 'The strong must take care of the weak. The rich must take care of the poor. We all need each other; the great need the small, the small need the great.'

In another letter he wrote a prayer: 'O God, make us children of quietness, children of peace.'

They seemed strange letters for someone in a prison camp to write. But Clement was able to think outside his prison, to think about others and to hope that one day people would live in peace, to hope that one day people would lead good lives, lives where everyone helped everyone else, lives lived as Jesus would have wanted them lived.

The workers in the prison camp read Clement's letters and felt optimistic, they felt full of hope that one day life would be better. It was a long time since some of them had felt any hope at all.

But the people in charge of the prison camp heard that Clement had been writing letters. They also heard that he had been talking to the others about Jesus. They were not pleased.

'He's never going to learn, is he?' they said amongst themselves. 'You'd think by now he'd give up all this talk of Jesus. But if he won't give it up, he'll have to die.'

They called Clement to a meeting with them.

'Are you going to stop all this talk of Jesus?' they asked.

'Are you going to stop writing these letters?'

'No,' said Clement. 'I can only do what I think is right. I think it is right to tell others about Jesus. I think it is right for me to write letters.'

'You will be killed if you don't stop,' said the guards. 'Will you stop?'

'No,' said Clement.

The guards took hold of Clement and pushed him down the hillside to the sea. They tied an anchor round his neck and put him in a boat. They sailed out to sea with him.

'Now will you stop talking about Jesus?' they asked.

'I'm sorry, but no,' said Clement.

The guards pushed him into the sea and he drowned.

But Clement was not forgotten. The words he wrote in his letters remained through the centuries and are still there for us to hear today.

'O God, make us children of quietness, children of peace. Let the strong take care of the weak, the rich take care of the poor. We all need each other. O God, make us children of peace.'

Saint Catherine of Alexandria

25 November

It is unlikely that Catherine ever existed – there is no evidence of her life and no record of her in early martyrologies – yet her legend is famous.

She is supposed to have been born to a noble family in Alexandria around the turn of the fourth century, and converted to Christianity after having a vision. Soon after this she spoke against the Emperor Maxentius and his persecution of the Christians, whereupon he confronted her with 50 philosophers and challenged her to put forward her argument. However, the philosophers were unable to win the debate and were executed for failing to do so.

Catherine was then imprisoned and tortured on a spiked wheel, but this broke, injuring several spectators but leaving Catherine unharmed. Catherine was then beheaded.

There are many English churches dedicated to St Catherine, and there are still in existence 170 medieval bells bearing her name. Her life is depicted in stained glass at York Minster and Balliol College Oxford. Catherine is the patron saint of young girls, students, the clergy, nurses, wheelwrights, spinners and millers.

Catherine and the Emperor Maxentius

Courage/standing up for what you believe to be right

Catherine of Alexandria was the cleverest girl in Egypt, where she lived nearly sixteen hundred years ago. Catherine was a Christian, at a time when many people did not know about the work of Jesus.

One day, the Emperor Maxentius ordered lots of poor people to be killed. He wanted to kill them in honour of his own god, but when Catherine heard what he wanted to do, she went straight away to his palace to tell him that it was wrong and cruel to kill innocent people.

'They have done nothing to deserve it,' she told Maxentius. 'You have no right to kill them. You say you want to kill them in honour of your own god, but you do not know the real God, the true God. The one true God teaches us that it is wrong to kill. He sent his Son, Jesus Christ, to show us that we should love one another. Set these people free.'

'How dare you speak to me like this,' shouted the Emperor Maxentius. 'You have no right to tell me what to do in my own Empire. Leave at once!'

But instead of being afraid of Maxentius as most other people were, and instead of leaving immediately as Maxentius had told her to, Catherine stayed where she was and tried to persuade him that she was right and that he was wrong to order innocent people to be killed. Maxentius became more and more angry.

'You shall pay for having the audacity to speak to me in this way. You think you are so clever. You think you can win with your words, then you shall show us all how clever you really are. You can put your arguments to fifty of my philosophers. Fifty of my thinkers. Fifty people who really know how to win with words. Then we'll see how clever you are!'

And Emperor Maxentius ordered fifty wise men to come immediately. He told them to argue on his behalf and to make sure that Catherine's arguments sounded silly and stupid and childish.

But the fifty philosophers lost the argument. They were not as clever as Catherine; and although she could answer all their questions, they could not answer hers. Some of the wise men were so impressed with her thoughts and ideas and words about Jesus, that they decided to become Christians themselves. The Emperor Maxentius became even more angry.

'She is nothing but a young girl. How can she beat my wise men in talk? But she will do as I say. She will accept my God and my laws. I shall make her marry me. Then she'll do as I say because I shall give her jewels and riches. I will give her anything she wants as long as she stops her talk about Jesus, and worships my God instead.

But to the surprise of Maxentius, Catherine would not marry him. 'I do not want your money and your jewels,' she said. 'I am a bride of Christ, not of yours.'

'Then you shall die,' said Maxentius, and he had Catherine thrown into a prison cell.

'I shall torture her,' said Maxentius. 'I shall kill her in front of everyone so that they can all see that I will not have people disobeying me. I will not have people arguing against my laws.'

Maxentius ordered a huge spiked wheel to be made and set up in the centre of the city. Then he had Catherine brought out of the prison cell. She was tied to the wheel.

'Now we'll see how clever you are,' he jeered. 'Now we'll see if your clever words help you out of this,' and he set the wheel turning.

But something had gone wrong with the machinery of the wheel and its huge frame. Suddenly, with a great grinding noise, the wheel broke into pieces. Splinters of wood showered into the crowd and some people were injured. Catherine remained unhurt. She was taken back to the prison cell.

'You will die,' said Maxentius as she was led away.

Twelve days later, Maxentius gave the order that Catherine should be beheaded, and she died soon after the order was given.

But Catherine's bravery and Maxentius's cruelty had made yet more people decide to become Christians. Catherine had not died in vain.

The date of Easter from 1995 to 2025

(Also shown are the dates of the movable feasts Ash Wednesday, Ascension Day and Whit Sunday.)

Year	Easter Day	Ash Wednesday	Ascension Day	Whit Sunday
1995	Apr 16	Mar 1	May 25	Jun 4
1996	Apr 7	Feb 21	May 16	May 26
1997	Mar 30	Feb 12	May 8	May 18
1998	Apr 12	Feb 25	May 21	May 31
1999	Apr 4	Feb 17	May 13	May 23
2000	Apr 23	Mar 8	Jun 1	Jun 11
2001	Apr 15	Feb 28	May 24	Jun 3
2002	Mar 31	Feb 13	May 9	May 19
2003	Apr 20	Mar 5	May 29	Jun 8
2004	Apr 11	Feb 25	May 20	May 30
2005	Mar 27	Feb 9	May 5	May 15
2006	Apr 16	Mar 1	May 25	Jun 4
2007	Apr 8	Feb 21	May 17	May 27
2008	Mar 23	Feb 6	May 1	May 11
2009	Apr 12	Feb 25	May 21	May 31
2010	Apr 4	Feb 17	May 13	May 23
2011	Apr 24	Mar 9	Jun 2	Jun 12
2012	Apr 8	Feb 22	May 17	May 27
2013	Mar 31	Feb 13	May 9	May 19
2014	Apr 20	Mar 5	May 29	Jun 8

Year	Easter Day	Ash Wednesday	Ascension Day	Whit Sunday
2015	Apr 5	Feb 18	May 14	May 24
2016	Mar 27	Feb 10	May 5	May 15
2017	Apr 16	Mar 1	May 25	Jun 4
2018	Apr 1	Feb 14	May 10	May 20
2019	Apr 21	Mar 6	May 30	Jun 9
2020	Apr 12	Feb 26	May 21	May 31
2021	Apr 4	Feb 17	May 13	May 23
2022	Apr 17	Mar 2	May 26	Jun 5
2023	Apr 9	Feb 22	May 18	May 28
2024	Mar 31	Feb 14	May 9	May 19
2025	Apr 20	Mar 5	May 29	Jun 8

(The information for this table is taken from The Alternative Service Book 1980.)

Chronology of saints

Michael the Archangel   no date
Anne   1st century BC
Joseph of Nazareth   1st century BC to 1st century AD
Matthew   1st century
Luke   1st century
John the Baptist   d. c. 30
Stephen   d. c. 35
James the Great   d. c. 44
Andrew   d. c. 60
Peter   d. c. 64
Mark   d. c. 74
Paul   c. 3–c. 67
John the Evangelist   d. c. 100
Clement   d. c. 100
Christopher   3rd century
Valentine   3rd century
Alban   d. c. 209
George   d. c. 250
Felix   d. c. 260
Crispin & Crispinian   d. c. 285
Helen   c. 255–c. 330
Martin   c. 315–c. 400
Nicholas   4th century
Blaise   d. c. 316
Sylvester   d. 335
Ambrose   c. 340–397
Jerome   c. 342–420
Patrick   c. 385–c. 461
Catherine   late 4th century

Brigid   c. 450–c. 525
Keneth   c. 6th century
David   c. 520–c. 589
Columba   c. 521–c. 597
Cadoc   b. c. 522
Gregory the Great   c. 540–604
Augustine   d. c. 605
Aidan   d. 651
Chad   620–672
Lambert   b. c. 635
Caedmon   d. c. 680
Oswald   c. 605–642
Hilda   614–680
Audrey (Etheldreda)   c. 630–679
Cuthbert   634–687
Bede   673–735
Boniface   c. 680–754
Swithin   c. 800–862
Ludmilla   c. 860–921
Wenceslas   c. 907–929
Hugh   1135–1200
Francis   1181–1226
Zita   1218–1278
Ignatius of Loyola   1491–1556
Francis Xavier   1506–1552
Theresa   1873–1897

Bibliography

A Calendar of Saints, J. Bentley, Macdonald & Co, 1988
Alternative Saints, R. Symonds, MacMillan Press, 1988
A Year of Festivals, G. Palmer & N. Lloyd, Frederick Warne, 1972
Cattern Cakes and Lace, J. Jones & B. Deer, Dorling Kindersley, 1992
High Days and Holidays, D. Self, Lion Publishing plc, 1993
In Search of Lost Gods, R. Whitlock, Phaidon Press Ltd, 1979
Legends of the Saints, H. Delehaye, translated by D. Attwater, 1962
Lives and Legends of English Saints, L. M. Shortt, 1914
Origins of Festivals and Feasts, J. Harrowven, Kaye & Ward
Saints, Birds and Beasts, M. Mayo, Kaye & Ward, 1980
Saints – Chambers Encylopaedic Guides, A. Jones, Chambers, 1992
Saints in the Calendar: Their Lives, Legends, Emblems and Dedications, G. J. Jenkinson, Robert Scott, 1915
The Book of Saints Canonised by the Catholic Church, A & C Black, 1989
The Christian Year, J. C. J. Metford, Thames & Hudson, 1991
The Oxford Dictionary of Saints, D. H. Farmer, Oxford University Press, 1992
The Penguin Dictionary of Saints, D. Attwater, Penguin Books, 1983
The Perpetual Almanac of Folklore, C. Kightly, Thames & Hudson, 1987
The Saints in Christian Art: Lives & Legends of the Evangelists, Apostles and other Early Saints, A. Bell, 1901
The Saints in Christian Art: Lives & Legends of the Great Hermits and Fathers of the Church, A. Bell, 1902
The Saints in Christian Art: Lives and Legends of the English Bishops and Kings, Medieval Monks and other later Saints, A. Bell, 1904

Alphabetical index of stories

A partnership with God
  Rogation Sunday   80
Aidan in Northumbria **31 Aug**   130
Alban and the Christian
  22 Jun   100
Ambrose and the emperor
  7 Dec   12
Audrey and the Isle of Ely
  23 Jun   102

Boniface and the great oak tree
  5 Jun   95
Brigid and the wolf **1 Feb   33**

Caedmon's song **11 Feb   42**
Catherine and the Emperor Maxentius
  25 Nov   169
Chad and the King of Mercia
  2 Mar   48
Clement prays for peace
  23 Nov   167
Columba sails to Iona **9 Jun   98**
Crispin and Crispinian **25 Oct   154**

David and the robber **1 Mar   46**

Felix and the spider **14 Jan   28**
Fishers of men **30 Nov   6**
Francis Xavier and the people of

Yamaguchi **3 Dec   8**
Herod kills the boy children
  28 Dec   71
Hilda, Abbess of Whitby
  17 Nov   163

Ignatius the soldier **31 Jul   117**

Jesus answers questions
  Holy Week   64
Jesus enters Jerusalem
  Palm Sunday   61
Jesus goes to the temple
  Holy Week   63
Jesus is alive **Easter Day   71**
Jesus is crucified **Good Friday   69**
Jesus is lost in the temple
  Mothering Sunday   51
Jesus is named **1 Jan   25**
Jesus is taken to the temple
  2 Feb   35
Jesus is tempted in the wilderness
  Ash Wednesday   40
Jesus returns to his Father
  Ascension Day   82
Joachim and Anne **26 Jul   115**
John and Jesus are promised
  Advent Sunday   3

Joseph of Nazareth **19 Mar**   56
Juliana and the festival of Corpus
    Christi **Corpus Christi**   87

Keneth and the gulls **1 Aug**   122
King Wenceslas **28 Sep**   140

Lambert does as he is told
    17 Sep   134
Luke the writer **18 Oct**   151

Mary met an angel **25 Mar**   60
Mary visits Elizabeth **31 May**   93
Matthew is called to follow Jesus
    21 Sep   136
Michael and the dragon **29 Sep**   143

Nicholas and the bags of gold
    6 Dec   10

Oswald and the silver dishes
    9 Aug   126

Peter heals a lame man **29 Jun**   106

Saint Augustine and the children from
    England **26 May**   91
Saint Blaise and the animals
    3 Feb   36
Saint Cadoc and the mouse
    25 Sep   138
Saint Cuthbert and the eagle
    20 Mar   58
Saint Francis tames a wolf
    4 Oct   149
Saint George and the dragon
    23 Apr   73
Saint Gregory and the angel
    3 Sep   133
Saint Helen and the True Cross
    18 Aug   128
Saint Hugh and the wild swan
    17 Nov   165

Saint James and the evil magician
25 Jul   112
Saint Jerome and the lion
30 Sep   145
Saint John and the band of robbers
27 Dec   19
Saint Mark and the great storm of
Venice **25 Apr**   75
Saint Martin and the beggar
11 Nov   161
Saint Patrick and the Christian fire
17 Mar   53
Saint Swithin's request
15 Jul   108
Saint Theresa of Lisieux
1 Oct   148
Saint Unknown and the goat
1 Nov   156
Saint Valentine and the Roman
emperor **14 Feb**   44

The birth of John the Baptist
24 Jun   104
The coming of the Holy Spirit
Whit Sunday   83
The conversion of Saul
25 Jan   30
The hermit of All Souls
2 Nov   158
The Lammas Day loaf
1 Aug   119
The Last Supper and the arrest of
Jesus **Maundy Thursday**   66
The legend of Saint Christopher
25 Jul   110
The pancake bell
Shrove Tuesday   38
The plot against Jesus
Holy Week   65
The stoning of Stephen
26 Dec   17
The world's special baby is born
25 Dec   15

Three disciples begin to
    understand **6 Aug**   124
Three in one **Trinity Sunday**   85
Timotheus' treasure **31 Dec**   23

Visitors from the East **6 Jan**   26

Zita the servant **27 Apr**   78

Theme index

The saints' stories have been listed under the thematic index, as teachers may well wish to use them to fit in with a particular theme or idea, almost regardless of the date of the feast, rather than in their own right on their specific day. However, it is not anticipated that teachers will wish to retell the stories of the principal festivals at any other time of year but their own, therefore these stories have not been included in the thematic index.

Appearances can be deceptive
Michael and the dragon **29 Sep** 143
Francis Xavier and the people of
    Yamaguchi **3 Dec** 8

Being Observant
Saint Cadoc and the mouse
    25 Sep 138

Caring
Saint Blaise and the animals
    3 Feb 36
Saint Valentine and the Roman
    emperor **14 Feb** 44
Jesus is lost in the temple **4th Sunday
    in Lent, Mothering Sunday** 51
Joseph of Nazareth **19 Mar** 56
Alban and the Christian
    22 Jun 100
Keneth and the gulls **1 Aug** 122
Oswald and the silver dishes
    9 Aug 126
Aidan in Northumbria **31 Aug** 130

Saint Gregory and the angel
    3 Sep 133
Saint Jerome and the lion
    30 Sep 145
Saint Francis tames a wolf
    4 Oct 149
Luke the writer **18 Oct** 151
The hermit of all souls **2 Nov** 158
Saint Martin and the beggar
    11 Nov 161
Hilda, Abbess of Whitby
    17 Nov 163
Clement prays for peace
    23 Nov 167
Nicholas and the bags of gold
    6 Dec 10
Saint John and the band of
    robbers **27 Dec** 19
Timotheus' treasure **31 Dec** 23

Cheerfulness
Saint Theresa of Lisieux **1 Oct** 148

Consideration for others
Brigid and the wolf **1 Feb**   33
Saint Valentine and the Roman
   emperor **14 Feb**   44
Jesus is lost in the temple **4th Sunday
   in Lent, Mothering Sunday**   51
Saint Gregory and the angel
   3 Sep   133
Luke the writer **18 Oct**   151
The hermit of all souls **2 Nov**   158
Saint Martin and the beggar
   11 Nov   161
Nicholas and the bags of gold
   6 Dec   10

Courage
Saint George and the dragon
   23 Apr   73
Saint Mark and the great storm of
   Venice **25 Apr**   75
Alban and the Christian
   22 Jun   100
Peter heals a lame man **29 Jun**   106
The legend of Saint Christopher
   25 Jul   110
Saint James and the evil magician
   25 Jul   112
Crispin and Crispinian **25 Oct**   154
Saint Martin and the beggar
   11 Nov   161
Saint Hugh and the wild swan
   17 Nov   165
Clement prays for peace
   23 Nov   167
Catherine and the Emperor Maxentius
   25 Nov   169
Ambrose and the emperor
   7 Dec   12
The stoning of Stephen **26 Dec**   17
Timotheus' treasure **31 Dec**   23

Doing your best
Caedmon's song **11 Feb**   42

Chad and the King of Mercia
   2 Mar   48
Joseph of Nazareth **19 Mar**   56
Zita the servant **27 Apr**   78
Juliana and the festival of Corpus
   Christi **10 days after
   Pentecost**   87
All is finished **25 May**   89
Boniface and the great oak tree
   5 Jun   95
Columba sails to Iona **9 Jun**   98
The legend of Saint Christopher
   25 Jul   110
The Lammas Day loaf **1 Aug**   119
Saint Jerome and the lion
   30 Sep   145
Hilda, Abbess of Whitby
   17 Nov   163

Envy
King Wenceslas **28 Sep**   140

Fair play
Brigid and the wolf **1 Feb**   33

Forgiveness
David and the robber **1 Mar**   46
Saint James and the evil magician
   25 Jul   112
Matthew is called to follow Jesus
   21 Sep   136
Crispin and Crispinian **25 Oct**   154
Saint Unknown and the goat
   1 Nov   156
The stoning of Stephen **26 Dec**   17
Saint John and the band of robbers
   27 Dec   19

Friendship
Felix and the spider **14 Jan**   28
Saint Blaise and the animals
   3 Feb   36
David and the robber **1 Mar**   46

Alban and the Christian
22 Jun   100
Saint James and the evil magician
25 Jul   112
Ignatius the soldier 31 Jul   117
Keneth and the gulls 1 Aug   122
Aidan in Northumbria 31 Aug   130
Saint Jerome and the lion
30 Sept   145
Saint Francis tames a wolf
4 Oct   149
The hermit of all souls 2 Nov   158
Saint Hugh and the wild swan
17 Nov   165

Generosity
Felix and the spider 14 Jan   28
Brigid and the wolf 1 Feb   33
Saint Blaise and the animals
3 Feb   36
Zita the servant 27 Apr   78
Oswald and the silver dishes
9 Aug   126
Aidan in Northumbria 31 Aug   130
Saint Unknown and the goat
1 Nov   156

Greed
King Wenceslas 28 Sep   140
Timotheus' treasure 31 Dec   23

Honesty
Columba sails to Iona 9 Jun   98
The Lammas Day loaf 1 Aug   119
Ambrose and the emperor
7 Dec   12
Saint John and the band of robbers
27 Dec   19

Humility
Caedmon's song 11 Feb   42
Chad and the King of Mercia
2 Mar   48

Joseph of Nazareth 19 Mar   56
Saint Swithin's request 15 Jul   108
Lambert does as he is told
17 Sep   134
Saint Theresa of Lisieux 1 Oct   148

Keeping your word
Saint Swithin's request 15 Jul   108
Joachim and Anne 26 Jul   115
Saint Helen and the True Cross
18 Aug   128
Saint John and the band of robbers
27 Dec   19

Kindness
Saint Valentine and the Roman
emperor 14 Feb   44
Chad and the King of Mercia
2 Mar   48
Joseph of Nazareth 19 Mar   56
Alban and the Christian
22 June   100
Keneth and the gulls 1 Aug   122
King Wenceslas 28 Sep   140
Saint Francis tames a wolf
4 Oct   149
Saint Unknown and the goat
1 Nov   156
The hermit of all souls 2 Nov   158
Saint Martin and the beggar
11 Nov   161
Saint Hugh and the wild swan
17 Nov   165
Francis Xavier and the people of
Yamaguchi 3 Dec   8
Nicholas and the bags of gold
6 Dec   10

Loyalty
Felix and the spider 14 Jan   28
Ignatius the soldier 31 Jul   117
King Wenceslas 28 Sep   140
Hilda, Abbess of Whitby
17 Nov   163

Obedience
Chad and the King of Mercia
 2 Mar   48
Jesus is lost in the temple **4th Sunday
 in Lent, Mothering Sunday   51**
Lambert does as he is told
 17 Sep   134
Saint Theresa of Lisieux **1 Oct   148**

Patience
David and the robber **1 Mar   46**
Juliana and the festival of Corpus
 Christi **10 days after
 Pentecost   87**
Audrey and the Isle of Ely
 23 Jun   102
Joachim and Anne **26 Jul   115**
Aidan in Northumbria **31 Aug   130**
Saint Cadoc and the mouse
 25 Sep   138
The hermit of all souls **2 Nov   158**
Timotheus' treasure **31 Dec   23**

Perseverance
David and the robber **1 Mar   46**
Juliana and the festival of Corpus
 Christi **10 days after
 Pentecost   87**
All is finished **25 May   89**
Saint Augustine and the children from
 England **26 May   91**
Boniface and the great oak tree
 5 Jun   95
Audrey and the Isle of Ely
 23 Jun   102
The legend of Saint Christopher
 25 July   110
Saint Helen and the True Cross
 18 Aug   128

Repentance
Columba sails to Iona **9 Jun   98**
Matthew is called to follow Jesus
 21 Sep   136

Responsibility
The Lammas Day loaf **1 Aug   119**
Hilda, Abbess of Whitby
 17 Nov   163

Setting an example
Zita the servant **27 Apr   78**
Ignatius the soldier **31 Jul   117**
Francis Xavier and the people of
 Yamaguchi **3 Dec   8**

Sharing
Felix and the spider **14 Jan   28**
Saint Blaise and the animals
 3 Feb   36
Saint Cuthbert and the eagle
 20 Mar   58
Zita the servant **27 Apr   78**
Oswald and the silver dishes
 9 Aug   126
Aidan in Northumbria **31 Aug   130**
Saint Gregory and the angel
 3 Sep   133
Saint Cadoc and the mouse
 25 Sep   38
The hermit of all souls
 2 Nov   158
Saint Martin and the beggar
 11 Nov   161
Saint Hugh and the wild swan
 17Nov   165
Francis Xavier and the people of
 Yamaguchi **3 Dec   8**
Nicholas and the bags of gold
 6 Dec   10

*Standing up for what you believe to be
 right*
Saint Valentine and the Roman
 emperor **14 Feb   44**
David and the robber **1 Mar   46**
Saint Patrick and the Christian fire
 17 Mar   53

Boniface and the great oak tree
    5 Jun   95
Alban and the Christian
    22 Jun   100
Peter heals a lame man 29 Jun   106
Michael and the dragon 29 Sep   143
Crispin and Crispinian 25 Oct   154
Saint Martin and the beggar
    11 Nov   161
Clement prays for peace
    23 Nov   167
Catherine and the Emperor Maxentius
    25 Nov   169
Ambrose and the emperor
    7 Dec   12
The stoning of Stephen 26 Dec   17
Timotheus' treasure 31 Dec   23

Temptation
Columba sails to Iona 9 Jun   98
The Lammas Day loaf 1 Aug   119
Michael and the dragon 29 Sep   143
Saint Unknown and the goat
    1 Nov   156

Thinking
Saint Helen and the True Cross
    18 Aug   128
Luke the writer 18 Oct   151

Tolerance
Conversion of Saul 25 Jan   30
David and the robber 1 Mar   46
Juliana and the festival of Corpus
    Christi 10 days after
    Pentecost   87
Saint Unknown and the goat
    1 Nov   156

Hilda, Abbess of Whitby
    17 Nov   163

Trust
The Conversion of Saul 25 Jan   30
Saint Patrick and the Christian fire
    17 Mar   53
Saint Cuthbert and the eagle
    20 Mar   58
Saint Mark and the great storm of
    Venice 25 Apr   75
Alban and the Christian
    22 June   100
Saint James and the evil magician
    25 July   112
Matthew is called to follow Jesus
    21 Sep   136
Saint Francis tames a wolf
    4 Oct   149
Saint Hugh and the wild swan
    17 Nov   165
Fishers of men 30 Nov   6
Saint John and the band of
    robbers 27 Dec   19

Working together
Joseph of Nazareth 19 Mar   56
Saint George and the dragon
    23 Apr   73
A partnership with God Rogation
    Days, 5 weeks after Easter   80
Ignatius the soldier 31 Jul   117
The Lammas Day loaf 1 Aug   119
Fishers of men 30 Nov   60
Saint John and the band of
    robbers 27 Dec   19